# Appearance and Power

# Dress, Body, Culture

Series Editor **Joanne B. Eicher,** *Regents' Professor, University of Minnesota*

Advisory Board:

Books in this provocative series seek to articulate the connections between culture and dress which is defined here in its broadest possible sense as any modification or supplement to the body. Interdisciplinary in approach, the series highlights the dialogue between identity and dress, cosmetics, coiffure, and body alterations as manifested in practices as varied as plastic surgery, tattooing, and ritual scarification. The series aims, in particular, to analyze the meaning of dress in relation to popular culture and gender issues and will include works grounded in anthropology, sociology, history, art history, literature, and folklore.

ISSN: 1360-466X

*Previously published titles in the Series*

DRESS, BODY, CULTURE

# Appearance and Power

*Edited by*

*Kim K. P. Johnson and*
*Sharron J. Lennon*

*Oxford • New York*

First published in 1999 by
**Berg**
Editorial offices:
150 Cowley Road, Oxford, OX4 1JJ, UK
70 Washington Square South, New York, NY 10012, USA

Berg is an imprint of Oxford International Publishers Ltd.

**Library of Congress Cataloging-in-Publication Data**
A catalogue record for this book is available from the Library of Congress.

**British Library Cataloguing-in-Publication Data**
A catalogue record for this book is available from the British Library.

ISBN   1 85973 298 4 (Cloth)
       1 85973 204 6 (Paper)

Typeset by JS Typesetting, Wellingborough, Northants.
Printed in the United Kingdom by WBC Book Manufacturers Ltd., Bridgend

Contents

Contents

# *Acknowledgements*

We thank Dr Joanne B. Eicher as the series editor for *Dress, Body and Culture* and Kathryn Earle as editor at Berg Publications for approaching us about the possibility of this book and getting us started on the process. We thank our colleagues who served as reviewers for each of the chapters: Louella Anderson – Logan, UT; Leslie Burns – Oregon State University; Christy Crutsinger – University of North Texas; Mary Lynn Damhorst – Iowa State University; Marilyn DeLong – University of Minnesota; Judith Forney – University of North Texas; Sally Francis – Oregon State University; Jane Hegland – New Mexico State University; Cynthia Jasper – University of Wisconsin at Madison; Susan Kaiser – University of California at Davis; Hilda Lakner – University of Illinois; Suzanne Loker – Cornell University; Kimberly Miller – University of Kentucky; Gwendolyn O'Neal – The Ohio State University; Elaine Pederson – Oregon State University; Nancy Rabolt – San Francisco State University; Margaret Rucker – University of California at Davis; Nancy Rudd – The Ohio State University; Nancy Schofield – University of Wisconsin at Menominee; Ann Slocum – Michigan State University; and Patricia Warner – University of Massachusetts. Their comments and suggestions were extremely helpful to authors.

# Notes on Contributors

**Elizabeth Anderson** is an instructor at San Joaquin Delta College in Stockton, California. She is also a graduate student in the Division of Textiles and Clothing at the University of California-Davis. Before returning to college to continue her formal education, she managed her own apparel company.

**Betsy Covell Breseman** is a graduate student in the Department of Consumer and Textile Sciences at The Ohio State University, Columbus, Ohio. Her research interests include obesity and attitude change, appearance management and coping strategies of obese women, and motivations involving surgery for obesity.

**Mary Lynn Damhorst, Ph.D.** is an Associate Professor in the Department of Textiles and Clothing at Iowa State University, Ames, Iowa. Her research interests include consumer involvement with appearances in the media and the role of dress in career development. She is co-editor of *Fashioning the Self in Cultural Context* and has published numerous articles in a variety of journals.

**Jane E. Hegland, Ph.D.** is an Assistant Professor in the Department of Family and Consumer Sciences at New Mexico State University, Las Cruces, New Mexico. Her research, publications, and teaching focus on dress, gender, and issues of power. Specifically, her research has examined topics concerning rape and dress, cross-dressing, dressing for the ritual of the high school prom, the use of dress in film, aesthetics related to dress and identity, and the effectiveness of public school uniforms and dress codes intended to control students' behavior.

**Kim K. P. Johnson, Ph.D.** is Professor and Director of Graduate Studies in the Department of Design, Housing, and Apparel at the University of Minnesota, St Paul, Minnesota. Her research interests include dress as a form of nonverbal communication and consumer behavior related to dress. She co-edited *Dress and Identity* and has publications in the *Clothing and Textiles Research Journal*, *Family and Consumer Sciences Research Journal*, and the

*Journal of Family and Consumer Sciences* among others. She teaches in the areas of retail merchandising and the social psychological aspects of dress.

**April Kangas** is employed as a Postgraduate Researcher in the Division of Textiles and Clothing, Davis, California. She is also completing her Masters of Business Administration in the Graduate School of Management at the University of California-Davis. Prior to graduate work, she held positions in both the apparel and entertainment industries.

**Sharron J. Lennon, Ph.D.** is a Professor in the Department of Consumer and Textile Sciences at The Ohio State University, Columbus, Ohio. Her research covers a variety of topics including (1) social perception and media analyses as related to purposeful manipulations of appearance, (2) the use of dress by the U.S. legal system, (3) cultural categories, body image, and self-esteem, (4) customer service within the context of television shopping, apparel market shows, and retail stores. She has published widely in a variety of journals.

**Jennifer Paff Ogle** is an Assistant Professor of Apparel and Merchandising at Colorado State University, Ft Collins, Colorado. Her research focuses upon social psychological aspects of appearance, with an emphasis upon socialization, body image, and satisfaction. She has published in the *Clothing and Textiles Research Journal*, *Family and Consumer Sciences Research Journal*, and *Journal of Fashion Marketing and Management*.

**Gwendolyn S. O'Neal, Ph.D.** is an Associate Professor of Consumer and Textile Sciences at The Ohio State University, Columbus, Ohio. Her research interests include African American aesthetic of dress, clothing and violence, and meanings assigned to apparel products and their impact on behavior. She teaches fashion merchandising, forecasting, and semiotics of apparel and related consumer products.

**Margaret Rucker, Ph.D.** is a Professor and Chair of the Division of Textiles and Clothing at the University of California-Davis, Davis, California. Her research interests include clothing preferences and problems of workers across a wide range of occupations – from managers and clerical employees to fire fighters and flight attendants. Other interests include international trade and gift giving. She is the author of two chapters on gift giving and one on pesticide applicators' attitudes and practices concerning clothing. She has published numerous articles in a variety of journals.

**Nancy Ann Rudd,** Ph.D., is an Associate Professor in the Department of Consumer and Textile Sciences at The Ohio State University, Columbus, Ohio. She teaches both undergraduate and graduate courses in the social/ psychological/cultural aspects of dress and in aesthetics. Her research focuses on the use of clothing and appearance management strategies for consumer groups that may be stigmatized by society on the basis of appearance. She has been published in *Family and Consumer Sciences Research Journal, International Textiles & Apparel Association Special Publications, Clothing and Textiles Research Journal, Semiotica, Journal of Homosexuality, and Journal of Ritual Studies.* She chairs the University Body Image and Health Task Force.

**Nancy A. Schofield** is a lecturer in the College of Technology, Engineering, and Management at the University of Wisconsin-Stout, Menomonee, Wisconsin. She teaches in the area of clothing and textile design, retail merchandising, computer-aided design, and computer application courses.

**Theresa Lennon Schulz** is an attorney specializing in employment law litigation with offices in Lake Elmo, Minnesota. She is licensed to practice in the state and federal courts of Minnesota, Wisconsin, and California. She has published numerous articles on employment law topics and is a weekly columnist with the *Minnesota Lawyer* newspaper.

**Suzanne Szostak-Pierce** is a graduate student in the Department of Design, Housing, and Apparel at the University of Minnesota, St Paul, Minnesota. Her research addresses the ways in which youth experience style in the formation and participation in social groups. Other interests include rave and techno-culture, skateboarding, and the swing scene.

**Malcolm Young,** Ph.D. read social anthropology on a Home Office Scholarship halfway through a 30-year police career. After ten years in CID as a detective, he eventually reached the rank of Superintendent, completed his doctorate, and spent the last decade of his working career also writing fieldnotes and analyzing police culture. He is now a freelance writer whose interests not unnaturally lie in the analysis of systems of power and control. He has written two books: *An Anthropologist in the Police (1991)* and *In the Sticks: Cultural identity in a rural police force.* He has also written several papers on gender and the rituals and symbolism of contemporary culture.

# Introduction: Appearance and Social Power

## Kim K. P. Johnson and Sharron J. Lennon

Our appearance is our most apparent individual characteristic. We are, in one sense, trapped inside our bodies. However, how we are packaged physically, tall or short, fair or dark, thin or heavy, tends to be programmed in our genes.[1] Thus, although we can exercise, diet, and change hair color and texture, barring cosmetic surgery, our physical packaging is somewhat immutable.[2] Accordingly, we are socialized not to judge others by their appearances because to acknowledge that appearances play a significant role in everyday life is counter to the democratic notion that they are or should be superficial because they are not freely chosen.

Yet, at the same time, relying on appearance to guide personal decisions and social interactions is not only natural, it is inescapable. In order to survive in and respond to massive amounts of stimuli in daily life (Hamilton, 1979), we sort people and other objects into similar groupings (Rosch, 1973). Because humans are highly visual,[3] we tend to use appearances to guide these judgments.[4] For example, perceptually, humans attend to novel, unusual, and complexly-patterned objects.[5] Because novel (Kaiser, Nagasawa, & Hutton, 1991; 1995), unusual (see Szostak-Pierce, this volume), or brightly-colored (O'Neal, 1998) looks may be created by people as they manage their appearances, dress and appearances will capture attention in social interactions. Thus, it is important to study the effects of appearance and dress within that context.

What do we mean when we use the term dress? Authors in this volume have for the most part, adopted Roach-Higgins and Eicher's (1992) definition of the term. They define dress as all the modifications made to the human body and supplements to the body (Roach-Higgins & Eicher, 1992). Using this definition, dress includes a long list of changes to the body which can be either permanent or temporary such as tattoos, straightened teeth, exercise, or permed hair as well as additions to the body like clothing or weight gain.

The authors in this volume directly address many different aspects of dress including weight gain, clothing, cosmetics use, and socially-derived aesthetic rules concerning dress.

People use dress to make inferences or to convey information about sex,[6] attractiveness,[7] group membership,[8] and power.[9] In fact, Damhorst (1990), in her analysis of the information conveyed by dress, found that dress communicated information about power[10] in nearly 45 per cent of the 103 published studies she reviewed. Investigations of the relationships between dress and power make important contributions to the study of dress and human behavior.

A prevalent definition of social power stems from the early work of French and Raven (1959). They defined social influence as 'a change in belief, attitude or behavior of a person – the target of influence, which results from the action, or presence of another person or group of persons – the influencing agent' (p. 218). Social power is the potential for such influence. They propose that people have social power due to resources they can utilize: reward, coercion, legitimacy, expertise, reference, and information. The authors in this volume directly or indirectly address all of these bases of social power.

Johnson, Hegland, and Schofield in the first chapter, explore how dress functions in a situation of coercive power, a rape. They give voice to the perspective of rape survivors, in contrast to much of the existing literature on rape and dress, and suggest that how survivors of rape use their dress is related to two sources of social power as defined by Raven: reward power and information power. They raise several questions for the reader: Who decides what appearance means, the wearer or the viewer? Although dress communicates information about the wearer, does it communicate consent to sexual intercourse? Does your appearance keep you safe from a rape?

Young uses a reflexive approach taking personal data and field material from a thirty-year police career to interpret how the uniform and image of the police reflect the cultural meanings and symbolic power that the police maintain. He asserts that the militaristic appearance in which symbols of power and control are increasingly presented to the British public conflicts with the proclaimed desire by that police force to be approachable and interactive with the public. He documents the change from the view of the role of the police officer as an integrated community member and friend in the neighborhood to a distant, alienated, law enforcer. He raises the question: Can the evolving police uniform communicate that the police are friends of the community?

In addition to Young, several authors (Rucker et al., Ogle & Damhorst, Lennon) explore relationships between social power and dress as they apply to the workplace. The workplace is a complex social environment where we expect that all types of social power (i.e. reward, coercion, legitimacy, expertise, reference, and information) might be exercised and subsequently visible in dress. In traditional male-dominated corporate environments, White men wore suits to establish a powerful image. Women, who were gaining entry into management for the first time in the 1980s, were repeatedly advised to adopt the appearance of their male counterparts and wear a suit in order to be perceived as professional and competent. The suit was dark in color, tailored, and worn with a conservative blouse, and low-heeled shoes. In many respects, these women were advised to look like men. The findings of numerous clothing and textile researchers supported this advice.[11] Women, however, found it difficult to adopt the cookie-cutter appearance of men in high-level corporate positions. They complained they wanted to appear feminine not masculine, because they were, after all, women (Kimle & Damhorst, 1997). As a result, they adopted dress that was something of a compromise.

As Rucker, Anderson, and Kangas point out, there has been a further shift away from traditional dress codes within many U.S. corporations to allow employees to adopt casual dress. The shift makes constructing a powerful image complex for all employees. In addition, women and other minorities are gaining access to corporate positions. As a result, Rucker, Anderson, and Kangas, in their direct investigation of the workplace, raise several questions about the new emerging role of dress in the workplace: Is staying with traditional clothing symbols of power a better strategy to take for advancement than adopting casual dress? Is a new symbol system developing for communicating power via clothing? Will clothing no longer communicate one's position and power within the workplace? In order that members of ethnic minorities fit in and move up the established power structure, is it important to adopt traditional clothing symbols or is a casual appearance equally effective? When casual clothing is worn in the workplace does it imply casual work relationships?

Ogle and Damhorst and Lennon in their chapters take into account the media and its impact on relationships between power and dress in the workplace. Echoing Rucker et al., Ogle and Damhorst note that the corporate dress code is changing. They examine one source of information about these rules, magazine and newspaper articles, which offered business-dress advice to men and women during the 1980s and 1990s. Because their research spans a timeframe when workplace roles for women were changing dramatically, the reader is able to ask whether the advice given was the same for both men and women. Was it consistent for both? Was there a 'uniform' developing for women similar to the traditional business suit that developed for men? Was anyone telling men to dress casual? Or was this advice directed only to women? Were men advised to move away from the traditional suit?

What reasons were given for the advice? What dress was considered to be powerful?

Lennon, looking at another form of media, contends that the use of dress in a television series reflects how the society that created that series uses and interprets dress. To illustrate her point, she analyzes how dress is used in the futuristic workplace of the television series '*Star Trek, The Next Generation*'. She asks what types of social power are present in this hypothetically egalitarian society? Have gender differences in power disappeared? What power do uniforms convey? Is such power contingent on sex of wearer? How and when is dress used to convey differences in social power? What types of power does the series itself exercise over audience members?

Television as well as other forms of media plays a role in the way women judge their appearances. In their research, Rudd and Lennon note that media influence is important in shaping evaluations of women's appearances and subsequent feelings of self-worth. People are reinforced and rewarded for having attractive appearances, which for women is commonly understood to mean being thin or at least not overweight. As a result, a woman's body size may function as a source of indirect power for women. But what happens to women who believe they are not attractive? What impact does this belief have on self-esteem? How do they learn they are not attractive? Is a woman's body image directly related to her social power? Do women feel powerless in social situations because they perceive themselves as unattractive? Are dieting, exercise, and grooming simply methods of increasing social power? What happens when these behaviors are taken to the extreme? Finally, if a thin body confers social power, then is an obese body equated to an absence of social power?

To explore the relationship between obesity and power, Breseman, Lennon, and Schulz reviewed social science sources, legal sources, and the popular press. They document the stereotypes, prejudice, and discrimination experienced by obese individuals. They also analyze relevant judicial decisions regarding obese individuals. In so doing, they convincingly argue that obese women are powerless. They leave the reader with the question of why, in this age of enlightenment, are companies still discriminating against the obese? Is there any legal recourse for such discrimination? Is obesity the last socially acceptable prejudice, and if so why?

O'Neal and Szostak-Pierce in their chapters address how cultural groups outside the mainstream achieve a sense of empowerment. O'Neal also addresses the power of style as she explores dress as a political instrument within African American culture. She draws upon both historical and contemporary examples to document the process of stylin' which she views as an act of resistance. Stylin' provides the African American a system of meaning within which to define the self and reject the 'normal' mode of dress imposed by the dominant culture. Stylin' allows one to take control or exercise power over how one is to be defined. She raises questions for the reader about the rationality and 'rightness' of the aesthetic rules that dominate mainstream culture and whether the process of stylin' is not unlike the processes engaged in by another cultural group – youth.

Szostak-Pierce focuses on youth and notes that style is a means of obtaining status for cultural groups. By using dress in ways that are markedly different from mainstream practices, the youth subculture is able to achieve a sense of empowerment. She documents this process through her observations of raves and ravers. She suggests that by using dress to symbolize their 'otherness' these young people feel powerful. But what happens when the mainstream adopts the clothing of the subculture? Is the subculture effectively stripped of the feeling of power? In order to maintain power, must the clothing symbolism be constantly in a state of flux, undergoing constant definition and redefinition?

## Summary and Synthesis

Socially-constructed aesthetic rules regarding dress influence the social power we feel and attribute to others. Lack of social power is associated with appearances, which do not conform to the rules, whether they are for mainstream ideas regarding co-ordinated clothing or youthful thin bodies. Some groups and individuals have assumed power by effectively resisting these imposed aesthetic rules, while others have yet to do so. Yet, in the context of the workplace the importance of these rules may be especially important for non-mainstream groups such as young workers, ethnic minorities, women, and obese individuals.

Whether in the context of the workplace or not, many authors echo the notion that for women, exuding sexiness is not powerful. This was true in the work-dress advice columns, in the workplace of the future, and in the lived experiences of rape survivors. Based on these chapters, women appear to be facing a dilemma. To experience reward power, they must not be obese or unattractive. Yet, if they are attractive and thin, they must take care not to dress in a sexy manner (e.g., not powerful). However, rape survivors have learned that gaining weight, not maintaining an attractive appearance, and dressing in an asexual manner, do not offer protection from rape. Is a powerful look for women a contradiction in terms, since power = not sexy = not feminine = masculine?

Taken together, authors acknowledge that dress affects social interactions, such as police interactions with the community and interactions in the workplace. Dress is used to establish characters and is associated with power on television. Uniforms of protective organizations tend to be associated with legitimate power, both in the media and in real life. Dress is discussed endlessly in advice columns, and for women, inconsistent advice abounds, perhaps because a *powerful woman* is an oxymoron. And finally, dress can be used as an instrument of power. Clearly then, dress influences attributions of power to others, personal feelings of power, and the assumption and negotiation of power.

## Notes

1. For example, Roberts, Savage, Coward, Chew, and Lucus (1988) studied energy expenditure and energy intake in infants of overweight and lean mothers. No differences were found in energy intake of the infants at three months; yet there was a significant difference in energy expenditure. At three months, infants born to overweight mothers expended less energy than the others; by twelve months, 50 per cent of infants born to overweight mothers were themselves overweight, while no infants born to lean mothers were overweight. In a study (Stunkard et al., 1986) of 540 adult adoptees, no relationship was found between their fatness and that of their adoptive parents; yet a strong correlation was found between the fatness of the adoptees and their biological parents. These results and other studies suggest that metabolic speed and body fatness are strongly influenced by heredity. In other research Rolland-Cachera and Bellisle (1986) found no correlation between food intake and body fatness in 2,440 children for whom food diaries were kept. See also Allen and Beck (1986) and Grady (1988) for similar results.

2. Both Major, Testa, and Bylsma (1991) and Bloch and Richins (1992) discuss striving to achieve an ideal appearance and the extent to which certain physical characteristics are mutable or immutable. According to Major et al. attractiveness is perceived to be immutable, whereas hair color is perceived to be mutable. In their discussion of the use of products to enhance appearance, such as cosmetics, hair coloring, or clothing, Bloch and Richins suggest that the use of such products may be related to traditional attitudes toward gender roles and may be a means of increasing self-esteem.

3. Even when instructed not to rely on sight, humans seem unable to comply. For example, in studies of fabric hand (e.g., evaluations of the tactile sensations of fabrics), researchers often use screens so that participants cannot inadvertently rely on the sense of sight (Brandt et al., 1998). Even when explicitly instructed to focus on tactile characteristics, participants may use visual characteristics to make their assessments if screens are not used (Kim & Winakor, 1996).

4. Based on her research, Buckley (1984–5) suggested that her participants may have relied on both (a) visually perceived structural features of dress and (b) an

assumed context in which an outfit is typically worn. DeLong, Minshall, and Larntz (1986) investigated how consumers evaluate sweaters. When asked, consumers mentioned both visual and tactile characteristics (fiber, color, softness, bulk), an inferred characteristic (warmth), and a contextual characteristic (worn in winter). Research shows that people categorize others as a function of their body types (Lennon, 1992). Lennon found that in a recall test people tended to confuse large-sized individuals with other large-sized individuals, but not with smaller individuals. In each of these instances, people have relied on visual characteristics in making judgments.

5. People attend to objects and people who are salient to them (McArthur & Post, 1977; Miller, 1982). Objects that are moving, spotlighted, novel, or complexly patterned are perceptually (i.e., visually) salient according to McArthur and Post. Miller used these ideas to create salient appearances for stimulus persons. Miller's salient stimulus persons wore brown and white plaid (i.e., complexly-patterned) clothing and hearing aids (i.e., a novelty in terms of appearance). Other types of novelty in appearance include newly introduced looks.

6. According to Cahill (1989) young children rely on hairstyle, clothing, or even bathing caps to assess someone's sex. In other research (Shakin, Shakin, & Sternglanz, 1985) adults were able to correctly identify the sex of infants through clothing cues. See also Leone and Robertson (1989).

7. Researchers (Buckley, 1983; Buckley & Haefner, 1984) have studied the role of clothing in judgments of physical attractiveness and the extent to which attractive clothing contributes to favorable first impressions (Lapitsky & Smith, 1981; Lennon, 1990).

8. Knowles and Bassett (1976) found that several similarly-dressed people were treated as a group by pedestrians. Schlick and Rowold (1991) found that high-school and university students from Indiana schools often wore 'senior cords' when they were in their senior year as a very personalized indicator of their status.

9. Since social power is defined (in part) to be the potential for a change in behavior of a person resulting from the presence of another, research which has investigated compliance to a request is relevant to studies of power. In research on compliance, Bickman (1974) concluded that a uniformed authority figure's power was likely based on legitimacy. In addition, Bushman (1984;1988) found that compliance was influenced by perceived authority as manipulated by clothing.

10. Damhorst's (1990) definition of power was broader and more inclusive than that of French and Raven (1959).

11. For example, results of experimental research indicate that stimulus persons wearing suits are perceived to have more occupational success (Johnson & Roach-Higgins, 1987b), to have a more professional image (Thurston, Lennon, & Clayton, 1990), to be more competent (Johnson & Roach-Higgins, 1987a) and professional (Lennon & Clayton, 1992), and to be more independent (Johnson & Roach-Higgins, 1987a) than stimulus persons wearing dresses. In addition, stimulus persons wearing suits in dark colors or with masculine design lines (Forsythe, Drake, & Cox, 1984) or clothing appropriate for an interview (Johnson & Roach-Higgins, 1987a; 1987b)

are perceived to be more likely to possess managerial traits than stimulus persons wearing dresses.

## References

Allen, D. O., & Beck, R. R. (1986). The role of calcium ion in hormone-stimulated lipolysis. *Biochemical Pharmacology, 35*, 767–72.

Bickman, L. (1974). The social power of a uniform. *Journal of Applied Social Psychology, 4*(1), 47–61.

Bloch, P. H., & Richins, M. L. (1992). You look "Mahvelous": The pursuit of beauty and the marketing concept. *Psychology and Marketing, 9*, 3–15.

Brandt, B., Brown, D. M., Burns, L. D., Cameron, B. A., Chandler, J., Dallas, M. J., Kaiser, S. B., Lennon, S. J., Pan, N., Salusso, C., & Smitley, R. (1998). Development of a method to measure the individual and joint effects of visual and tactile perceptions of fabrics. *Journal of the Textile Institute, 89*(2), 65–77.

Buckley, H. M. (1983). Perceptions of physical attractiveness as manipulated by dress: Subjects versus independent judges. *Journal of Psychology, 114*, 243–48.

Buckley, H. M. (1984–5). Toward an operational definition of dress. *Clothing and Textiles Research Journal, 3*(2), 1–10.

Buckley, H. M., & Haefner, J. E. (1984). The physical attractiveness stereotype using dress as a facilitator. *Journal of Consumer Studies and Home Economics, 8*, 351–8.

Bushman, B. (1984). Perceived symbols of authority and their influence on compliance. *Journal of Applied Social Psychology, 14*(6), 501–8.

Bushman, B. (1988). The effects of apparel on compliance: A field experiment with a female authority figure. *Personality and Social Psychology Bulletin, 14*(3), 459–67.

Cahill, S. (1989). Fashioning males and females: Appearance management and the social reproduction of gender. *Symbolic Interaction, 12*, 281–98.

Damhorst, M. L. (1990). In search of a common thread: Classification of information communicated through dress. *Clothing and Textiles Research Journal, 8*(2), 1–12.

DeLong, M. R., Minshall, B., & Larntz, K. (1986). Use of schema for evaluating consumer response to an apparel product. *Clothing and Textiles Research Journal, 5*(1), 17–26.

Forsythe, S., Drake, M. F., & Cox, C. (1984). Dress as an influence on the perceptions of management characteristics in women. *Home Economics Research Journal, 13*, 112–21.

French, J. R. P., & Raven, B. (1959). The bases of social power. In D. Cartwright (Ed.), *Studies in social power* (pp. 150–67). Ann Arbor: University of Michigan.

Grady, D. (1988, March 7). Is losing weight a losing battle? *Time, 59*.

Hamilton, D. L. (1979). A cognitive-attributional analysis of stereotyping. In L. Berkowitz (Ed.), *Advances in experimental social psychology* (Vol. 12, pp. 53–84). New York: Academic Press.

Johnson, K. K. P., & Roach-Higgins, M. E. (1987a). Dress and physical attractiveness of women in job interviews. *Clothing and Textiles Research Journal, 5*(3), 1–8.

Johnson, K. K. P., & Roach-Higgins, M. E. (1987b). The influence of physical attractiveness and dress on campus recruiters' impressions of female job applicants. *Home Economics Research Journal, 16*, 87–95.

Kaiser, S. B., Nagasawa, R. H., & Hutton, S. S. (1991). Fashion, postmodernity and personal appearance: A symbolic interactionist formulation. *Symbolic Interaction, 14*(2), 165–85.

Kaiser, S. B., Nagasawa, R. H., & Hutton, S. S. (1995). Construction of an SI theory of fashion, part 1: Ambivalence and change. *Clothing and Textiles Research Journal, 13*, 172–83.

Kim, H., & Winakor, G. (1996). Fabric hand as perceived by U.S. and Korean males and females. *Clothing and Textiles Research Journal, 14*(2), 133–44.

Kimle, P. A., & Damhorst, M. L. (1997). A grounded theory model of the ideal business image for women. *Symbolic Interaction, 20*(1), 45–68.

Lapitsky, M., & Smith, C. M. (1981). Impact of clothing on impressions of personal characteristics and writing ability. *Home Economics Research Journal, 9*, 327–35.

Lennon, S. J. (1990). Effects of clothing attractiveness on perceptions. *Home Economics Research Journal, 18*, 303–10.

Lennon, S. J. (1992). Categorization as a function of body type. *Clothing and Textiles Research Journal, 10*(2), 18–23.

Lennon, S. J., & Clayton, R. (1992). Age, body type, and style features as cues in nonverbal communication. *Semiotica, 91*(½), 43–55.

Leone, C., & Robertson, K. (1989). Some effects of sex-linked clothing and gender schema on the stereotyping of infants. *Journal of Social Psychology, 129*(5), 609–19.

Major, B., Testa, M., & Bylsma, W. H. (1991). Responses to upward and downward social comparisons: The impact of esteem-relevance and perceived control. In J. Suls and T. A. Wills (Eds), *Social comparison: Contemporary theory and research* (pp. 237–60). Hillsdale, NJ: Lawrence Erlbaum Associates, Publishers.

McArthur, L. Z., & Post, D. L. (1977). Figural emphasis and person perception. *Journal of Experimental Social Psychology, 13*, 520–35.

Miller, F. G. (1982). Clothing and physical impairment: Joint effects on person perception. *Home Economics Research Journal, 10*, 265–70.

O'Neal, G. S. (1998). African-American aesthetic of dress: Current Manifestations. *Clothing and Textile Research Journal, 16*(4), 167–75.

Roach-Higgins, M. E., & Eicher, J. B. (1992). Dress and identity. *Clothing and Textiles Research Journal, 10*(4), 1–8.

Roberts, S. B., Savage, J., Coward, W. A., Chew, B., & Lucas, A. (1988). Energy expenditure and intake in infants born to lean and overweight mothers. *New England of Medicine, 318*, 461–6.

Rolland-Cachera, M., & Bellisle, F. (1986). No correlation between adiposity and food intake: Why are working-class children fatter? *American Journal of Clinical Nutrition, 44*, 779–87.

Rosch, E. (1973). On the internal structure of perceptual and semantic categories. In T. M. Moore (Ed.), *Cognitive development and the acquisition of language* (pp. 111–44). New York: Academic Press.

Schlick, P. J., & Rowold, K. L. (1991). Senior cords: A rite of passage. In P. A. Cunningham & S. V. Labs (Eds), *Dress and popular culture* (pp. 106–24). Bowling Green, OH: Bowling Green State University Popular Press.

Shakin, M., Shakin, D., & Sternglanz, S. (1985). Infant clothing: Sex labeling for strangers. *Sex Roles, 12*(9/10), 955–63.

Thurston, J. L., Lennon, S. J., & Clayton, R. V. (1990). Influence of age, body type, currency of fashion detail, and type of garment on the professional image of women. *Home Economics Research Journal, 19*(2), 139–50.

# 1

# *Survivors of Rape: Functions and Implications of Dress in a Context of Coercive Power*[1]

## Kim K. P. Johnson, Jane E. Hegland, and Nancy A. Schofield

The dress of an individual consists of all the modifications made to the human body and/or supplements to the body (Roach-Higgins & Eicher, 1992). Using this definition, dress includes a long list of direct modifications to the body such as pierced ears, tattoos, as well as supplements to the body like clothing and jewelry. Dress functions as a modifier of body processes and as a medium for nonverbal communication. Both body supplements and modifications can alter body processes as they serve as microphysical environments and as interfaces between the body and the larger physical and social environments in which humans live.

Dress functions as an interface when it protects the human body. Examples include hats or lotions that are worn to prevent sunburn, shoes worn to cover the feet, or sweaters worn for warmth. Items of dress are worn not only to protect the body from its physical environment but items, such as amulets and charms, can be worn as a psychological defense from bad luck or evil spirits (Gmelch, 1978). This last type of interface is between the individual and his or her socio-cultural environment, rather than physical environment, and implies that dress is imbued with social power. For example, in the case of rape survivors, specific items of dress may be adopted because survivors believe wearing the item will protect them from future rapes.

When dress functions as a medium of communication, Roach-Higgins and Eicher emphasize the use of dress to communicate information about the self. They define self as a 'composite of an individual's identities communicated by dress, bodily aspects of appearance, and discourse, as well as the material and social objects that contribute meaning to situations for social interaction' (Roach-Higgins & Eicher, 1992, p. 2). An individual can have a number of identities that comprise the self. Dress can be manipulated to communicate information about the self to a general audience or to a select few. Unfortunately, in the case of rape survivors, a myth exists that they manipulate their dress intentionally to communicate a specific message (e.g., they are interested in sexual intercourse). This myth may function to bias people in favor of the perpetrator and against the survivor.

One piece of information that can be communicated by or associated with dress is social power. Social power, as used in this chapter, refers to the influence that someone or something has that results in some form of change (e.g., opinion, behavior, goals, needs, values) in another person (French & Raven, 1959). Six primary bases of social power have been identified: reward, coercive, legitimate, referent, expert, and information (Raven, 1992). These categories are not mutually exclusive and an individual's social power can stem from many sources. However, using these categories allows us to talk about power with respect to dress. Three of these bases of social power – reward, coercive, and information power – are particularly relevant in our discussion of rape and dress.

People who have reward power have the ability to grant honors and awards or grant personal approval of another. Dress may be imbued with reward power if you believe that wearing a certain object (e.g., amulet, charm) will bring you good luck, or prevent bad things from happening to you. People who have coercive power have the ability to decide punishments and can threaten rejection or social disapproval. The business suit of an executive might announce coercive power to an employee because the executive can fire employees. The power of information is based on the knowledge or logical argument that the influencing agent can present. As compared to other sources of power, the changed behavior as a result of information is maintained without dependence on the influencing agent. Fashion consultants or advice columnists who provide advice on which clothing styles are appropriate for specific social settings may have information power.

In this chapter we present the results of an investigation of the functions of dress within a context of coercive power (e.g., rape) in the United States. According to the Department of Justice, rape is defined as carnal knowledge[2] or attempts at carnal knowledge through the use of force or the threat of force (Harlow, 1991). According to the National Crime Victimization Survey,[3] each year, during 1992 and 1993, there were half a million sex crimes committed against women in the United States. These included 310,000 rapes or attempted rapes and 186,000 other sex crimes (Schafran, 1995).

Brownmiller (1975) posits that rape is an expression of social power that has little to do with sexual urges. She contends that rape is nothing more than a conscious process of intimidation, a type of coercive power, by which all men keep all women in a state of fear. This position is amplified by Kennedy (1992) who notes that sexual abuse is 'disciplinary' in the sense that it 'functions to enforce patriarchal social norms' (p. 1311). To maintain the belief that a woman's dress spurs otherwise decent men to rape is to further empower men and disenfranchise women.

How widespread is the belief that a woman's dress invites, provokes, or serves as implied consent to sex? A U.S. survey reported in *USA Today* revealed that nearly a third of those who responded believe the dress or behavior of a person who is raped can contribute to attacks (Snead, 1990). A subsequent survey of 500 adults revealed that 28 per cent of 18–34 year olds, 31 per cent of 35–49 year olds, and 53 per cent of individuals aged 50 and over agreed with the statement that a woman who is raped is partly to blame if she dresses provocatively (Gibbs, 1991). Statements such as: 'She asked for it. She was advertising for sex. We felt she was up to no good [by] the way she was dressed' ("Jury: Woman in Rape", 1989, p. A20) reflect this viewpoint. Rapists claim women use clothing to communicate their availability for sex (Feild, 1978; Schram, 1978; Scully & Marolla, 1984). The U.S. legal system also supports the belief that a woman's clothing may signal consent to sexual intercourse because in most states clothing is allowed as evidence of consent and consent to sex is a primary defense against charges of rape (Lennon, Lennon, & Johnson, 1993).

Researchers interested in understanding the relationships between women's dress and their victimization have found that people, primarily people who have never been raped, think a woman's clothing plays a role in her assault (Cahoon & Edmonds, 1989; Edmonds & Cahoon, 1986; Feild, 1978; Feldman-Summers & Palmer, 1980; Mazelan, 1980; Muehlenhard & MacNaughton, 1988; "Rape Victim", 1988; Terry, 1981; Terry & Doerge, 1979; Vali & Rizzo, 1991). These researchers, who utilized various subject populations, consistently demonstrate that many people *believe* women who wear body-revealing clothing are more likely to be sexually violated than women who wear non-revealing clothing. In addition, people are willing to blame victims of sexual violence for their assaults because of their clothing (Alexander, 1980; Cahoon & Edmonds, 1989; Edmonds & Cahoon, 1986; Kanekar & Kolsawalla, 1981; Lewis & Johnson, 1989). In these studies, participants were asked to indicate the responsibility of a hypothetical victim of sexual violence. When the woman was described or depicted as wearing body-revealing clothing, she was consistently rated as more responsible for her rape than when she was described or depicted as wearing non-revealing clothing. It is not surprising, with these findings, that defense lawyers would want to introduce into evidence the rape survivor's clothing if it was body revealing.

Accepting the belief that a woman's clothing contributes to whether or not she is sexually assaulted leads to the conclusion that women who do not want to put themselves at risk for sexual violence, should not wear clothing that is body revealing. However, there is no clear evidence that women who wear body-revealing clothing are at any higher risk for rape than any other woman. In fact, Richards' (1991) theoretical analysis suggests that women who wear body-concealing clothing may be more at risk than women who wear body-revealing clothing.

Rape survivors, whether or not they accept the myth that dress was one of the contributing factors to their experience, may subsequently change their appearances for several reasons. They may change in an attempt to prevent similar incidents from occurring in the future or to shield themselves from the inferences and assumptions drawn about women who wear body-revealing dress. They may manipulate their appearances in an attempt to protect themselves. Evidence that people believe clothing can be used as a form of protection is found in advice given to female travelers. For example, in order to avoid harassment or injury, women readers of *Traveler Magazine* in 1993 were advised to keep a low profile, to avoid showy jewelry, to avoid behavior that draws unwanted attention, and to dress discreetly.

## Clothing and the Courts

To prove a charge of rape, the prosecutor must demonstrate that the defendant engaged in sexual intercourse without consent (Black's Law Dictionary, 1990). To win acquittal for the defendant, the jury or judge must believe that the person charging rape consented. In their discussion of clothing and consent to sexual intercourse, Lennon, Lennon, and Johnson (1993) pointed out in court cases, clothing has been used for the purpose of documenting consent.[4] In addition, newspaper accounts report cases in which the survivor's clothing appeared to play a significant role in the outcome of the case although the clothing was not always introduced as evidence of consent. In a 1977 Wisconsin rape case, a 15-year-old defendant was given a probated sentence for raping a 16-year-old girl. The judge voiced the following rationale:

I'm trying to say to women stop teasing. There should be a restoration of modesty in dress and elimination from the community of sexual-gratification businesses. Whether women like it or not, they are sex objects. Are we supposed to take an impressionable person 15 or 16 years of age and punish that person severely because they react to it normally ("Rape and Culture", 1977, p. 41).

In addition, jurors in a rape case in Florida noted the survivor's clothing when they acquitted a man accused of kidnapping and raping her. The outfit she wore at the time of the rape consisted of a short, white lace skirt, a brief top, a leather belt, and no underwear. One juror commented that the outfit was an important factor. Apparently the defense held that the complainant was a prostitute and the jurors were convinced that she was, in part, by her clothing. The defendant was later convicted of kidnapping and raping a Georgia woman ("Jury: Woman in Rape", 1989).

In William Kennedy Smith's rape trial, defense attorneys indicated that the lack of damage to the victim's bra was a critical piece of evidence (Pesce, 1991). The pictures of the bra that were used as evidence clearly showed the Victoria's Secret label. In an unsuccessful attempt to stop the introduction of the bra into evidence, the prosecutor argued that the bra might suggest to jurors that someone who wears Victoria's Secret underwear could not possibly be a victim of rape but rather was a willing participant in consensual sex.

To date there are five states, Georgia, Alabama, Florida, New York, and Louisiana,[5] that have statutes that address the admissibility of clothing as evidence in rape trials. The statutes of Georgia and Alabama follow the criterion that evidence of a person's dress cannot be admitted at trial unless it supports an inference that the accused could have reasonably believed that the complaining witness consented to the conduct (Ala. Code 12-21-203 (a)(3) 1991; Ga Code Ann. 24-2-3 (a)(b), 1992). The Florida statute specifies that 'evidence presented for the purpose of showing that manner of dress of the victim at the time of the offense incited the sexual battery shall not be admitted' in a rape prosecution (Fla. Stat. Ann 794.022 (3)1992). The New York statute does not allow any evidence of the manner in which the victim was dressed into a rape trial unless such evidence is deemed by the judge to be relevant and admissible (N.Y. Crim. Pro. Sec. 60.48, 1994). Louisiana does not permit the admission of dress as evidence if it is used to show that a person encouraged or consented to the offense (La Code of Evid. Art. 412.1 1996). Thus, Georgia, Alabama, New York, and Florida even with their statutes still permit (albeit under specific circumstances) the introduction of clothing to demonstrate there was consent to sexual intercourse.

The courts – and perhaps the general public – may view dress as nonverbal consent to sexual intercourse. People clearly implicate dress as a contributing factor in sexual assaults, implying dress indicates consent. Numerous researchers have documented the nonverbal communication process that can occur via dress by investigating the types of information and inferences perceivers make about real and hypothetical survivors of rape. In this way the view of the perceiver in the communication process has been privileged. However, researchers have not studied the types of information survivors of rape actually *encoded* in their clothing. We do not know whether rape survivors intentionally wore clothing or manipulated other aspects of their appearance to communicate their consent to sexual intercourse. Therefore, in this research project, we determine the functions of dress from the perspective of women who have survived rape. Specifically, we explore and analyze whether these women thought that their clothing or other aspects of their appearance might be used to communicate consent to sexual intercourse and whether, after having been raped, their use of clothing changed.

## Method

Participants were solicited through an advertisement placed in local newspapers. The advertisement indicated that we were interested in interviewing women who had been raped, that each participant must have sought counseling prior to the interview, that they would be paid for the interview, and that their names would not be associated with their responses. Forty-one female adults answered the ad and volunteered for a one-time interview composed of open-ended questions.

The participants' ages at the time of the interviews ranged from 20 to 60 years old, with the average age of 33.9. The participants' reported ages at the time of their rapes ranged from 5 to 39 years. Most of them were Caucasian (87 per cent) but there were also African Americans (5 per cent), and Native Americans (5 per cent). One participant did not provide her ethnicity. The highest percentage of participants had completed a bachelor's degree (49 per cent), the next highest had some college (23 per cent), the next were high school graduates (15 per cent), and the lowest percentage had a graduate degree (13 per cent).

This research represents sixty-seven incidents of rape. Twenty-five of these incidents happened before the survivor was eighteen. While the majority of participants had been raped once (54 per cent), eight reported they had been raped twice, two said they had been raped three different times, one indicated she had been raped five times, and one indicated seven rapes. Five women indicated the same man had raped them at different times. However, the participants did not discuss each of these incidents. These rapes were committed by men in the following relationships to their victims: acquaintance (45 per cent), stranger (37 per cent), someone they had just met (12 per cent), or a family member (6 per cent). Rapes by a family member occurred when the survivor was a child. Several of the rapes occurred while couples were on dates (28.4 per cent).

To explore rape survivors' opinions concerning the functions of dress, we asked them the following questions: How do people consent to engage in sexual intercourse? Do people use any aspect of their appearance to consent to sexual intercourse? If yes, what aspects do you believe people use? If no, why not? Do you believe that people use clothing to consent to sexual intercourse? Why or why not? Describe your appearance when you were raped. Was this appearance similar or different from your normal appearance? Did you purposefully change your appearance after you were raped? If yes, what aspects did you change? Why did you change? Participants' interviews were tape-recorded and transcribed. We were unable to transcribe two interviews due to the quality of the recordings, therefore, the final data set consisted of thirty-nine interviews.

After transcription, we read each of the interviews as a whole several times. We analyzed the interviews to identify the major themes and concepts that occurred in participants' responses to each of the questions. Because the questions were open-ended and the participants were asked if they wanted to add anything, it was possible for them to make comments about a topic at a time other than when a specific question was asked. These responses were noted. In addition, a number of topics emerged that were not directly related to specific questions. Major concepts and pertinent information were identified by a selective approach in which we underlined and noted essential phrases (van Manen, 1990) in the transcribed text.

We used Q.S.R. NUD.IST Software for Qualitative Data Analysis (1995) to sort and code the interviews. The participants' responses were arranged into sections by question number. Additional, out of sequence, responses that had been identified were added to those in the appropriate section. All responses to a specific question could then be examined together. Our knowledge of the interviews was helpful in keeping the responses in context and in locating relevant information. For each question, we attached codes to the data to group together the information referring to the same concepts. The concepts were used as categories (e.g., their dress when they were raped was categorized by garment as jeans/dress/nightgown). If a concept emerged repeatedly, it was identified as a theme. After the first coding, some concepts were recoded into broader themes (e.g., the clothing was recategorized as jeans/work clothes/sleep wear).

Coding reliability was established by having two of the researchers read the same set of responses to each question. Inconsistent codings were negotiated until agreement was reached and adjustments were made to categories and themes.

## Findings

In the subsequent paragraphs, we include responses to the questions asked of each participant in the order they were asked. The quotations incorporated into the text were selected to provide the reader with the range of responses, as well as to reflect major themes and concepts, both of which emerged in our analysis and interpretation of the interviews.

1  *How do people consent to engage in sexual intercourse?*
Many participants were challenged by this question. Some were bewildered and expressed uncertainty as to how to respond. However, no one generated the idea that clothing was ever used to indicate consent to sexual intercourse. Three of the participants stated that they did not know how people consented to engage in sexual intercourse.

> I think it's different for different people and that's what makes it an uncertain, precarious, big thing. I can't answer that.

Some participants suggested that one might never really know whether someone's consent was given, but one would definitely know if consent was *not* given. Numerous respondents noted that consent would be given verbally, would be mutual, and that there was confusion on the issue of communicating consent versus communicating interest in someone. Many participants indicated that people *had to be verbal* and say yes in order to indicate their consent. Some also noted various nonverbal aspects to saying 'yes.'

> How do they consent? Well. With words. They talk around the subject. They both participate in foreplay. That's consenting.

> If it's consensus, two people have to be very attracted to each other and have to ask each other if they want to. It has to be totally open and honest in every aspect. Whereas, he asked me, actually he told me, and I said 'no' and he didn't care.

Participants suggested that consent was given through active and passive actions. Those who noted that consent was active cooperation talked about the existence of a set of behaviors, almost like a ritual, that are a part of culture, and that a person consents to sexual intercourse by going through certain steps with both verbal and nonverbal aspects. Some participants noted that consent could be given passively because you were going along with it, being passive about the entire process of intimacy, or because of a series of things that you were *not* doing. It was clear from many of these responses that these women accepted the commonly held belief that it was a woman's responsibility to make the final decision concerning sexual intercourse.

> I have no idea. It would usually come from making out. .... I think it's partially true that it's the female who decides, whether this is a yes or not, because the guy is certainly never going to say no.

> By not saying, 'this is making me uncomfortable,' by not giving out the verbal signals, or pushing somebody back or directly blocking. By being responsive, ... not saying 'wait a minute', not stepping back. I think that is as good as consenting or encouraging in my estimation.

A few of the participants suggested circumstances under which there was no consent. Their responses reflected a combination of verbal and nonverbal details, but key to their descriptions was saying no.

> Well more than words. If there's a pulling away, if there's a 'no,' ... I mean if a woman's saying: 'No, don't do this to me, don't,' that's non-consenting.

2   *Do you believe that people use clothing to consent to sexual intercourse?* Participants overwhelmingly said no to this question. There were several explanations for why clothing did not indicate consent. Participants questioned the idea that clothing could always reliably predict someone's future behaviors and whether it could communicate a specific sexual behavior. Several participants reiterated that consent was something given verbally. They reasoned since clothing could not talk, it could not possibly provide consent.

> It has nothing to do with it. Clothing has to do with your own person, not about your interactions with others. It can show people what you wish them to think about you, but it doesn't specify what type of behavior you wish to engage in with other people.

> Not really. It has to be verbal . . . I just cannot buy that . . . what anyone is wearing is going to instigate someone to do what . . . that guy did to me.

> No. Why not? Unless it actually has a sign on the dress, or something that says: 'Give me a good lay' or something. I'm saying that with as much sarcasm as I can because this is really, it gets me. Clothes can't talk.

Participants acknowledged that clothing is used to be sexually attractive, but that trying to be sexually attractive was not the same as communicating your consent to sexual intercourse. Their responses indicated that clothing was a medium that addressed a general audience. How then, could consent to sexual intercourse, which is a very specific communication, given on an individual basis, be transmitted using a medium that was intended to address a general audience?

> I think it can be . . . a sign they may be interested in having sexual intercourse. If I'm dressed provocatively, that does not mean that if you ask, if you decide you want to have sex with me; I'm going to have sex with you no matter what. I don't think it's a fair assumption to say just because I'm dressed provocatively or sexually I want to have sexual intercourse with every person I see.

> Thinking about that, it's like that sort of means consent to sex with anybody, at anytime, anywhere and that's just ridiculous. If clothing was consent, the logical assumptions would be that the decision to have sex was made when the woman got dressed and she can't change her mind.

> From my experience, most of the women that wear a lot of makeup, wear really tight clothes, wear a lot of jewelry, the kind that guys typically think of as easy, I think they don't feel good about themselves and this is a way for them to feel better about themselves and to make others attracted to them. . . . They just want to attract people to them and they think that's the only way they can do it. And I think wanting to attract somebody and wanting to have sex with somebody are different things.

One participant noted that for her, clothing could never mean consent because she used clothing as a layer of protection.

> Because, for me clothing has always been the first line of defense. It's protected people from knowing who I am and my pain. So I wouldn't take my first line of defense and strip it away like that.

Several participants simply noted there is no relationship between clothing and consent. The idea that one had anything to do with other was ridiculous. One participant noted that if such a relationship really existed between specific items of dress and consent to sexual intercourse, then clothing should be sold with warning labels attached. Another noted that women were more likely to be following fashion than consenting to sex with their appearance. In addition, one participant noted that clothing does not mean consent to sex because rape is not about sex, it's about power.

> I think people want to be sexually attractive but that's not consent to sexual intercourse. And I think fashion changes, you know. . . . I see in *Vogue* these thigh-high socks that used to be on hookers, that they're suggested for office dress. I

don't think the designers or people wearing them are saying these are consent to sexual intercourse.

I think men will see a woman in a miniskirt . . . and assume because she is wearing . . . a short skirt that means she wants to have sex. . . . You can't make the leap from wanting to look appealing to saying: 'Here I am, have sex with me.' That's too big of a leap to make in terms of someone's clothing.

Participants indicated that clothing is not consent because, if dressing provocatively meant 'yes' to sex, then dressing the opposite should mean 'no,' but it does not. They also suggested that sexy clothing should mean the same for both genders but because it does not, the idea of clothing meaning consent is gender discrimination.

I do remember dressing once for a guy I did not want to be intimate with. . . . It didn't work. So even if you are going to dress against it, it is still no guarantee it's going to work. If the guy wants to have sex with you, it doesn't matter what you have on.

Because what you wear shouldn't make a difference. . . . If a guy is in tight shorts, is he asking for it too?

3   *Do people use any aspect of their appearance to consent to sexual intercourse?*
When asked about appearance, participants' responses centered on clothing to the exclusion of other visual aspects. The overwhelming response to this question was no, appearance is not a method used to communicate consent either real or implied. There were several different reasons provided concerning why appearance could not be used to communicate consent. Key to several of these explanations was the idea that the meaning of appearance varies from person to person; that is, one appearance could mean something to one person and something different to another, regardless of what the wearer intended.

Appearances can't talk . . . because you may have your hair down, that doesn't mean you want to have sex, because you may have eyeshadow on, that doesn't mean you want to have sex, the way you sit and cross your legs, that doesn't mean you want to have sex. . . . There could be one woman in a room of five million different men and they could all get a different idea.

Well you can't really unless you have a shirt on that's saying: 'I want sexual intercourse.' You can't.

Some participants indicated that to say a woman's appearance caused the rape is just a convenient excuse for the perpetrator.

No . . . well because I don't want to buy into the 'she wants [it], you can tell by looking at her' type of thing or 'look at those tight shorts' . . . Men use it a lot as a defense because they know it works. . . . I know that the way I dress or when I choose to dress in a short skirt, I'm not saying: 'I want to get laid so I'm going to wear this short skirt'. . . . I get harassed on the street just as much when I am wearing a pair of blue jeans and a sweatshirt as when I am wearing this . . . which is a short skirt and sweater. . . . So it doesn't matter [at] all what I'm wearing [for] how much I get harassed. All I have to do is be a woman.

Participants questioned why appearance could *ever* be used to assume so much about a person sexually.

I just wonder what happened in a society where we have to ask all these questions in the first place, what happened? What got so out of whack between men and women and communication that just by the way somebody looks, they assume so much about a person . . . sexually. . . . Where did that come from? What generation of fashion? What happens in the minds of these boys [as they are] growing up that tells them somehow that because a woman wears a skirt or doesn't wear a bra, that means she wants to have sex?

Two of the participants' responses suggested that, although their appearance did not communicate their consent, they understood the potential for confusion over the 'meaning' of a woman's appearance. They noted women may want to appear attractive to men but that was separate from being sexually available to them. Some of the participants talked about body language and/or clothing being used to communicate general interest in the opposite sex. They noted that communicating interest in the opposite sex in general was different from being interested in a specific individual.

I dress so I will feel good about myself when I'm having a conversation. I feel confident, I feel attractive, I wear lingerie so I feel good about me. I certainly want my date to think I am attractive.

Although all participants acknowledged that clothing did not signify consent, when pressed for specific details about an appearance that could possibly designate consent, three participants noted they were aware of a 'prostitute image.'

It could be something tight, or it could even be something loose. Loose could be seen as more convenient. A lot of clothes that are supposedly easy to get in and out of could be taken as maybe consent; *Could* [italics added] be, but not *should* [italics added] be. The more made-up look. The more prostitute look – generally. But you should be able to dress and say and do what you want without anything being taken as consent unless you out and out say [yes].

There are some women out there to get it and you look at the hookers on the street; yeah, definitely they are dressed to entice. They are not out there just to meet people and socialize, they are definitely dressed to entice, but I think that is the extreme . . . people who get raped aren't generally dressed like hookers.

One participant reiterated that appearance (like clothing) could not communicate consent because consent was a very distinct message directed at a single individual.

No, because I think consent is a really specific thing. And I think that you, a lawyer, whatever, can make the case that a woman was saying to the world she's interested in relationships where that is a possibility. . . . But I think that's really different from saying: 'I want to do that right now with you.' I mean it's ridiculous to think it's the same thing.

Another participant noted that the meaning of clothing is tied to context, that using clothing to signify sexual interest (not consent) was tied to particular conditions; and those different forms of dress are more or less attractive to different people.

In a close relationship, something long-standing, long-term, I think that sometimes dress does affect –. You know, you get home before your significant other does and you're sitting there in a sexy nightgown, or whatever, that's going to lead the other person to believe that you probably are interested in doing something, but I don't think if there's a woman walking down the street who's dressed in a skin-tight dress, just because she's dressed like that means she wants to have sex with the next guy who comes up and talks to her. It's context-related.

4  *When you were raped, was the appearance you described similar or different from what you normally wore?*
Participants supplied general descriptions of what they were wearing when they were raped for fifty-eight of the sixty-seven rapes represented in this research. Twenty outfits described included jeans. Five rapes occurred when the survivors were in bed or getting ready for bed. Their descriptions reflect what they usually slept in (e.g., t-shirts and underwear, a nightshirt, a nightgown). Four rapes occurred when the survivors were wearing uniforms or other clothing that they wore to work. There were forty-eight responses to the question of whether the clothing worn when raped was similar to clothing

that was regularly worn. Forty descriptions represented clothing that participants indicated they regularly wore. Seven participants indicated their clothing was not 'regular' because they had dressed up for a date. Three of those indicated that their goal in dressing up was to be attractive. One indicated she had dressed specifically to attract attention. None indicated they dressed to consent to sexual intercourse. Thus, most of the women in the study were raped while wearing clothing they wore routinely. Several indicated they had worn the very same clothing other times without similar results. Even those who indicated that they were 'dressed up' were not wearing something extraordinary.

Some participants expressed self-blame for their rapes, often blaming behaviors such as drinking alcohol. Six participants included aspects of their dress as a reason to feel blame. One participant *still* blamed herself for what she wore.

> I don't think that the way I was dressed had any trigger effect, because he was so used to seeing me. He'd probably seen those clothes plenty of times.

> It was like dressing to go to church. You wore your nicest thing. And it was also not revealing.

## 5 *Did you purposely change your appearance after you were raped?*

Twenty-three participants reported that they did change their appearance after they had been raped and sixteen said they did not. Of the sixteen who said no, four of them, in responses to other questions, revealed they did, in fact, make a change. For example, when we asked the survivors to recall their appearance when they were raped, participants talked about how they had been raped while wearing a specific type of clothing or while wearing a particular color. They frequently followed with a comment such as: 'I don't wear T-shirts any more,' or 'I still don't wear the color green.' Therefore, we concluded that 69 per cent of all of the participants altered some aspect of their appearance after they had been raped. Of those participants who had been raped more than once, 72 per cent indicated they changed their appearance, whereas 62 per cent of those who had been raped once changed their appearance. Of the participants who indicated they had made a change, the majority acknowledged the change was permanent, while three said they were in the process of reverting back to how they appeared and dressed prior to the rape. Most participants altered their appearance in more than one way.

6  *Of those survivors who altered their appearance, what aspects did they change?*

In order to present this information we classified changes in appearance made by survivors into four broad categories: body modifications, body attachments, total appearances, and attitudinal. Changes in a body modification included weight gain or loss, and alterations to the body's surface such as cutting or coloring hair. Changes in a body attachment included changing how clothing was worn, changing the colors worn, or eliminating a particular style or a specific garment from the wardrobe. A change to total appearance signified that the participant remade her image from head to toe. A change in attitude reflected participants' raised consciousness of what they wore and how others might relate to it, or no longer dressing to please others.

Reported changes to the body consisted of weight gain and body odor. One participant gained fifty pounds and another woman increased from a size 7 to a size 10. While one woman thought the process of weight gain was unconscious, another said that for several years after the rape, she put on between five and ten pounds per year. When participants talked about body modifications, they talked primarily about changing their hair. They frequently mentioned altering its color or cutting it into a short style. One participant indicated that after the rape she did *not* want to have a hairstyle at all; that she simply let her hair 'go.' Another participant noted a change in her hygiene routine as well, abandoning her regular practice of bathing.

> I gained a bunch of weight. . . . I don't know if that was purposely but it might have been. . . . I just never wanted to be overpowered like that again.

> I cut off all my hair because I felt like that was a way that nobody could recognize me. . . . And also because people always focused on that. . . . People were always making comments about my hair. I hated it. I cut it off.

> At the time I had very long hair, and probably within three weeks, a month, I started slowly cutting my hair. . . . I didn't wash it very often, I mean, I wore a lot of perfume. I remember my mother yelling at me to go take a bath and I can't cover up my smell with perfume.

Changes in body attachments reported by participants consisted of clothing style, fit, color, accessories, and makeup. Changes in style included always wearing one type of clothing, (e.g., always wearing slacks), adopting new clothing (e.g., wearing a bra), or discontinuing a specific style (e.g., no longer wearing a bra). Changes in fit involved wearing loose clothing or clothing that covered the body. Several individuals talked about always wearing baggy clothing after they had been raped.

After this first happened, I wore sweat pants and baggy T-shirts and I didn't do my hair and I didn't do my makeup and I didn't go anywhere for about two years. I would say just this summer is when I started actually to socialize again. I do wear my hair in ponytails with the little ribbon things around my ponytails. I wear earrings faithfully now. I do put my makeup on now again. But I still wear extremely baggy clothes. Baggy shorts, baggy T-shirts, or baggy jeans and a baggy shirt. Everything totally baggy. I dress cutesy now like 'little kid' cutesy instead of like a 25-year-old woman should dress.

Before I was wearing really short, not tacky type things, but short and some slinky things. And afterwards, no way. . . . I wore skirts that came down to my ankles. Even then I wore tights underneath. I didn't want anybody to think I was asking for anything.

Changes in color included no longer wearing a specific color, switching to wearing exclusively one color, or wearing very bright colors. Changes in accessories meant wearing fewer accessories or wearing eyeglasses instead of contact lenses. Changes in makeup consisted of wearing less makeup or none at all.

The color of clothes – they were all black and dark – and it was summer – and I never wear black. Before that I had very little black in my wardrobe. After – that was all I looked at. After – it was very loose – hidden. Very non-revealing for a long time.

I started working out, figured I might as well dye my hair bright red, starting wearing really bright colors. And it's almost like I courted. . . . It was like, 'I dare you. I dare you.'

Changes in participants' total appearances involved altering an entire image (i.e., body and dress), rather than just a few aspects. Participants noted that they altered their overall appearance, resulting in a dressier, conservative image, or in a sloppy appearance. Many of the alterations they discussed were subtle, while some participants spoke of creating a new image for themselves.

Clothes I wear to the movies, the frumpiness I talk about, my hairstyle, and my lack of appreciation for keeping my hair neat, I think that has a lot to do with my lack of self-esteem from those experiences I've had.

I thought guys like to see girls dressed pretty, and I thought at parties – that's what parties were for. I thought of it more as a dress-up costume thing rather than looking sexy or anything like that. But after, I guess I did start to dress a little more conservative. After, when I'd go to parties – I don't wear silver dresses and silver shoes and all that kind of stuff. I just wear something, you know, simple.

The last category reflects participants' changes in attitude from being unaware of potential reactions to their appearance to becoming conscious of what they wore, and from pleasing others with what they wore to no longer dressing to please others.

I think maybe I'm more conscious as to how things fit, but I don't think it was something I purposely changed. I think I'm just more conscious of the way I dress, the way I'm presenting myself to other people; I'm more conscious of that, but it's not something I've changed. It's just a reaction, the way my mind works, to what happened.

As a result of the experience, my thinking patterns changed; my whole personality basically. I matured a lot. I basically . . . became more myself in dress. I used to try to look nice or cute or whatever . . . and after this I decided I was going to be who I am. I wear jeans and a t-shirt all the time.

7 *What reasons did rape survivors give for changing their appearance?*
The survivors who changed any aspect of their appearance emphasized self-protection. They also acknowledged the communicative power of dress. Participants who dress for self-protection talked about trying to protect themselves from future rapes and to protect themselves from the comments of others. Those that acknowledged the communication function of dress noted they wanted to present an image that was not sexy or attractive. Several participants indicated they changed their appearance after they were raped because they no longer wanted to be noticed. They spoke about wanting to be invisible, trying not to call attention to themselves, and putting on a mask. Others spoke of attempting to appear asexual, which was typically linked with not looking female, in order to protect them from unwanted sexual attention.

When I walk out the door, I have to make sure I am not wearing anything revealing at all because if I walk down the street, I'm going to get hassled by everybody anyway. . . . I have to dress according to what I feel is asexual so that no one will say anything.

I think after that incident I kind of fell back into wearing slacks. . . . I don't feel attractive when I wear slacks and so maybe others aren't going to see you that way either 'cause it's that factor that seems to be what people are always bringing up when they want you to do you know what: 'You look so good.'

If I had to walk outside, I would wear a coat . . . be aware so I wouldn't get hassled, I didn't want anyone to notice.

Some comments indicated participants changed their appearance because they wanted to present a different image. One woman made a conscious attempt to remake herself into a powerful being so others would perceive her differently than they did before the rape.

I felt and have since called her, this thing in myself, the Amazon woman. She is strong, beautiful, with long red hair . . . a sexual powerful woman who squashes men. . . . So I sort of became obsessed with looking like that.

## Implications

As we stated at the outset of this chapter, one of the primary functions of dress is as a means of nonverbal communication (Roach-Higgins & Eicher, 1992). Clothing and other specific aspects of appearance have the potential to communicate valuable information about the wearer. Participants did note that clothing could be used to communicate a general interest in the opposite sex. However, these rape survivors were unanimous in their conviction that appearance cannot, should not, and does not communicate *consent* to sexual intercourse. Consent is something that can be granted or taken away at the very last moment prior to sexual intercourse and therefore cannot be embodied in an action or a decision concerning dress that was made earlier in time. In addition, if appearance or dress could be used to communicate consent, there would need to be significant consensus in a society about what aspects of dress and appearance constitute consent.

Communication is a two-way process through which information *encoded by the sender* needs to match information *decoded by the perceiver*. It is highly improbable that a society could reach consensus about which forms of dress or what appearance would incontrovertibly mean that one is consenting to sexual intercourse. The styles and practices that comprise dress are themselves continually changing. Although dress is a form of communication, the meanings tied to dress are continually negotiated and renegotiated. They vary dramatically from culture to culture, context to context, and person to person.

According to participants in this study, consent to engage in sexual intercourse is – at best – nebulous issue. Many participants believed consent must be verbalized before acted upon. If either party becomes unwilling to progress at any point in the interaction, consent has been withdrawn and neither party has the right to proceed to sexual intercourse. It is only through words, actions agreeable to both parties and voluntary participation that mutual consent to sexual intercourse occurs, not through dress.

Participants commented about what they thought a woman's dress could communicate: that you feel good about yourself, confident, attractive, and that you are fashion conscious. These are messages of a general nature intended for diverse audiences, not messages sent to specific individuals. However, are there circumstances where women clothe themselves to communicate to a specific man that they are consenting to sex? None of the participants in this research shared that view when they decided how they were going to appear prior to their rapes, their dress was selected to indicate their interest in sex, let alone, their consent to sex. A few participants, when pressed for specific details about an appearance that could possibly designate consent, noted they were aware of a 'prostitute image.' Still in their conversations they did not suggest that prostitutes through their appearance were *consenting* to sex to all that viewed them.

Participants indicated that women might want to use dress to communicate interest in others, to encourage attention from others, or to show interest in a relationship that may lead to sex. However, a vast difference exists between a woman who looks sexually attractive and a woman creating an appearance that communicates consent to sex to anyone, at any time, in any location. The latter type of appearance does not exist. No one – regardless of how sexually promiscuous she or he may be – is sexually available to all people at all times; none of us is willing to relinquish personal freedom of choice in such matters. The defense against rape that women ask for 'it' (i.e., to engage in sexual intercourse) because their appearance nonverbally conveys this message to men, has been used successfully by some lawyers to acquit some men accused of rape. If women ask for 'it,' then it is not a rape. This defense is merely an excuse, which allows rapists to avoid responsibility for their behavior.

Despite the fact that these survivors of rape fervently believed their dress was not *consent* to sexual intercourse, a majority altered significant aspects of their dress in the days and years following their experience. If participants believed there was little relationship between the clothing worn and their experience of rape, why did they change their appearance? When queried about reasons for the changes, participants' responses indicated changes were made for protection. Survivors noted that they did not want to be reminded of the incident. Their changes in appearance may also have been their futile attempt to try to do *something* to gain back a sense of control over what happened to them. Even knowing rationally that there is nothing they could have done concerning their appearance to prevent their rape, participants may have believed that if they do not wear those clothes it will not happen again. They gave clothing, in a sense, reward power. It may also be that they changed their appearance due to informational power or persuasion. The myth that clothing invites rape is pervasive in the United States. Participants, then, may have altered their dress due to their understanding of current modes of thinking perhaps doubting what they know in their experience to be true, that is, rapists rape regardless of appearance.

A major issue with equating changes in dress to protection from rape is the difference between feeling safe and being safe. For several participants to appear less visible, unattractive, or asexual *felt safe*, but none indicated they believed this new practice actually reduced their risk of rape. We concur that changes in dress will not protect women from rape.

Although it is clear that many people *believe* dress plays a role in whether or not a woman is sexually assaulted, there is limited research on what appearance cues rapists use in selecting their victims. Although there is one published study in which a convicted rapist used the victim's body-revealing clothing (e.g., the woman wore tight black clothes without a bra) in defense of his behavior (Scully & Marolla, 1984), there is limited research on the relationships between women's dress and the rapist's motives and choices. Future work could be directed at answering these questions. In addition, educational efforts should be directed at dispelling the myths about the role of women's dress in rape.

## Notes

1. We take this opportunity to express our heartfelt thanks to the forty-one women who volunteered to share their experiences with us. Although it was clearly painful and difficult for the women to relive their experiences of rape during the interviews, their generosity of time and spirit has been sincerely appreciated. This research was supported in part by a Faculty Grant-in-Aid from the University of Minnesota and by Minnesota Agriculture Experiment Station Grant #053-048.

2. Also known as sexual intercourse.

3. The National Crime Victimization Survey is conducted annually and reports the interviews of 100,000 people. It is intended to uncover crimes that are not reported to the police as well as provide additional details of reported crimes.

4. Lennon, Lennon, and Johnson (1993) noted that determining how often clothing is introduced in court cases is nearly impossible since evidence is introduced at the trial court level and transcripts from these courts are not typically accessible.

5. There is also legislation pending in Oregon that addresses the issue. The proposed legislation in Oregon, if passed, would forbid dress as evidence if used to show consent or incitement (Oregon House Bill No. 2349, 1997).

# References

Ala. Code Sec. 12-21-203 (a) (3) (1991).

Alexander, C. (1980). The responsible victim: Nurses' perceptions of victims of rape. *Journal of Health and Social Behavior, 21*, 22–33.

*Black's law dictionary*. (6th ed.). (1990). St. Paul, MN: West Publishing Co.

Brownmiller, S. (1975). *Against our will: Men, women and rape*. New York: Simon and Schuster.

Cahoon, D., & Edmonds, E. (1989). Male-female estimates of opposite-sex first impressions concerning females' clothing styles. *Bulletin of the Psychonomic Society, 27*(3), 280–1.

Edmonds, E., & Cahoon, D. (1986). Attitudes concerning crimes related to clothing worn by female victims. *Bulletin of the Psychonomic Society, 24*(6), 444–6.

Feild, H. S. (1978). Attitudes toward rape: A comparative analysis of police, rapists, crisis counselors, and citizens. *Journal of Personality and Social Psychology, 36*(2), 156–79.

Feldman-Summers, S., & Palmer, G. (1980). Rape as viewed by judges, prosecutors, and police officers. *Criminal Justice and Behavior, 7*, 19–40.

Fla. Stat. Ann. Sec. 794.022 (3) (1992).

French, J. R. P., & Raven, B. (1959). The bases of social power. In D. Cartwright (Ed.), *Studies in social power* (pp. 150–67). Ann Arbor: University of Michigan.

Ga. Code Ann. Sec. 24-2-3 (a) (b) (Michie Supp. 1992)

Gibbs, N. (1991, June 3). When is it rape? *Time*, 48–55.

Gmelch, G. (1978). Baseball magic. *Human Nature, 1*(8), 32–9.

Harlow, C. W. (1991). Female victims of violent crime. Washington, DC: US Department of Justice. Office of Justice Programs. Bureau of Justice Statistics.

Jury: Woman in rape case 'asked for it'. (1989, Oct. 5). *Atlanta Constitution*, p. A20.

Kanekar, S., & Kolsawalla, M. (1981). Factors affecting personality attributed to a rape victim. *The Journal of Social Psychology, 113*, 285–6.

Kennedy, D. (1992). Sexual abuse, sexy dressing, and the eroticization of domination. *New England Law Review, 26*, 1309–93.

La Code Evid. Art. 412.1 (1996).

Lennon, T. L., Lennon, S. J., & Johnson, K. K. P. (1993). Is clothing probative of attitude or intent? Implications for rape and sexual harassment cases. *Law & Inequality: A Journal of Theory and Practice, 11*(2), 391–415.

Lewis, L., & Johnson, K. K. P. (1989). The effect of dress, cosmetics, sex of subject, and causal inference on attribution of victim responsibility. *Clothing and Textiles Research Journal, 8*, 22–29.

Mazelan, P. M. (1980). Stereotypes and perceptions of the victims of rape. *Victimology: An International Journal, 5*(2–4), 121–32.

Muehlenhard, C., & MacNaughton, J. (1988). Women's beliefs about who "lead men on." *Journal of Social and Clinical Psychology, 7*, 65–79.

New York Crim. Pro. Sec. 60.48 (1994)

Oregon House Bill No. 2349 (1997).

Pesce, C. (1991, Oct. 31). Delicate bra is permitted as evidence. *USA Today*, p. 3A.

Q. S. R. NUD.IST (1995). Software for qualitative data analysis (Rev 3) [Computer software]. Melbourne, Australia: Qualitative Solutions & Research Pty Ltd.

Rape and culture: Two judges raise the question of victim's responsibility. (1977, Sept. 12). *Time*, 41.

Rape victim partly at fault, many students say in survey. (1988, July 23). *Dallas Times Herald*, p. 1A.

Raven, B. (1992). A power/interaction model of interpersonal influence: French and Raven thirty years later. *Journal of Social Behavior and Personality, 7*(2), 217–44.

Richards, L. (1991). A theoretical analysis of nonverbal communication and victim selection for sexual assault. *Clothing and Textiles Research Journal, 9*, 55–64.

Roach-Higgins, M. E., & Eicher, J. B. (1992). Dress and identity. *Clothing and Textiles Research Journal, 10*(4), 1–8.

Schafran, L. H. (1995, August 26). Rape is still underreported. *The New York Times*, p. 15.

Schram, D. D. (1978). Rape. In J. R. Champman & M. Gates (Eds), *The victimization of women* (pp. 53–79). Beverly Hills, CA: Sage.

Scully, D., & Marolla, J. (1984). Convicted rapists' vocabulary of motive: Excuses and justification. *Social Problems, 31*(5), 530–44.

Snead, E. (1990, April 19). Do women's clothes invite rape? *USA Today*, p. 6D.

Terry, R. (1981). Contextual similarities in subjective probabilities of rape and other events. *Journal of Social Psychology, 113*, 293–4.

Terry, R., & Doerge, S. (1979). Dress, posture and setting as additive factors in subjective probability of rape. *Perceptual and Motor Skills, 48*, 903–6.

Vali, D., & Rizzo, N. (1991). Apparel as one factor in sex crimes against young females: Professional opinions of U.S. psychiatrists. *International Journal of Offender Therapy and Comparative Criminology, 35*(2), 167–81.

van Manen, M (1990). *Researching lived experience*. New York, NY: State University of New York Press.

# 2

# Dressed to Commune, Dressed to Kill: Changing Police Imagery in England and Wales

## Malcolm Young

'A force that talks like TESCO and dresses like NATO'[1]

(Kohn,1994).

## Structures of Feeling and Symbolic Power

Social anthropology increasingly uses autobiographical data in its reflexive studies (Geertz, 1988; Hobbs & May, 1993; Okely & Calloway, 1992). In this chapter the subjective self is used in a reflexive way as an analytic tool (see Okely, 1975; 1996), taking personal data and field material from a thirty-year police career to interpret how the uniform and bodily image of the police reflects the cultural meanings and symbolic power which the police maintain. Following Bourdieu (1991), I define symbolic power as a system of social knowledge inculcated by a dependent familiarity or habitus and which institutions and organizations such as the police rely on to impose and sustain their position in the order of things.

The analysis also reflects on how technological and managerial change, the amalgamations of police forces, and other socio-political pressures have combined to undermine what Loader (1997, p. 2) describes as the 'prominent place the police currently occupy within the extant English "structures of feeling".' These structures of feeling (Williams, 1976) operate supportively within the wider collective consciousness. Evincing deep emotional commitment, they give an order to the world, helping to sustain an ontological security, which in turn gives rise to an integrated sense of cultural identity.

As such, they inform an inchoate sense of self, which Loader (1997, pp. 3–5) argues the police clearly use. Taking advantage of affinities which exist between police and nation, he suggests the police have long understood how to evoke and deploy various hallowed traditions of British policing, such as those encompassed in the terms, 'the village bobby,' 'citizens in uniform,' and 'policing by consent.'

Despite this apparent success, I suggest policing now demonstrates what amounts to a growing psycho-social malaise. For within its defensive and semi-closed and bounded arenas, there exists a burgeoning sense of what might metaphorically be defined as a 'social schizophrenia,' and in which managers and operatives strive continuously to weld together the paradoxical and conflicting elements of 'force' and 'service' (Stephens & Becker, 1994). What we are witness to is a publicly proclaimed desire at managerial levels for an integrated 'community policing,' based on an interactive police/public consultation which sees shirt-sleeved officers walk and talk to the population across the towns and shires of England and Wales. However, this clearly conflicts with an increasingly militaristic appearance in which bodily symbols of power and control are increasingly presented for the public gaze.

Even as the organization continues to promulgate an ideal form of community policing, which would see officers working closely with the public in a range of activities designed jointly and communally to suppress crime and maintain order (e.g., police/parish meetings, juvenile liaison panels, victim support schemes, local consultative groups, quality assessment evaluations, and the like) (See Fielding, 1995), so this 'soft glove' implementation of shared power and control sits somewhat uncomfortably with the symbols, rituals, and imagery associated with a visible drift towards a militaristic domain.[2] In this alternative world, helicopter surveillance, body armor, an increasing use of firearms by armed response units, riot shields, CS sprays,[3] DNA databases, the introduction of longer, side-handled truncheons, CCTV (close-circuit T.V.) systems, and a drift towards compulsory I.D. cards, all impinge upon the public at every turn (Davies, 1996).

The softer image contained within the pre-existing structures of feeling seems to demand a world in which aspects of service and control can be melded together; and to some extent the police have managed to sustain this as they engage in the production and reproduction of the idea of order and security. This is only possible, however, because of their symbolic power (Bourdieu, 1991), which is inculcated through instruction, habit, and routine (i.e., Bourdieu's 'habitus,' 1977; 1990) to the point that it is largely taken for granted because of a police entitlement and capacity to speak about the world and thus create a range of 'institutional truths.'[4]

A reflexive approach then, to how amalgamations of the various police units and changes in their organizational, social and technological formats have been constructed, reveals how the body of the police has been dressed and presented as a primary cultural reflection of these same underlying changes in police modes of thought, belief, and practice. The discourse thus gives some indication as to how these extant structures of feeling of support for the police could well become diluted and even destroyed.

## The Body as A Medium of Expression

The body and the way it is clothed and presented is a primary medium of expression (Benthall,1976; Benthal & Polhemus, 1975; Foucault, 1977; Goffman, 1971; Hebdidge, 1979; 1988; Polhemus, 1978), for it makes communicative statements on the condition of society itself (Barnes & Eicher, 1992; Blacking, 1977; Douglas, 1973; Mauss, 1935). In the police the body has always been of enormous import. This occurs, as I have written elsewhere, because

> a police world always values uniformity, for as the language infers it embodies the essentials of a system obsessed with physical and ideological concepts of order and discipline. Massively symbolized by the uniform itself, as Douglas (1973, p.16) indicates, this obsession tends to focus on the body, for the 'more value people set on social constraints, the more value they set on symbols of bodily control' (Young, 1991, p. 72).

In this situation the ontological gap between a preferred representation demanded by some socio-political necessity, and an alternative reading of that same reality, can often be observed on the body and the way it is dressed. It is precisely in the disparities in body imagery that the dilemma currently facing the police can be detected, for even as the organization sets out to sustain a presentation which would argue they are a service which works with its public – and thus reassure those who foot the bill – so, at the same time, they are coerced by events beyond their immediate control. For example, this has seen Lincolnshire police (a rural force with a low crime rate) join its larger, urban contemporaries in purchasing and then almost immediately using CS spray at two insignificant public order incidents. These, it can be argued, would previously have been handled without recourse to an imagery of riot control, or use of weaponry of this nature. The resulting media alarm and apology by the Force to those innocents caught up in these events can also be viewed as part of the paradox involved in a move to hard-line, pro-active initiatives which amend the body and the way it is dressed and presented (Maguire & John, 1995). Such events, I suggest, threaten the remnants of a sentimental model of policing that still exists for a large section of the public.

For 20 per cent of the population are older than the author, and thus have deeply instilled recollections of the 'softer' era (described below), which cascade down to imbue those structures of feelings Loader (1997) outlines. Dress and appearance thus becomes a communicator of 'power, agency and experience' (Littlewood, 1997, pp. 7-8), so that as the concept of 'service' comes hard up against the reality of expanding 'force,' this can be observed in the way the body is dressed and presented.

## The Recent Past: The 'Softer' and Ubiquitous Foot Patrol

A police career in England and Wales is generally considered to be of thirty years duration in one particular force area. Officers on some course, for example, almost immediately ask their contemporaries 'What force are you with?' and 'What service have you got in?' For this instantly defines who you are and what your police work entails (i.e., a metropolitan background, a medium-sized town, or a life 'In the Sticks' (Young, 1993). I entered this world when I joined a small city force (Newcastle upon Tyne City Police) in the mid-1950s (see Young, 1979; 1991) at a time when policing might crucially be described as structured 'from the bottom up.' (Figure 2.1) By this I mean the essential form was concerned with the public presentation of foot patrols as a visible deterrent, and was organized around historically defined geographic beats delineated on a map of the city. This primary unit, pursuing historic principles relating to the preservation of public order and the prevention and detection of crime, was supported by a small detective department, a token traffic unit, as well as a handful of other specialists (e.g., Scientific Aides, Courts/Summons officers, and Administration). However, since 1836 when the force had been created, the basic, most visible and essential unit for these tasks had always been the uniformed foot patrol.

Newcastle Police was then one of 150 city, borough, or county forces in England and Wales (Reiner, 1991, p. 4), and was organized on three divisions, with eighteen foot beats in each. Lack of specialization, as well as reduced supervisory or managerial hierarchies to those which followed a spate of amalgamations in the early 1970s made for maximum foot-patrol visibility from the establishment of 678 men and 44 women (Young, 1991; 1992; 1995). Indeed, colloquial nicknames for the police give some indication as to how an extant imagery helped generate those structures of feeling outlined previously. 'Bizzies,' 'Bluebottles,' 'Plods,' or 'Flatfoots' (Partridge, 1972, p. 710) were semi-affectionate terms, which, in their jocular way, suggest the ubiquitous presence of 'bizzy-bodying' flies who plodded and perambulated with collapsed arches. What is crucially important, however, is that the names deny any semantic vision of some powerful enemy who represents an omnipresent threat.

**Figure 2.1.** Map showing the constituent forces which made up Northumbria
Police prior to the amalgamations of 1967, 1969, and 1974.

Between 1958 and 1964 my duties occasionally required me to list 'patrol details', an administrative measure to mark up all beat patrols for the following 28-day period, matching officer to patrol area or beat. A reflexive approach (following Okely 1975; 1996) now suggests just how ubiquitous the visibility of the actual and semantic body of the police was at this time. This omniscient presence, I believe, occurred for the following reasons: (a) an unquestioned 'habitus' meant all beats had to be manned when the public was around. Thus large numbers of men walked the beats across twenty-four hours; and smaller beats in the city center might be covered fifty or more times in an eight-hour shift. In effect, the public saw up to twenty-four men in each division during each eight-hour period, plodding round the beats. (b) Additional 'day patrols' on busy thoroughfares were manned by elderly constables on a permanent foot patrol. Such elder statesmen were often those Reiner (1992b) has recognized as being work-shy 'uniform carriers,' nevertheless they were also a source of police bodies available for scrutiny by the public. (c) Point duty created another visible police presence. The city center then had ten long-service constables at busy crossroads, waving their arms at traffic, or standing on main thoroughfares on what would eventually become pedestrian crossings. (d) Officers mostly traveled to and from work by bus in full uniform, and thus the bodily presence of policemen was again enhanced. (e) Discipline codes created offenses of 'idling your time on duty' or 'being off your beat without authority.' Much supervisory time was spent in trying to catch beat officers in pubs, in 'tea spots,' or other locations affording a brief spell off the beat. Indeed the demand for men to be visible was such that until just before I joined, the refreshment break for a beat officer was split into two twenty-minute periods, to be taken at pre-arranged times in police boxes placed at strategic intersections of two or more beats. The perception that men should be out and about was so central to the order of things that in my beat days, constables would be ordered from the main police station in the city center if they came in two minutes before their 45-minute sandwich break was due. In addition, discipline charges could follow should you be found on the wrong side of a street looking in a shop window at 3:00 a.m., when the beat boundary ran down the other side of that same street (cf. Brogden, 1991). Then again, in this world of the 'Dr. Who' police box, men on eight of the eighteen beats in the city center started and finished on the beat, near the box. I thus spent many consecutive shifts with only the 45-minute sandwich break in the warmth and comfort of the main police station. (f) Finally there were court appearances. Officers were then obliged to attend as witnesses in every case, even when their evidence was unchallenged. With five or six courts operating per day, often with 200 defendants in total, citizens saw streams of uniformed police constables traveling to and from court by bus, further adding to the visible body count described above.

## The Body Communal

Despite this collective police presence, each officer was essentially an island, and largely unconnected to much of what went on around him. It seems possible to suggest this has considerably influenced the extensive 'discretion' about which so much is written in relation to the British police officer. For each officer followed long precedent which held it to be axiomatic that you were without immediate access to advice or assistance. Indeed, we walked the beat simply as we stood, in a good quality serge jacket and trousers, and uniformed cap, presenting an image little changed since the force was founded, when 'the uniform was ... blue with white buttons and white lace [and] [T]he buttons bore the shield of the town arms and the words Newcastle Police' (Newcastle City Police, Commemorative booklet, 1969).

This same commemorative booklet has a photograph taken in 1899, of a constable wearing an identical uniform to the one I was issued sixty years later. However the caption reveals that by 1899 the rattle of earlier days had given way to a police whistle on a chain, while the high hat of 1867 with glazed leather top – which was 'invariably dislodged in a struggle' (Newcastle City Police, 1969, p. 8) – had been supplanted by our highly significant 'guards style peaked cap,' for that standard symbol of the British police – the helmet – was not for us in Newcastle (see Young, 1991, p. 72). Indeed, the helmet was despised, for it stood as a prime symbol of those other adjacent forces which we always used to set ourselves against when we contrasted our own superiority as 'real polices,' against what we saw as their ambiguity and lower social status (see Young, 1991, chap. 3). In this instance, and before political correctness denied such overt discrimination, the Newcastle force required its men to be at least 5' 10" tall, and rarely took anyone under 6' 0." Helmets were, therefore, said to be 'for those dwarfs on the other (south) bank of the River Tyne in Gateshead Borough force,' or for 'the woolly-back sheep-shaggers in Northumberland County police' (Young, 1991, pp. 72–3) to the north. And so, armed with only a 12" wooden truncheon slipped into a special pocket in the uniform trousers, and a pair of snips (a type of handcuff which could be opened without a key, and not only by the officer!), the beat man walked his patch in a manner

> forced on constables by the general practice of solo patrol, punctuated only by brief contact with supervisors at 'fixed points.' The negotiating skills to resolve trivial incidents and minor conflicts were necessary survival techniques. Technical means of assistance were seldom available, so situations, which would today

provoke a heavy response, posing dangers of confrontation, were resolved without help (Fielding, 1995, p. 37).

Elsewhere I have described why this system of negotiated justice and the ways of avoiding such conflict were essential (Young, 1986, pp. 278–9); for the beat box always seemed to be at the other end of the beat to some incident; and to call for assistance thus meant leaving the scene to run perhaps half a mile to phone the divisional station. The result was

> this technological gap helped generate self-reliance and produced a style of policing which required the foot patrol to calm and dispel disorder, and created . . . a certain reluctance to call for assistance. Calls for help suggested you were incapable of resolving local problems, so although . . . arrests . . . were justified, the gratuitous arrest of those who could have been 'talked into going home' was not always looked on favorably. Calls for 'the van' could seriously interfere with the activities of the inspector, the station sergeant, and the shift driver, who might well have a game of dominoes interrupted (Young, 1986, pp. 278–9).

Moreover, each division was furnished with just one van and one saloon car; and each shift had only one officially listed driver, usually a long-service constable who would chauffeur supervising inspectors or sergeants and attend with the van if you rang from a beat box with an arrest. Of course, when you rang he could well be delivering stationery to some section house, and you could wait some time with your prisoner. Thus everything was geared to suggest all was well within society, that known disorder and calamity was contained within acceptable [and manipulated] statistical terms . . . [for] there was little opportunity in such a system for the isolated patrolling officer to present a tough crime-busting image (Young, 1986, p. 279).

Finally, in these days of a self-contained patrolling, even the vaguely militaristic uniform jacket gave way to the softer presentation of 'shirt-sleeve order' in warmer weather; but not before May 1st or after September 30th. Force Orders specified these dates and required everyone to discard the jacket in unison – no discretion was sanctioned. In the circumstances, any crime-busting image was negated by the actuality, for a softer appearance had existed for decades. Those now completing a thirty-year career in the late 1990s can thus be said to have entered this world just as it was vanishing, leaving behind only those deep structures of feeling that the format undoubtedly had helped generate and sustain.

## A Change of Pace

In the late 1960s and early 1970s politically motivated acts generated a wave of amalgamations, and reduced the numbers of forces in England and Wales from 150 to 43. Newcastle Police was joined with eight or nine of its neighbors to form Northumbria Police. This swept away some tightly woven force identities in which a set of thirty-year service officers, all of whom knew each other, had spent a lifetime in one circumscribed and bounded location. Furthermore, this destruction of the idea of a 'sense of place' was allied to other techno-structural changes that would significantly and irrevocably alter the imagery and style of policing.

The first concerned the introduction of a personal radio, so that each beat officer was suddenly in constant and immediate contact with his station, with neighboring patrol officers, with his vehicle support, and with other specialists. A second was generated by the politically driven 'Unit Beat Policing' system. This saw the British police abandon its foot patrol beat system after some 130 years, and move into new beat or panda cars (small, marked patrol cars) intended to replace the foot-patrol function described above. A motorized officer with personal radio could now be dispatched to most incidents, and response times became a crucial factor – and remain a primary measurement of efficiency up to the present time. In essence a section or sub-division would be split into two or three panda-car units, each believed capable of handling a statistical workrate of incidents per eight-hour shift (although no standard number has ever been agreed upon). One immediate impact was to free up numbers of men for specialist departments which concomitantly seemed imperative in the newly amalgamated units. These new forces suddenly needed enhanced drug squads, fraud squads, burglary teams, crime intelligence units, shop-lifting squads, community-affairs and school-liaison teams, collators, crime prevention departments, stolen-vehicle squads, firearms units, driving schools, and the training sections necessary to support these. The numbers of supervisors also soared as management systems burgeoned, so, for example, the rank of Chief Superintendent became a norm, even though it had not existed in any of the constituent forces.[5] Then again, supervisory stages between constable and chief officer expanded, so even though police numbers doubled between the 1960s and the 1990s, to 120,000 officers, the ubiquitous visibility of the officers described above simply vanished.

Moreover, as men now traveled to work in civilian clothing and most now owned a vehicle, it became possible to transfer officers around to pursue a proclaimed policy of integration, and thus break the keenly-felt sense of place they had created for their own territories or 'patch' (Young, 1993, pp. 16–30); and which I believe inhabited and impelled their own structures of feeling. Within a decade it became rare for men to spend a whole shift on foot; for now they wandered in and around the station waiting the next call, as the fixed locations and bounded beat system vanished – along with the semantic ideals which ensured such a system could be sustained.[6]

In 1977 I returned to uniform policing after spending three years at university and the previous decade as a detective in the CID (Criminal Investigation Department) and on Crime Squads (see Young, 1991). The same division I had started in nineteen years earlier now averaged only nine or ten uniformed constables on a normal shift. Moreover, there were no officers on point duty, no elder statesmen cozily patrolling main streets, and no foot-patrol system was in place – though beats were still mapped so that incidents could be classified and located for statistical purposes. This was a moot change that occurred across the length and breadth of Britain. As Tony Judge, a police superintendent, said in commenting on such changes

> I joined in 1963, left to join the Army in '65, and came back and rejoined in 1968, and the world had changed. Before, I walked out on some pretty tough streets [in Manchester] with only me gob[7] for support, and never thought a thing about it . . . Today we've got body armor, the side-handled baton, and CS sprays on the belt (T. Judge, May 1997).

## Public Order and the Politics of Dissent

In 1977, A. C. Germann, writing in the *Police Journal*, described how an ideology of macho power was becoming adulated to the extent it denied the softer world of communal contact. In this situation, he argued, action and ideology seemed destined to lead irrevocably to a nightmare scenario lying just over the horizon, where a legalistic criminal justice system is pursued to its logical and ultimate conclusion; and in which

> the police assume, unilaterally, all decision making authority for social control and apply immediate, massive force in any situation where [they] are not awarded instant deference and obedience . . . the police continue their close affinity with conservative and . . . very right wing movements and philosophies . . . incoming recruits are more intensively screened to eliminate socially sensitive probationers and those who would question traditional procedures and postures. . . . Crime continues to increase in numbers . . . citizens become ever more panicked and angry. The police . . . ask for more manpower, facilities and equipment, and suggest to the public that the 'war on crime' be intensified (pp. 340–7).

This seemed ominously prescient, for in 1979 Mrs Thatcher came to power determined to curb union power. Immediately, and significantly, she increased police pay, then set a political agenda for the next decade and a half which would not only see the gap between rich and poor widen, but would make police imagery synonymous with support for right-wing philosophies. By 1981 there was rioting in Brixton, in London, and in Liverpool, and later in Handsworth in Birmingham, when entire city blocks burned to the ground

(Cowell, Jones & Young, 1982). These urban riots were, as Reiner (1991, p. 167) suggests, without parallel in recent British experience, and caused the police a profound shock.

Lord Scarman's Report (1981) on the Brixton riots criticized the increasing separation of the police from the public, and identified hard-line policing tactics and an excessive response to incidents as a cause of events. And though the report was a 'catalyst for a climate of [police] re-orientation and reform' (Reiner, 1991, p. 166), which saw 'Community Policing' with consultative groups established throughout the country, it also led the police to train and equip extensively to meet the divisive forces which the politics of the moment were generating. Moreover, it saw the government encourage the use of police mutual aid (between individual forces), finance the purchase of protective equipment, and sponsor public-order training (Scraton, 1985, p. 144). The influences of the riots are detailed in Reiner (1991, chap. 8) where chief officers reflect on their difficulties with the problem of public order, and of conflicting and often irreconcilable expectations in society. On the one hand society wishes to see its police act within the law and use a strategy of minimum force (Reiner, 1992a, p. 765), yet, on the other hand, it wants calm and thus encourages the police to immediately and irresistibly stem any dissent and contest.

The Thatcherist pursuit of individualism and wealth, with its denial of the concept of society, saw the police become increasingly embroiled in actions which, at another time, might well have been resolved by some alternative political or civil process, and thus avoided police involvement (such as in demonstrations about the disposal of nuclear waste). Yet despite an alleged growing reluctance of chief police officers to be involved in such overt socio-political matters (Reiner, 1991, pp. 210–19), reaction in these contests has generally been to clamp down and enforce waves of new legislation. This has criminalized public protest, making demonstrations harder to organize – as if Thatcher's allegedly non-existent society was still able to engage with some threatening outside force in huge conspiracies.

In these contests, in which Mrs Thatcher's cry was 'are you one of us?' the tone was set to create an unacceptable vision of 'otherness,' in which the police, as a first line of state response, increasingly appeared in 'hard' enforcement riot gear as 'the militarisation [sic] of policing proceeded apace . . . [and] the traditional unarmed image of the British bobby . . . faded' (Reiner, 1992a, pp. 766–7).

However, it was the twelve-month period of the Miners' Strike of 1984–5 which provided the most graphic example of police and worker conflict, for across this time phalanxes of policemen faced picketing miners; and stretched the niceties of legal correctness by operating road blocks often many hundreds of miles from the mines themselves. Throughout this period, as a result of a massive nationwide operation co-ordinated through a National Reporting Center at Scotland Yard, a de facto national force appeared nightly on TV newsreels, in heavy armor, fighting a working class who were making a last-ditch attempt to prevent the politically engendered demise of their industry (see Fine and Millar, 1985; Green, 1990).[8] As Brake and Hale (1992, p. 68) record, police in riot gear were to be seen ferociously charging pickets, using horses, batons, dogs, and vehicles, and were thus identified as an arm of government determined to break union power. A regrettable partiality of the police in the long conflict is inferred by the ever-circumspect Reiner (1991, pp. 182–92), whose interviews with most of the country's Chief Constables reveal that

> while the official version of events, which denies any central pressure to conform to the national policing operation, was maintained by all the chiefs during the recorded interviews, it is clear that such interventions did occur in fact . . . [and] I was told anecdotes outside the formal recorded interview which confirmed the existence of overt central pressure when voluntarism did not produce the required goods (pp. 190–1).[9]

Reiner goes on to describe how Prime Minister Thatcher wanted a secret Intelligence Unit staffed with Special Branch and CID men to infiltrate and monitor groups which threatened her vision of public order, and how this was agreed to by the chief officers. As this was occurring at much the same time as Cathy Massiter, the civil servant, was blowing the whistle on how MI5 (the arm of the Security Service concerned with internal dissent) was spying on trade unions and others on the political left, we should not be surprised; for during these same years the police were also set against similarly dispossessed groups which had been hit by the results of the dogma of a free-market monetarist political system.

For example, they were clearly arraigned against disenfranchised youth epitomized in that amorphous classification of 'New Age Traveler' (NATs) (Judge, 1994).[10] These NATs were vilified as a 'band of Medieval brigands' by the Home Secretary, then badly beaten up by police in Hampshire at the 1985 'Battle of the Beanfield' (Davies, 1985), and subsequently defined in satanic terms when, in 1992, they arrived for a Bank Holiday rave at 'Castle Morton Common' in Worcester (Judge, 1994). Yet this modern variant of the 1960s hippy or counter culture never remotely threatened society or disturbed its prominent structures. As marginals, however, they experienced the police road blocks perfected during the Miners' Strike, as well as the quasi-legal application of what Judge (p. 36) calls 'the creative use of bail conditions,' when police agreed or denied bail applications to suit. Moreover, they faced the concerted might of those 'Darth Vaders' of modern police imagery. Yet, as Judge clearly shows, the NATs committed little or no crime, and merely came to 'play loud music, drink, dance, take drugs; and then disperse' (pp. 49–65). As I have written elsewhere on this need by the forces of control to name and identify new criminal classes (Young, 1991, p. 259),

> we could easily find police hegemonies using their powers to generate even more disciplined structures than those which exist at the moment. For in an institution whose *raison d'etre* is to exercise power and control, the only truth necessary to its own continuity lies in its chance to expand and demand even more control and more authority (Douglas, 1987, p. 92).

This, I fear, can only lead the criminal justice system to move closer to the Orwellian vision described by Germann (1977), who clearly understood 'there is one peril that requires more than science and technology and concern: [and that is] the peril of excessive social control' (p. 340). This, I believe, can only bring the police into an increasing conflict with those weaker members of society, who they might well be expected to protect.

### Dressed To Kill – Symbolic Power and Institutional Truths

By 1987 I was in the twenty-ninth year of a police career, and almost due to retire. I was therefore somewhat surprised to be nominated for the Intermediate Command Course at the Police Staff College in Hampshire, where thirty-five other Superintendents from various forces gathered for a relatively prestigious ten-week (fifty-day) Home Office-approved course. As was the norm, I asked a colleague who had just been on the course what I might expect. Given that policemen are gossips, I was somewhat surprised when he replied that he could not speak about it. This was intriguing, and I decided to take field notes, not the least because this would be the last covert data I would be able to make about such an occasion. I cannot replicate all the notes here, though the structure of the course and its tutelage came as something of a surprise; and, I suggest, reflects on matters central to this chapter.

The first surprise was to find ex-military officers ran the course. The overall academic director was an ex-lieutenant colonel, and the academic tutor for my syndicate of twelve superintendents was an army captain from what I suspect – but could never prove – was military intelligence, and on 'rest leave' from Northern Ireland. On the first day we were warned not to talk about the course outside the confines of the college, and we then played a tactical war game. Of the following forty-nine days, one was spent at a military establishment enacting a tactical resolution game based on an IRA incident, and another twenty-five days were spent with 270 senior military men (and one woman) playing war games at the Army Staff College. The scenario here was one in which public order was said to have broken down, so that the civil police had to call in the military to restore peace in a MACP game.[11] Entitled 'Early Resolution,' this would see the military would go in hard and fast, and restore tranquillity by force. More than 50 per cent of the course was engaged by this and other war games. Only two days were spent on 'community policing,' and one on public finance and accountability – matters then riding high on the agenda of police management for the rank of superintendent.

I finished the course somewhat perturbed; for the supposed enemy in this ferociously hard-line game of 'Early Resolution' was centered on the students in a make-believe university; and we simply ignored the complex political events allegedly creating the social disorder. To train senior commanders on such a straightforward hard-line basis of control, I believe, was to ignore what John Vidal (1997,G2, p.3) describes as the fact that 'governments have . . . problems. The first is image. For a variety of reasons, police forces have been semi-militarized. Faceless menacing-looking thugs dressed as for war do not compare well in Middle England with cheerful, passionate students.'

The prevalence of this appearance of power is such, that an ideological imagery of being 'dressed to kill' rather than 'dressed to commune' now seems to be lodged within the collective consciousness, and this is being reinforced at every turn. In the six months following initial correspondence on this chapter, I collected a stream of newspaper photographs of police officers in riot gear from only one national broadsheet, noting how each was virtually interchangeable with the next. Only the caption, and an occasional variation in the spelling of the word 'Police' on the riot shield told in which country the incident was situated (e.g., Israel, Albania, Bosnia, France, Britain, Turkey, Italy, South Korea, Columbia, Argentina, the USA, and so on). This new and global cultural anonymity is, I suggest, an important issue. For the walking-talking officer of the 1950s and 1960s was an identifiable and idiosyncratic human being, often known as much for his peculiarities as for his abilities (see Young, 1991; 1995). Today, however, the technocratic warrior-image means the officer himself vanishes, and thus becomes synonymous with an offensive profile, so that he (and the images are always masculine) literally, symbolically and metaphorically presents an appearance and potential for death and destruction.

This vision was exemplified in the *Independent on Sunday* (Gillie, 1991), following riots in Newcastle, when the newspaper graphically illustrated a move from 'Roman Legionary to Robocop.' This new warrior-cop was said

**Figure 2.2.**

to have evolved from a 1981 Brixton model, who, it was regretted, had been relatively unprepared for warfare. By now, however, history had allowed the police to take the Roman legionary of Pons Aelii [Newcastle], AD 101 as its model for defense and attack (Fig. 2.2).

'I studied the half-suits used by the legionaries,' said Mr. Stott (Managing director of ICL Technical Plastics who planned a range of modern body armour [sic]). The Romans knew that the shin and the knee are the most vulnerable parts … the body armour [sic] is worn together with what the police call 'babygro' – a boiler suit made of flame-retardent [sic] material. The armour [sic] itself is made from ABS, a type of light but strong plastic which means that it is much less heavy than the steel used by the conquistadores [sic] and tougher than the hardened leather used by the legionaries. Its efficiency is increased by a backing of shock-absorbent foam … most helmets used by the british [sic] police [use a] shell of glass fiber or ABS plastic. They have features such as a neck curtain and visor reminiscent of ancient armour [sic], but they also have the potential for a major technical advance – the in-helmet radio.[12]

As the article indicates, the warrior/officer with the helmet radio, the lexan polycarbonate shield 250 times stronger than toughened glass, the rubber seals to protect against petrol attack, the steel-capped boots, and the knee and shin guards, is supplemented by a vast range of accouterments. This Robocop image exudes symbolic power (Bourdieu, 1991, p. 170), which

Loader argues (1997) has 'the power of legitimate pronouncement: a power to diagnose, classify, authorize, and represent . . . and have this power of 'legitimate naming' [for the population, by the institution] not just taken seriously, but taken-for-granted' (p. 3). Such legitimization, I would suggest, must be scrutinized and demystified. In the journal *Policing Today* (Young, 1994), I parodied a proposal that patrol officers should also carry a tape deck to record the exact replies of those arrested for some offense. Encumbered with all the paraphernalia listed above, and with night- vision intensifiers, a Heckler and Koch sub-machine gun, and the like, this – my tongue-in-cheek article and cartoon suggested (Fig. 2.3) – was truly an Orwellian domain: but one in which some constable in a reflexive mood might just, for one moment, regret the passing of the days of the whistle and the police box. That others regret this drift to para-militarism is apparent, for when *Police Review* (1997, March 7) carried a cover photo captioned 'Turning the Tide: Fighting Crime on the Thames,' David Pallister pointed out in the *Guardian* newspaper (1997, March 8) that this had been released to the magazine by the police, to 'illustrate an article on the unarmed maritime special operations team' (p. 9). However, he went on to reflect that

> six paramilitary police officers with flak jackets, steel helmets and goggles aiming Heckler and Koch machine guns at the camera, was not the sort of impression that Scotland Yard wanted for its new anti-crime boat unit on the River Thames . . . 'we don't want the public to feel that that is what police officers do everyday,' said a Yard spokeswoman (Pallister, p. 9).

The item also earned the ire of the *London Evening Standard* (1997, March 7) which accused the 'London bobby of harboring SAS (Special Air Service) delusions' ("Marine Blues," 1997). A month later, when the IRA was making a stream of mostly hoax bomb calls in the run-up to the General Election, a Liverpool newspaper front page reported 'Armed Cops on Allerton Road: Crackdown on Terrorist Threat' (Varley, 1997, p. 1), alongside a picture of armoured [sic] officers with 'Heckler and Coch' [sic] sub-machine guns, and carrying side-arms. That such patrols would almost certainly never come in contact with the guerrilla format of an IRA cell seemed not to have occurred to the Merseyside police spokesman, who told the newspaper they were 'cracking down on the terrorist threat.' It had a different response from the public, however, as

> one woman out shopping with her two year old son said 'I was absolutely terrified when I saw them coming towards me with the guns. I wondered what on earth was happening.' Another said: 'I nearly died when I saw them, the officer saw the shock on my face and winked at me (Varley, 1997, p. 1).'

**Figure 2.3.**

Yet, as the police spokesman also commented: 'High visibility policing, including armed officers, is in line with our commitment to public safety and public re-assurance (Varley, 1997, p. 1).' This untested claim of a commitment to public reassurance, is I contend, another 'institutional truth' of the kind the police consistently indulge in (Young, 1991, chap. 5; 1993, chap. 9; 1995a). In these ritual events, statements are made and positions adopted that broach no argument. Thus, for the police they form a striking part of the 'symbolic power' by which they legitimize their actions. No alternative reality is allowed to cloud these representations of events, which often have the enabling strength of institutional history to support a vision of total objectivity. For example, claims of cost-effective operational success for expensive helicopter purchase and deployment is only one area in which these institutional truths cascade around; while the appearance of armed patrols in body armor, or the lauded yet dubious value of multi-million pound CCTV surveillance systems (Davies, 1996; Norris & Armstrong, 1999) could be argued to be mobilizations of similar police symbols. Bourdieu (1991, p. 75) emphasizes there can be no symbolic power without this symbolism of power, and Loader reaffirms this, pointing out that these handcuffs, riot shields, helicopters and so forth 'connect with and re-articulate dispostions [sic] towards, and fantasies of, policing that already pertain within the wider culture (see Sparks, 1992)' (1997, p. 4).

This is a world of effective ritual, which, as Bourdieu argues (1991,126), only preaches to the converted. In recent times the symbolic stance of the organization has been transformed, generating an appearance of being dressed to kill which it might well come to regret. In this situation the pre-existing and deeply imbued structures of feeling which the public appears so keen to maintain may well be threatened; for as Loader cogently warns

> we need . . . to take stock of the stubbornly high levels of support evinced across the social spectrum for more 'bobbies on the beat.' Despite mounting evidence of the limited effectiveness of beat patrolling, the public demand for visible police protection persists unabated (1997, p. 2).

### Conclusion

An appearance of power on our highways and byways increasingly seems to be lodged in the body of a heavily armed and armored Robocop. In this drift to mechanization the police seem to be increasingly trapped by their own institutional truths and an intense symbolic power. This escalates them, taking them away from community contact on a human basis, and into cars, armored vehicles and helicopters; and all the while dressed in a uniform which is so uniform that it is now completely inter-changeable with those worn by other paramilitary units across the world.[13]

Driven by a high-profile divisive political dogma, and the glamour of instant communication and information technology, a standardized image proposed by the Uniform Project Group of the Association of Chief Police Officers (ACPO) (Rose, 1996) is to 'be seen throughout Britain by 1998 [when] Magic T-shirts worn next to the skin will stop a bullet [fired from a .375mm pistol], or a knife (p.6).' At this time, both the old-style helmet and the flat cap will vanish to give way to 'the new round, cycling-style helmet, in polystyrene and plastic, [which] will have a built-in radio microphone and . . . [be able to] resist the force of a base-ball bat (Rose, 1996, p. 6).' (Fig. 2.4). Assistant Chief Constable Hughes of West Yorkshire Police, and leader of this uniform project group, emphasized the new look would 'give the service 'a corporate image', eliminating the existing differences between the forty-three separate forces (Rose, 1996, p. 6).' There is no mention here of any human scale, with some idiosyncratic officer walking and talking with the public. For everything is aimed to generate a single corporate vision, governed by a centralized managerial format, which denies the idea of any heterogeneity in

Early Victorian
Police Uniform .c.1840-50

Mid-Victorian
Uniform of the 1870's

1950's-60's
"bobbies on the beat"

Helmet
Goodbye old Prussian helmet (in service since 1863). Hello cycling style poly-styrene and plastic hard hat, with radio link and eye shield.

'Magic T-Shirt'
The 'covert protective vest' will stop a bullet or knife attack. It is light, flexible and barely visible under a shirt.

Jacket
Out: Hated old-fashioned button-up tunic. In: Fleecy water-proof blousons, as worn by mount-aineers.

Shirt
Gone is the see-through style so despised by WPCs. In comes a new thicker weave.

Belt
Updated utility belt with just handcuffs and the recently issued long-handled baton.

Trousers
No more shivering on the beat. The new trousers have a breathable water-proof membrane.

Boots
New lightweight pair to prevent tripping - leg and ankle injuries cost English & Welsh forces £5.5m in lost work days every year.

Figure 2.4.

its target populations. The growing cultural diversity of British society seems to be ignored by this proposal, and another institutional truth appears about to be created. Yet, as an editorial in the *Guardian* warns

> The most worrying development in policing is its growing militarism. A force, which wants to be known as a service, has become too enamoured [sic] with the trappings of force. Part of this is understandable. Confrontations have become more violent. Heavy armoury [sic] does provide more protection: body armor, fireproof overalls, helmets with visas, bigger shields – longer truncheons. Yet there is a paradox. A more heavily protected force generates less inhibition among protesters ready to throw things. It might even invite missiles. The Dutch police went through a similar cycle in the 1970s. Disarmament was finally seen to be a better way of defusing confrontations. In a pluralist society, policing cannot operate without consent ("Police on the Old Beat," 1996, p. 10).

This paradox, I suggest, is something that might well be reflected upon, for it is exactly because of these heterogenic cultural differences and variable forms that we have created what Reiner (1992b) and others have noted is an exceptional public acceptance of the police in Britain; and this has clearly been sustained by those deeply inculcated structures of feeling which Loader (1997) points us towards. We would destroy it at our peril.

## Notes

1. TESCO, a nationwide British supermarket chain, pursues a policy of customer involvement, which offers rewards for loyalty. NATO is the North Atlantic Treaty Organization, formed for the military defense of the West.

2. See, for example, the typical 1995/96 Annual Report of the South Yorkshire Metropolitan Force. In forty-eight pages it includes fourteen pictures of police officers with children, at schools, at carnivals, and sports events. In contrast, only one image infers force, with a small picture showing two smiling officers armed with machine guns on page 45, alongside a paragraph on the work of the Armed Response Teams.

3. Named after Carson and Stoughton, the chemists who first discovered it's properties in the 1920s, CS gas leaves its victims with an intense burning pain. Particularly sensitive to the eyes and face, other effects of CS include blistering and dermatitis. The introduction of CS spray has polarized many police officers. In a six month pilot scheme in 1996, 3,818 were equipped with canisters, resulting in the gas being discharged 726 times and 585 medical reports submitted with details of those who had been cross-contaminated with the spray (Kliman, 1998, p.8).'

4. Among police activities which seem to generate a stream of these institutional truths and deny alternative readings of events, are (a) Police Establishment Reviews (see Young, 1993); (b) claims for helicopters as a cost-efficient and effective item

(White, 1995); (c) the effective use of informants, which closely follows designated Home Office guidelines (see Dunnighan and Norris, 1996); (d) that computerized Crime Recording systems are efficient and cost effective (see Young, 1993). In this same vein I explored one piece of research on a Mobile Police Canteen (Young, 1995a), describing the creation of a machine costing upwards of £60,000. This was never used, yet was claimed to be a great success. Weatheritt (1986) describes much of the research processes surrounding many of these institutional truths as lying in the realms of 'foregone conclusion research.'

5. By the mid-1990s the rank of chief superintendent was again being dispensed with, with chief constables arguing this would allow them to use the cash savings to appoint more constables for beat work, in accordance with demands of the public. However, as one Superintendent (still serving and thus wishing to remain anonymous) has pointed out in a personal communication (Anonymous, May 1997) 'the rank has gone, yet the constable establishment is lower than it was, and the superintendent rank is now graded to replicate what went before.' The chief constable's pronouncement might thus be seen as another example of an institutional truth.

6. Ex-Commander Keith Hunter (1997, p. 17) reflecting on 'the loss of [an] effective preventive patrol' points out that 75 per cent of all resources were committed to such priorities until the 1960s, when adjustments 'led to the virtual abandonment of those objectives. Today's police managers will consider themselves lucky to have 5 per cent of their resources available for foot patrol.' Across a 30-month operational command in West Mercia Police in the mid-1980s, I noted (Young, 1993, p. 151) we averaged 42 per cent of an 83-uniform constable establishment per 24-hour period. This was on a sub-division covering three medium-sized towns (each with a population of 25,000), just to the south-west of Birmingham city. On night shift (10p.m.–6a.m.) we usually deployed five or six constables in beat-patrol cars and two in a Response vehicle across the three towns. Elected local-authority members asked to estimate patrol strengths in each of the three towns one Thursday night hazarded guesses ranging from 'around seventeen' (for the most southerly of the towns), to 'at least one hundred on foot, plus cars' (for that closest to Birmingham).

7. Gob is an English slang term for mouth with the meaning here being to talk his way out of trouble.

8. During the Miners' Strike, my sub-divisional establishment of Local Beat Officers (the force name for the Resident or Community Beat officer) would go off as part of a Police Support Group to Nottingham, Derby, or elsewhere, for seven days at a time. Having spent months building a public vision which described them as running their own beats in full cooperation with local community leaders, they then spent the best part of a year outside the force, taking full-riot gear with them for activities which, to a large extent, denied community harmony, and were mostly a matter of contest and armed antagonism.

9. The silence of chief constables about the dubious legality of some police activities during the Strike was notable. Cressida Dick, then a young probationary constable, was one of the few insiders to publicly question events (Dick, 1985). A decade later she holds the rank of Superintendent, and might not now be able to be so critical in

view of her inclusion in the realms of hierarchic power. (For a media analysis of Supt. Dick's philosophies, see David Rose, 1998.)

10. New Age Travelers (NATs) are difficult to define. Essentially they are a loosely and occasionally inter-acting group of young, itinerant travelers, who move around – mostly across southern England – in a range of buses, vans, caravans and trucks, in which they live. As the NATs themselves eschew definitions, and many deny main-stream social conventions to follow lives that are only marginally interconnected to the tenets of sedentary society, they cannot be described as a homogenous unit. Some NATs follow new age religions, others pursue alternative economic and environ-mental lifestyles. Occasionally, such as at the time of the summer solstice, groups of NATs will band together at Stonehenge to celebrate; or will come together – as at Castle Morton Common mentioned in the text – to dance, drink and make music at some summer festival which denies any attempt to organize it for a commercial profit motive.

11. Reiner (1991, p. 179) describes the process of Military Aid to the Civil Police (MACP).

12. In 1997, in Scotland, Stott was fined £1000 when his firm was found to have been involved in the illegal exportation of electric stun batons to Middle Eastern regimes. There they had allegedly been used in the torture of political prisoners.

13. The impact of such symbolic power and associated symbols of power was brought home in 1994, when I attended a European Network of Policewomen conference in Brussels, Belgium. There the hosting Gendarmerie set out to convince us they had moved (in the two years since 1992) from a paramilitary format to a community-based policing system. We learned, however, they still held 76,000 assault rifles for a 14,000 establishment; while their barracks was entirely based on the army model, providing a salutary vision with a parade ground filled with rows of mobile water cannon and armored personnel carriers. However, it was the gold metal shoulder flash and lapel badge (replicated on the stationery and envelope franking system) that truly symbolized those structures of feeling which guided this ex-paramilitary unit; for it was explained this ball-like object with flaming comet tail was modeled on an exploding nineteenth century hand grenade. One current recruiting test, we were told, required an applicant to be able to throw the modern equivalent a specified distance – a unisex measurement, which, it seemed, had eliminated most women applicants.

# References

Barnes, R., & Eicher, J. B. (Eds). (1991). *Dress and gender: Making and meaning.* Oxford: Berg Publishers.

Benthall, J. (1976). *The body electric: Patterns of western industrial culture.* London: Thames and Hudson Academic Press.

Benthall, J., & Polhemus T. (1975). *The body as a medium of expression.* London: Allen Lane.

Blacking, J. (Ed.). (1977). *The anthropology of the body.* London: Academic Press Ltd.

Bourdieu, P. (1977). *Outline of a theory of practice.* Cambridge: Cambridge University Press.

Bourdieu, P. (1990). *The logic of practice.* Cambridge: Polity Press.

Bourdieu, P. (1991). *Language and symbolic power.* Cambridge: Polity Press.

Brake, M., & Hale, C. (1992). *Public order and private lives: The politics of law and order.* London: Routledge.

Brogden, M. (1991). *On the mersey beat: Policing Liverpool between the wars.* Oxford: Oxford University Press.

Burke, M. (1997, March 7). Marine blues. *Police Review, 105,* 1, 20–1.

Cowell, D., Jones, T., & Young, G. (Eds). (1982). *Policing the riots.* London: Junction.

Davies, N. (1985. June 9). Inquest on a rural riot. The *Observer,* p. 3.

Davies, S. (1996). *Big brother: Britain's web of surveillance and the new technological order.* London: Pan Books.

Dick, C. (1985, Oct. 18). Implications of the miners' strike. *Police Review, 93,* 2111–13

Douglas, M. (1973). *Natural symbols: Explorations in cosmology.* Harmondsworth: Pelican.

Douglas, M. (1987). *How institutions think.* London: Routledge and Kegan Paul.

Dunnigham, C., & Norris, C. (1996). A risky business: The recruitment and running of informers by English police officers. *Police Studies, 19*(2), 1–27.

Fielding, N. (1995). *Community policing.* Oxford: Oxford University Press.

Fine, B., & Millar, R. (1985). *Policing the miners' strike.* London: Lawrence Wishart and the Cobden Trust.

Foucault, M. (1977). *Discipline and punish: The birth of the prison.* London: Allen Lane Penguin Books.

Geertz, C. (1988). *Works and lives: The anthropologist as author.* Cambridge: Polity Press.

Germann, A. C. (1977, October). Law enforcement: A look into the future. *Police Journal, 50*(4), 340–7.

Gillie, O. (1991, Sept. 15). From Roman legionary to robocop. The *Independent on Sunday.*

Goffman, E. (1971). *Relations in public: Microstudies of the public order.* London: The Penguin Press.

Green, P. (1990). *The enemy without: Policing and class consciousness in the miners' strike.* Milton Keynes: Open University Press.

Hebdige, D. (1979). *Subculture: The meaning of style.* London: Methuen.

Hebdige, D. (1988). *Hiding the light: On images and things.* London: Routledge.

Hobbs, D., & May, T. (Eds). (1993). *Interpreting the field: Accounts of ethnography.* Oxford: Oxford University Press.

Hunter, K. E. (1997, May 28). (Untitled letter to the editor). The *Guardian,* p. 17.

Judge, A. J. (1994). *An analysis of the implications for policing, in England and Wales, of the contemporary profile of new age travellers.* Unpublished master's thesis, Leicester University, U.K.

Kohn, M. (1994, February 27). Trouble with funny hats. *Independent on Sunday.*

Littlewood, R. (1997). Military rape. *Anthropology Today, 13*(2), 7–16.

Loader, I. (1997). Policing and the social: Questions of symbolic power. *British Journal of Sociology, 48*(1), 1–18.

Maguire, M., & John, T. (1995). Intelligence, surveillance and integrated approaches. *Crime detection and prevention series No. 64, Police Research Group.* London: Home Office Policy Directorate.

Mauss, M. (1935). Les techniques du corps. Journal de psychologie normal et pathologique, 32. (1973. trans. B. Brewster. *Economy and society.* 2/1. February pp. 70–88.)

Newcastle City Police (1969). *Commemorative Booklet,* 1836–1969.

Norris, C., & Armstrong G. (in press). CCTV and the rise of mass surveillance. In P. Carlen and R. Morgan (Eds), *Crime unlimited.* Basingstoke: MacMillan.

Okely, J. (1996). *The self and scientism. Own or other culture.* London: Routledge. (originally publ. 1975. in *The Journal of the Anthropological Society of Oxford,* 6(3), 171–88.)

Okely, J., & Calloway, H. (Eds). (1992). *Anthropology and autobiography.* London: Routledge.

Pallister, D. (1997, March 8). Crack river force fails first publicity test. The *Guardian,* p. 9.

Partridge, E. (1972). *The Penguin dictionary of historical slang.* Harmondsworth: Penguin Books.

Police on the old beat: Divided society is still the issue. (1996, May 6). The *Guardian,* p. 10.

Polhemus, T. (Ed.). (1978). *Social aspects of the human body.* Harmondsworth: Penguin Books.

Reiner, R. (1991). *Chief constables.* Oxford: Oxford University Press.

Reiner, R. (1992a). *The politics of the police.* (Rev. ed.). Brighton: Harvester.

Reiner, R. (1992b). Policing a postmodern society. *Modern Law Review, 55*(6), 761–81.

Rose, D. (1996, October 20). New look fits the bill. The *Observer,* pp. 1, 6.

Rose, D. (1998, January 18). PC Plod, The *Observer,* p. 7.

Scarman, L.(1981). *The Brixton disorders.* Comand # 8427. London: Her Majesty's Stationery Office.

Scraton, P. (1985). *The state of the police.* London: Pluto Press.

South Yorkshire Police (1996). *Annual report for 1995/96.*

Sparks, R. (1992). *Television and the drama of crime.* Buckingham: Open University Press.

Stephens, M., & Becker, S. (1994). *Police force, police service.* Basingstoke: MacMillan.

Varley, C. (1997, April 24). Armed cops on Allerton Road. *South Liverpool Mersey Mart,* p. 1.

Vidal, J. (1997, March 6). Flying the freedom flag: The rise of people power against creeping state repression. The *Guardian,* sec. 2, p. 3.

Weatheritt, M. (1986). *Innovations in policing.* London: Croom Helm.

White, R. (1994). Service at the highest level. *Policing Today, 1*(3), 28–9.

Williams, R. (1976). *The long revolution.* Harmondsworth: Penguin Books.

Young, M. (1979). Pigs 'n prigs: A mode of thought, experience, and practice. In *Working Papers in Social Anthropology, No. 3*, 67–167. Dept. of Anthropology, University of Durham.

Young, M. (1984). Police wives: A reflection of police concepts of order and control. In H. Callan & S. Ardener (Eds), *The incorporated wife* (pp. 67–88). London: Croom Helm.

Young, M. (1986). An anthropology of the police: Semantic constructs of social order. Unpublished doctoral dissertation, University of Durham, U. K.

Young, M. (1991). *An inside job: Policing and police culture in Britain.* Oxford: Oxford University Press.

Young, M. (1992). Dress and modes of address: Structural forms for policewomen. In R. Barnes and J. B. Eicher (Eds), *Dress and gender: Making and meaning* (pp. 266–85). Oxford: Berg Publishers.

Young, M.(1993). *In the sticks: Cultural identity in a rural police force.* Oxford: Oxford University Press.

Young, M.(1994). Pseudonymously as "Pencarrow": Never mind the tape cassette, bring  back the whistle. *Policing Today, 1*(2), 23–4.

Young, M.(1995). Getting legless, falling down, pissy-arsed drunk: Policing men's leisure. *The Journal of Gender Studies, 4*(1), 47–61.

Young, M.(1995a). Risk avoidance in police research. Unpublished manuscript.

# 3

# Clothing, Power, and the Workplace[1]

## Margaret Rucker, Elizabeth Anderson, and April Kangas

From the 1950s through the 1980s, discussions of clothing and power in the workplace were commonly based on observations that White men most often held the superordinate positions in the world of work (refer to McCracken, 1985; McLeod & Damhorst, 1996). As noted by McCracken, men at work were supposed to be serious, reliable and disciplined. As a reflection of these attributes, clothing at work was supposed to be plain, dark and tailored. White men who wished to climb the corporate ladder were advised to wear somber formal attire to work; all others who wished to be assimilated into the executive hierarchy were urged to conform to this code and acquire a wardrobe of power suits (McLeod & Damhorst, 1996; Molloy, 1975, 1977; Solomon & Douglas, 1985).

Several factors have made dressing for success in the 1990s more complicated than it has been in previous decades. One is the increase in diversity of the workforce. A comparison of 1980 and 1990 census data indicates that White employees in the U.S. workforce have declined from 88 to 83 per cent while there has been a concomitant rise in the percentage of employees in other ethnic groups (Bureau of the Census, 1980; Bureau of the Census, 1990). This shift has implications for power systems and power symbols. As Hofstede (1983, 1984) has reported, preferred distance or difference between levels of power is one major dimension along which cultures may be distinguished from one another. Some societies elect to maximize distinctions among different levels of power or socio-economic status whereas others choose to minimize the differences. The way a culture or subculture deals with differences in power is apt to be reflected in attitude toward business-dress norms.

A shift in corporate dress codes in the direction of casual dress has also made constructing a powerful image complex. According to Maycumber (1998), research sponsored by Levi Strauss & Company showed a substantial rise in the percentage of U.S. white-collar workers who reported being able to wear casual clothes to work every day in recent years. The figure was 33 per cent in 1995 and 53 per cent in 1997, an increase of 20 per cent. When business-dress codes call for relatively informal dressing, either at the end of the week or all week long, the suit can no longer be depended upon as the basis for constructing a powerful image.

The intent of the present chapter is twofold. One is to provide a historical perspective on clothing and power in the workplace by reviewing previous literature in some detail. The other is to present new data on views of work clothing power and career advancement in the 1990s, with a focus on effects of minority status and relatively casual work environments.

## Clothing in the workplace

For a number of years, researchers have been asking questions about the role of clothing in the workplace (e.g., Form & Stone, 1955; Joseph & Alex, 1972). The majority of these questions fall into two general categories – what attitudes and practices are affected by differences in clothing and what characteristics or dimensions of clothing are responsible for these effects.

An early example of a focus on the social significance of occupational dress is the work of Form and Stone (1955). These researchers investigated how men in different occupational categories felt about clothing – how important they thought clothing was (a) in their current position and (b) for upward occupational mobility. Their research and subsequent studies of the importance of 'appropriate' or 'proper' occupational attire (Johnson & Roach-Higgins, 1987; Kwon, 1994a, 1994b; Kwon & Farber, 1992) indicated that such attire generally had a positive impact on overall assessments of potential and current employees as well as on ratings of individual traits. Furthermore, the benefits of appropriate occupational attire with respect to making favorable impressions on others were widely acknowledged, at least for white collar and managerial positions. In contrast, as Form and Stone noted, while appropriate clothing was also considered important for blue-collar workers, concerns here centered on durability of the clothing and whether it enhanced work performance.

Other researchers have gone beyond global assessments of appropriate attire to ask what dimensions of dress are most salient vis-à-vis the business image and what characteristics of the clothing make an outfit appropriate or effective in a given work environment. Most of these investigators have focused on female employees, with the assumption that dress codes for male employees were already well known whereas dress codes for women were not (e.g., Solomon & Douglas, 1985).

Given the focus on female employees and associated concerns about helping women succeed in male-dominated work environments, it is not surprising to find that the majority of the studies compared apparel and grooming attributes associated with masculine roles with those associated with feminine roles. As outlined in previous literature on gender roles (e.g., Gottdiener, 1977; McCracken, 1985; Roberts, 1977; Workman & Johnson, 1993), these distinctions included dresses versus suits, light versus dark colors, and soft curved versus sharp angular lines.

When researchers compared relatively masculine appearances with relatively feminine appearances, results have tended to support the proposition by Solomon and Douglas (1985) that to succeed in a traditionally male-dominated environment, women should adopt male props or symbols. They should not, however, abandon evidence of femininity to the point of gender norm violation. For example, in a series of studies by Forsythe and her colleagues (Forsythe, 1988; Forsythe, Drake & Cox, 1984, 1985; Forsythe, Drake & Hogan, 1985), outfits evaluated as moderately masculine were best at conveying images of being forceful, self-reliant, dynamic, aggressive, and decisive as well as eliciting the most favorable hiring recommendations. In only one of the studies by Forsythe (1990) did an extremely masculine outfit receive ratings that were as positive as the moderately masculine outfit.

Reports by other investigators also indicated that male symbols such as dark or cool colors, jackets and an overall plain, tailored appearance tend to garner higher ratings on work-related scales, although some differences by sex of the respondent were found (Cash, 1985; Damhorst & Reed, 1986; Scherbaum & Shepherd, 1987). While Scherbaum and Shepherd found no significant effect for sex of respondent, Damhorst and Reed as well as Cash found male respondents to have more consistently positive responses than did female respondents to masculine appearance cues. Again, however, research by Johnson, Crutsinger, and Workman (1994) indicated that women should be careful to avoid extremely masculine appearances. They compared the effects of a necktie, a scarf, and an open-collared blouse and found that subjects rated a woman in the scarf as more likely to be promoted than the same woman wearing either a necktie or an open-collared blouse. Furthermore, it should be noted that variations around traditional male business dress symbols, at least in terms of colors and design details, appear to have become more acceptable in the 1990s than in previous decades as women have moved into responsible positions in the business world and as norms for dress in general have been challenged, resulting in an increased number of choices for every occasion (Damhorst & Fiore, 1993; Kimle & Damhorst, 1997). For example, Damhorst and Fiore found that when personnel interviewers evaluated 100 color photographs of women's skirted suits, many different collar styles, garment materials, and garment colors were reported to be acceptable.

In related work that specifically addressed de-emphasizing sexuality through layering and minimizing skin exposure (Dillon, 1980; Rucker, Taber & Harrison, 1981), it was found that covering up the female form tends to be viewed positively in assessments of business dress. As Kimle and Damhorst (1997) reported finding in their interviews with businesswomen, skin exposure and body-hugging garments often are associated with sexiness, and projecting sexiness in a work environment is apt to be viewed as a major faux pas. Interviews conducted by Gottdiener (1977) supported the proposition that working women can benefit from de-emphasizing femininity and sexuality. For example, a female photographer reported wearing man-tailored clothes in order to be taken seriously and a model noted that when she wore Western wear to a job, the mannish appearance attracted less unwanted attention from men on the street.

As noted by Kimle and Damhorst (1997), another important dimension of a woman's business image is an innovative versus conservative appearance. A few investigators have explicitly considered innovative fashion details or trendy clothing versus conservatively-styled apparel in relation to images of women in the work environment. Data from both business people judging women's dress and the women themselves showed a negative relationship between innovative styles and projection of a professional image (Douglas & Solomon, 1983; Kimle & Damhorst, 1997; Thurston, Lennon & Clayton, 1990). As Kimle and Damhorst noted, an unchanging image tends to convey a sense of stability, which is highly valued in most business environments. In another study that examined the relationship between women's attire on the job and their actual career advancement (Gorden, Tengler & Infante, 1982), conservative dress was found to have a positive association with a number of promotions. However, Kimle and Damhorst caution against ignoring fashion altogether; going to this extreme could convey insensitivity to changes in the general cultural milieu and a lack of social savvy.

Conformity versus creativity is another dimension of business attire that has received some attention in the literature. Kimle and Damhorst (1997) found that expressing creativity through artful arranging of clothing and accessories was important to the women in their sample, although they were aware of the danger of taking creativity to the point of eccentricity. In contrast, the African American men in the study by McLeod and Damhorst (1996) felt comfortable with a relatively high level of occupational dress conformity, viewing it as important for successful job-role performance.

Powerful-weak is not mentioned by Kimle and Damhorst (1997) as a separate dimension of business dress although they do allude to its importance in their discourse on attractiveness. In fact, there are very few empirical works on business dress in which power is specifically mentioned.[2] One exception is the study by Damhorst and Reed (1986) in which color was considered in relation to power. In this study, male subjects were found to rate models in dark jackets as more powerful than models in light jackets.

A book by Rubinstein (1995) combines both empirical and theoretical work from a variety of different sources with her own observations to suggest ways in which clothing signs can facilitate exercising authority and wielding power. In chapters entitled 'The Image of Power' and 'The Image of Authority' she cites the work of Joseph and Alex (1972) on various functions of uniforms. Then she adds what are apparently her own views about rights reflected by various elements of appearance such as the right to enforce policy, the right to interfere with ongoing action, the right to control access, and the right to exercise force. Historical data starting with ancient Mesopotamia and Imperial Rome are presented to suggest that indicators of wealth such as gold, jewels, and layers of expensive fabric have traditionally been associated with higher levels of both power and authority.

In addition to academic works, there are a number of books and articles in the popular press that deal with power in the workplace and offer proscriptions for creating a powerful image through dress (e.g., Book, 1996; Hayes, 1996; Korda, 1975; Molloy, 1975; 1977). Unfortunately, these works provide little or no information on any empirical bases for their recommendations so that their usefulness is difficult to evaluate.

Even setting aside works in the popular press, though, it appears that there is a sizeable knowledge base regarding clothing in the workplace, including some information about clothing and power. However, much of the theory has assumed a predominantly White male power structure and much of the data has been drawn from predominantly White female samples. Furthermore, most of the data were collected before the dramatic changes in business dress codes that have been occurring in the 1990s. As corporate dress codes have shifted to include casual styles and the workforce has become ethnically diverse, it is important to reconsider elements of apparel as they relate to perceptions of power. Constructing a powerful appearance is apt to require different strategies when dress codes are relatively casual as compared to relatively formal. Regarding ethnic and cultural diversity, as noted earlier, Hofstede (1983; 1984) found that not all cultures have the same standards for the appropriate distance to maintain between levels of power. For example, people from the United States were found to prefer relatively small power differences whereas people from Mexico were found to prefer relatively large differences. Given this variation in preference for power distances, it was anticipated that ethnic groups might differ in their attitudes toward casual versus formal dress on the job and the importance of dressing to make a powerful impression as well as advance in their careers. Finally, the 'dress-down dilemma' may be more unsettling for men than for women since until recently the typical man has had relatively little experience in experimenting with dress codes.

This study was designed to determine the attitudes of working men and women from diverse ethnic backgrounds about business attire and power. It was also intended to explore how appearance was managed to create a powerful image under conditions of more and less formal business dress codes.

## Method

Respondents for this study were selected from staff directories of a local university. Data provided by campus administrators indicated that, based on self-identification information, the staff was ethnically diverse with 69 per cent White employees, 12 per cent Hispanic, 11 per cent Asian, 8 per cent Black and 1 per cent American Indian.[3] A systematic sampling method was used to select names of potential respondents. As explained by Babbie (1998), systematic sampling and simple random sampling produce virtually identical results and systematic sampling is an easier method to use. Samples were drawn from both the Hispanic Staff Association directory and the general staff directory to ensure that there would be sufficient diversity to permit meaningful comparisons across different ethnic groups. Hispanic staff employees were chosen as a comparison group because they were the largest ethnic minority on the campus and had an easily accessible staff association directory. Furthermore, although this ethnic group is increasing in size in the United States, its needs and preferences have been largely overlooked by consumer researchers (refer to Solomon, 1996).

The decision to conduct the study with university employees was based on the assumption that managerial, technical and clerical jobs are similar across institutions, so it should be possible to generalize the findings across work venues. Furthermore, it was thought that university employees would be relatively willing to participate in a research project, thus producing a satisfactory response rate. Of course, a limitation is that university work climates in general tend to be somewhat more casual than the work climates in the business sector. Nevertheless, our respondents seemed to have little difficulty relating to questions about dress-up versus dress-down situations.

A total of 118 employees were chosen for contact via telephone about participating in interviews. Of these, twenty-five were not reachable due to no longer holding an identifiable staff position on the campus. Of the ninety-three who were contacted, ninety agreed to be interviewed. In most cases, employees agreed to be interviewed in person where they worked and have the session taped. For the nine employees who were not able to schedule in-person interviews, telephone interviews were conducted and taped using the two-way recording feature of a digital telephone answering system.

The interview schedule developed for this project included items on the importance of appropriate work clothing for career advancement for university employees in general and for oneself in particular. Respondents were asked to provide ratings on seven-point scales ranging from very important (1) to very unimportant (7) and then provide reasons for the ratings. To compare perceptions of the need to emphasize power differences versus the need to minimize them, respondents were asked to rate how often it was important for them to dress to make a powerful impression and how often it was important for them to dress to mask or reduce differences between themselves and other employees. Five-point scales were used for these two items, with a range from never (1) to very often (5). To examine how the symbolic consumption of career clothing might be affected by shifting dress codes, respondents were asked to describe what they would wear in situations in which they needed to make a powerful impression. They were then asked to compare and contrast power outfits for dress-up days, when formal business clothing is expected, and dress-down days when casual, relaxed dressing is permitted. In addition to being interviewed about clothing for work, respondents filled out one page of demographic information. Demographic items included age, sex, level of schooling completed, number of years on the current job, and job level. A self-report item on ethnic identity was also included as the basis for classifying respondents into ethnic groups. The same questions were asked of all respondents and in the order indicated above.

Frequency distributions of the background information were used to characterize the sample. Two-way analyses of variance were used to test the ratings for significant differences between men and women, and between White and Hispanic employees. To analyze the qualitative data, transcripts of the interviews were read for themes that had been reported by previous authors as well as additional themes that emerged from the current data. This variation of 'interpretive tacking' (Geertz, 1983; Hirschman & Holbrook, 1992; Sherry, McGrath & Levy, 1995), or moving back and forth between models developed in other contexts and new data, was intended to highlight any ethnic and gender differences. It was also utilized to compare attitudes toward formal dress codes for work with attitudes toward casual dress codes.

## Results and Discussion

### Background Information

Analysis of the background information indicated that all but seven respondents self identified as either Hispanic or White. The seven who checked categories other than Hispanic or White were eliminated from subsequent analysis since there were not enough in the other categories for meaningful comparisons. The final sample consisted of 16 Hispanic men (HM), 23 Hispanic women (HW), 14 White men (WM) and 30 White women (WW). The age range of the final sample was from 25 to 66 with a median of 46. The sample was relatively well educated, with 82 per cent having at least some college and 40 per cent having completed college. About two-thirds of the sample had managerial positions with the rest about evenly divided between technical and clerical positions. Years in the current job ranged from 9 months to 33 years with a median of 10 years.

### Clothing and Advancement

With respect to clothing being important for the advancement of employees in general, the analysis of variance indicated that neither the main effects for sex, ethnicity, or the interaction term were significant. For the ratings of importance of clothing for personal advancement, however, there was a significant main effect for ethnicity, $F(1,78) = 12.65$, $p < .001$. On average, the Hispanic respondents rated clothing as more important ($M = 2.48$) than did the White respondents ($M = 3.33$).

Comments that helped explain the differences included references by Hispanic respondents to being a man or woman 'of color' and therefore having to be twice as good at everything. The comments were similar to some reported by McLeod and Damhorst (1996) in their study of African American male executives. In that sample, a number of the men reported feeling that they were judged more critically than White employees and therefore had to pay attention to their appearance.

A comparison of responses to the general question with responses to the personal question indicated that respondents saw clothing as more important for advancement of employees collectively ($M = 2.39$) than for their own advancement ($M = 3.01$). A repeated measures analysis of variance indicated that this difference was significant, $F(1,78) = 6.79$, $p < .05$. Several factors seemed to account for this effect. One was the phenomenon noted previously that when people were asked about occupational attire in general, its import-ance was widely acknowledged. Sentiments expressed in response to the item about employees in general included the point that people who looked like they did not care about their appearance probably did not care about their job responsibilities either. Also, appropriate clothing showed respect for one's position and one's co-workers. As a respondent expressed it:

> I think it [being dressed up for work] shows that you pay attention to detail or delivering a good package like the services that you provide. If you are all sloppy then I feel that people will think that the service you provide is kind of sloppy, too. (HW)

Another factor that appeared to elevate the general ratings was a tendency for respondents to answer this question in terms of one particular place where dress is relatively formal, the campus administration building. There was no evidence of an opposing effect. That is, no respondent mentioned consideration of locations in which dress was especially casual when they discussed campus employees as a group and the importance of appropriate attire.

Contributing to the discrepancy between ratings for employees in general and ratings for self were several common themes that seemed to result in lower importance ratings when respondents were questioned about their own personal situations. Most of the themes could be classified under the headings of either job activities or job life cycle.

Both men and women commented on how certain job activities, or lack of those activities, led to less concern with power dressing. One activity was interaction with students. Some comments illustrating the impact of this activity on work attire are as follows:

> Probably not that important, closer to unimportant. Maybe because the kinds of positions that I have advanced in are more student orientated positions, working with students. Casual attire is acceptable. (WW)

> Counselors have to be presentable but non-threatening, so I wear non-bureaucrat casual. (HM)

In contrast, both male and female employees acknowledged that appropriate dress became relatively important when dealing with customers outside the department or the general public, or when representing the department at a meeting with employees from other units. When their jobs did not involve much contact with outside audiences, employees tended to downgrade the importance of their work attire.

When the job requirements included a good deal of physical labor, working in a dirty environment, or both, importance ratings were sometimes low but not always. Consistent with the findings of Form and Stone (1955) some men in technical or blue collar positions saw appropriate clothing as very important because of its relationship to work performance. As one male employee explained:

> I have to be comfortable for one thing in my physical world. Also, it is kind of rugged work around farm equipment and that sort of thing, so they have to be durable. (WM)

Comments about having advanced as far as possible or desirable, and getting close to retirement were counted as job life cycle themes. Only women mentioned impending retirement as a factor in their dressing for work, in spite of the fact that age distributions for the two sexes were similar and therefore there should be little difference in time to retirement. Furthermore, the women indicated that not wanting to struggle with the components of female career apparel seemed to be the main issue leading to downplaying power dressing upon approaching retirement. Comments included:

> I don't care now because I am nearing retirement and I dress to be very comfortable now. (WW)

> I choose to be comfortable. As I have gotten older, nylons, high heels, skirts, and all that stuff just hangs me up. My boss told me that I was the best dressed [job title] on campus, but that is no longer the case and that is why. (WW)

It should be noted that even when retirement was not an immediate consideration, some women were willing to risk advancement for the sake of comfort. As one respondent explained:

> I work pretty much non-stop from the time I get to work until I go home, and I do not want to be uncomfortable. I don't want to have to think about these panty hose are pinching me or these pants are too tight or these shoes are uncomfortable. (WW)

On the other hand, themes of not seeing opportunities for advancement or being content in the current position were found only among the Hispanic respondents. Again, however, the two respondents who associated advancement with the need to wear less comfortable clothing were women. They discussed their feelings as follows:

> I'm content where I'm at. I like to be comfortable. I don't care to wear heels and struggle. (HW)

> [At] this point in my career, I am really winding down. There is no place for me to go, so I am enjoying myself! (HW)

While the majority of respondents answered the advancement questions in terms of external factors such as requirements of the job or impressions of supervisors and clients, a few spoke of the internal psychological effects of one's appearance at work. These psychological effects were thought to influence performance, which in turn affected advancement. For example, the disenchantment of some women with power dressing was balanced by the positive feelings that others expressed regarding the sense of personal competence and empowerment that can come with the knowledge that one is well dressed. Some examples of statements about these feelings are as follows:

> It has made me feel better so that I feel like I am more competent. Whether it is just a psychological thing or not, I'm not sure. But if I feel like I look nice, I feel better about myself. I do a better job. (HW)

> It makes me feel better, and I just work better. If I feel good about what I am wearing and how I look . . . [it] has an effect. I don't know – if I am wrinkly and yucky, I'm going to feel wrinkly and yucky. (HW)

> It makes you feel better and when you feel more professional, you act more professional. (WW)

A few of the male respondents also remarked on the psychological comfort that can be derived from being well dressed for the job. Furthermore, they also believed that feeling good was apt to be reflected in better job performance.

### Clothing and Power

*Dressing for power and dressing to fit in*   Analysis of ratings regarding dressing to make a powerful impression showed a significant main effect for ethnicity, $F(1,78) = 4.04$, $p < .05$. The Hispanic respondents reported needing to dress to make a powerful impression on average between 'sometimes' and 'fairly often' ($M = 3.34$) whereas the White respondents' average fell between 'sometimes' and 'rarely' ($M = 2.84$). Similarly, the only significant effect for dressing to fit in was the main effect for ethnicity, $F(1,78) = 6.55$, $p < .05$. Again, Hispanic respondents more often found it important to dress to fit in ($M = 2.39$) compared to the White respondents ($M = 1.61$). It appears from these findings that the Hispanic employees may be sensitive to power distances and the use of clothing to de-emphasize as well as emphasize such distances.

*Personal powerful impressions*   There was a high level of agreement among the male respondents regarding the style of attire that should be selected to make a powerful impression. The classic men's business uniform of a suit and tie, or at least a sports jacket and slacks was mentioned by about two-thirds of the men as the type of clothing they would wear to make a powerful impression. Furthermore, there was unanimous agreement that the suit should be dark whereas the sports coat could be light and still be part of a powerful image.

This finding is consistent with the contention by Solomon and Douglas (1985) among others that there is an established dress code for the male executive, with more or less flexibility depending on the type of unit in which he works. In this study, there seemed to be more agreement about what a very formal power suit should look like than what a less formal power sports coat and slacks should look like. When even casual styles of dress were mentioned, there was generally an accompanying explanation for the deviation from the traditional view of an executive uniform or a power suit. These explanations included both physical activities and social interactions that made the wearing of a suit problematic. For example, one man's job required a high level of contact with farmers in the area. Therefore, he tended more toward the 'Wrangler' rather than the 'Van Heusen' look for a powerful image.

Accessories were rarely mentioned, although a few men did comment on the importance of dress (leather) shoes. Three men added a belt to their descriptions and one spoke of cuff links as a power accessory.

Almost three-fourths of the female respondents also mentioned a suit or blazer with a dress or skirt as the style they chose when desiring to project a power image. They were far from unanimous, however, regarding what constituted powerful colors. Some women felt that neutrals such as black, navy blue or taupe were the best choices whereas others opted for brights such as red and royal blue. A few women were explicit and specific about not wanting to look like a male clone. As one woman commented:

> I don't think in terms of a business suit that looks like a man. There are certain colors that I like to wear, and they are . . . fuchsia, royal blue, or red, purple, teal. I am not into being in the navy and brown and dark colors that look like a man. (WW)

These findings are consistent with those of Damhorst and Fiore (1993), that is, variety in the color of women's business attire is more acceptable in the 1990s than it was in the 1980s.

For women, accessories were frequently mentioned as an important part of a powerful image. Jewelry was the accessory described most often, with an emphasis on simple items made of expensive materials. This is consistent with the observation of Rubinstein (1995) that display of expensive materials such as gold, diamonds, and pearls on the body has been a traditional signal of power and authority.

Shoes were discussed by over half of the female respondents, with general agreement that one should not wear flat heels if one wants to command attention. Although heels of at least an inch or more were touted as an essential part of power dressing for women, five of the women stated they themselves would not wear pumps out of concern for the effects on their feet. As one woman exclaimed, 'heels hurt!'

Adding a scarf to complete a power look was mentioned by only four of the female respondents. The lack of appreciation for this accessory was somewhat surprising given the association with promotability reported by Johnson et al. (1994). However, as one of the respondents implied, adding a scarf to a woman's outfit is not as simple as adding a tie to a man's outfit. There is one basic formula for adjusting a tie and most men master the technique through repeated practice in their teens. With scarves, there are a greater number of aesthetically pleasing and acceptable arrangements on the body but there are also a greater number of unpleasant possibilities. Consequently, a woman is apt to feel she does not have the knowledge or the time to use a scarf to her best advantage. It requires less time and effort to slip on a necklace or clip on a pin.

*Formal and casual symbols of power*   When asked to describe a typical 'power outfit' for dress-up conditions versus dress-down conditions, our respondents had little difficulty with the dress-up condition. Most repeated the comments they made when asked the general question about what they wore to make a powerful impression.

Generating power symbols for dress-down conditions was another matter. Almost 20 per cent of the sample could not connect power with casual. They made comments such as the following:

I have no idea. I can't even imagine what that would be. (WM)
I can't think of a dress-down [power] outfit. (WW)
There wouldn't be one. (WW)
I don't care for dress down. Jeans are for housecleaning! (HW)

Contrary to expectations based on previous literature regarding women's affinity for manipulating aesthetic codes (Kimle & Damhorst, 1997; McCracken, 1985; Solomon & Douglas, 1985), the percentage of women who could not describe a dress-down power outfit was approximately equal to the percentage of men who could not envision such an outfit. Instead, the

**Figure 3.1.** A female respondent demonstrates clothing she would wear to make a powerful impression when formal attire is appropriate. Here she is shown in a black wool suit with simple gold jewelry, softened with a pale blue sweater.

**Figure 3.2.** The same respondent constructs a powerful image for days when office norms call for casual dress. In this case, she has added a jacket in a powerful color (red) and her simple gold jewelry to a casual black sweater and jeans.

differences fell along ethnic lines. The White respondents were appreciably resistant or incapable of imaging a dress-down power outfit. One possible explanation for this difference could be that, as Aaker and Dean (1993) have observed, minorities have had to be sensitive to all kinds of social cues in order to get along and advance in a White-dominated social system. Therefore, they might have additional cues to draw on in creating casual images of power. This proposition would not, however, explain why women could not envision such images.

Among those respondents who could propose a dress-down image, the strategy seemed to be to take formal power cues and reinterpret them in a casual situation. For example, dark colors were frequently mentioned, especially black slacks or jeans. Some respondents added that wearing a belt with the slacks would enhance the image. Reliance on well-known brands and casual styles in relatively expensive materials such as silk, linen, and leather, suggested an appreciation of the connection between indicators of wealth and power as described by Rubinstein (1995). Several respondents commented on appropriate shoes for the dress-down outfit – loafers and boots, but not sandals that exposed too much skin. The comments about boots, either as part of a Western ensemble or as a separate item, were reminiscent of the report by Gottdiener (1977) that Western wear seems to convey masculine power. Adding a jacket to an otherwise casual outfit was another popular strategy for creating a power look.

There were also some interesting idiosyncratic comments that were consistent with previous writings on dress codes and power. For example, one female respondent described using a vest rather than a jacket to add a second layer to a blouse and thereby enhance the power of a casual outfit. A male respondent talked about his keys, tape measure, and beeper as power symbols. For this person, keys seemed to represent the right to control access as described by Rubinstein (1995). As he stated it:

> carry a tape measure around and look important. Not that you'd even use it but [carry] your beeper, your set of keys jingling on your side. Then the students know, 'Ah, somebody's here, they got a lot of keys.' (HM)

## Conclusions

This study offers support for the observation made by McLeod and Damhorst (1996) in their study of African American male executives that clothing symbols are especially potent for members of ethnic minorities as they use them to fit in and move up in the established power structure. In the present study, Hispanic employees rated clothing as significantly more important for personal advancement than did their White counterparts. In addition, they saw the need to dress to make a powerful impression significantly more often than White employees.

Previous studies on gender role requirements have brought to light a number of problems experienced by women trying to construct an effective business image, including conflicts between looking feminine and looking professional (e.g., Kaiser, Schutz & Chandler, 1987; Kimle & Damhorst, 1997). The present study contributes to that literature by demonstrating that both looking feminine and looking professional may conflict with the need to be comfortable, especially among older women. Our respondents expressed this point repeatedly and forcefully, finding fault with restrictive skirts, panty hose that pinched, heels that hurt and 'all that stuff [that] just hangs me up.'

Finally, the study provides a sense of how employees are dealing with the changing dress codes at work. As is often the case with change, there seemed to be a mix of resistance and creative renegotiations of clothing symbolism; responses ranged from an enthusiastic acceptance of the casual look, including jeans, to the heartfelt complaint that 'jeans are for housecleaning!'

## Notes

1. The authors would like to express their appreciation to staff from the local university who contributed their time to this research project.

2. The meta-analysis of impression formation studies by Damhorst (1990) suggests that consideration of 'power' is fairly common in dress research in general. However, her power category is more inclusive than the meaning of power in the present study, that is, the ability to influence others at work.

3. These designations were selected for this study based on their common usage on university forms and reports at the time data were being collected.

## References

Aaker, J. L., & Dean, J. (1993). *The non-target market effect: Associated feelings of acceptance, alienation or apathy.* Paper presented at the annual meeting of the Association for Consumer Research, Nashville, TN.

Babbie, E. (1998). *The practice of social research* (8th ed.). Belmont, CA: Wadsworth.

Book, E. W. (1996). The style of power. *Fortune, 134*(a), 96–105.

Bureau of the Census. (1980). *1980 Census of Population and Housing.* Washington, DC: Bureau of the Census.

Bureau of the Census. (1990). *1990 Census of Population and Housing*. Washington, DC: Bureau of the Census.

Cash, T. F. (1985). The impact of grooming style on evaluation of women in management. In M. R. Solomon (Ed.) *The psychology of fashion* (pp. 343–55). Lexington, MA: D. C. Heath.

Damhorst, M. L. (1990). In search of a common thread: Classification of information communicated through dress. *Clothing and Textiles Research Journal, 8*(2), 1–12.

Damhorst, M. L., & Fiore, A. M. (1993). Evaluations of women's suits by male and female personnel interviewers. In J. A. Costa (Ed.) *Gender and consumer behavior: Second conference proceedings* (pp. 58–60). Salt Lake City, UT: University of Utah Printing Service.

Damhorst, M. L., & Reed, J. A. P. (1986). Clothing color value and facial expression: Effects on evaluations of female job applicants. *Social Behavior and Personality, 14*(1), 84–98.

Dillon, L. S. (1980). Business dress for women corporate professionals. *Home Economics Research Journal, 9*(2), 124–9.

Douglas, S. P., & Solomon, M. R. (1983). Clothing the female executive: Fashion or fortune? In P. E. Murphy et al. (Eds) *AMA Educators Proceedings*, No. 49, 127–32.

Form, W. H., & Stone, G. P. (1955). *The social significance of clothing in occupational life* (Technical Bulletin 247). East Lansing, MI: State College Agricultural Experiment Station.

Forsythe, S. M. (1988). Effects of clothing masculinity on perceptions of managerial traits: Does gender of the perceiver make a difference? *Clothing and Textiles Research Journal, 6*(2), 10–16.

Forsythe, S. M. (1990). Effect of applicant's clothing on interviewer's decision to hire. *Journal of Applied Social Psychology, 20,* 1579–95.

Forsythe, S. M., Drake, M. F., & Cox, C. E. (1984). Dress as an influence on the perceptions of management characteristics in women. *Home Economics Research Journal, 13*(2), 112–21.

Forsythe, S. M., Drake, M. F., & Cox, C. E. (1985). Influence of applicant's dress on interviewer's selection decisions. *Journal of Applied Psychology, 70*(2), 374–8.

Forsythe, S. M., Drake, M. F., & Hogan, J. H. (1985). Influence of clothing attributes on the perception of personal characteristics. In M. R. Solomon (Ed.) *The psychology of fashion* (pp. 267–77). Lexington, MA: D. C. Heath.

Geertz, C. (1983). *Local knowledge: Further essays in interpretive anthropology.* New York: Basic Books.

Gorden, W. I., Tengler, C. D., & Infante, D. A. (1982). Women's clothing predispositions as predictors of dress at work, job satisfaction, and career advancement. *The Southern Speech Communication Journal, 47,* 422–34.

Gottdiener, M. (1977). Unisex fashions and gender role-change. *Semiotic Scene, 1*(3), 13–37.

Hayes, C. (1996). How to dress when moving up the ladder. *Black Enterprise, 27*(3), 131–4.

Hirschman, E. C., & Holbrook, M. B. (1992). *Postmodern consumer research: The study of consumption as text.* Newbury Park, CA: Sage.

Hofstede, G. (1983). The cultural relativity of organizational practices and theories. *Journal of International Business Studies, 14*(2), 75–89.

Hofstede, G. (1984). The cultural relativity of the quality of life concept. *Academy of Management Review, 9*(3), 389–98.

Johnson, K. K. P., Crutsinger, C., & Workman, J. E. (1994). Can professional women appear too masculine? The case of the necktie. *Clothing and Textiles Research Journal, 12*(2), 27–31.

Johnson, K. K. P., & Roach-Higgins, M. E. (1987). Dress and physical attractiveness of women in job interviews. *Clothing and Textiles Research Journal, 5*(3), 1–8.

Joseph, N., & Alex, N. (1972). The uniform: A sociological perspective. *American Journal of Sociology, 77*(4), 719–30.

Kaiser, S. B., Schutz, H. G., & Chandler, J. L. (1987). Cultural codes and sex-role ideology: A study of shoes. *American Journal of Semiotics, 5,* 13–34.

Kimle, P. A., & Damhorst, M. L. (1997). A grounded theory model of the ideal business image for women. *Symbolic Interaction, 20*(1), 45–68.

Korda, M. (1975). *Power! How to get it, how to use it.* New York: Random House.

Kwon, Y.-H. (1994a). Feeling toward one's clothing and self-perception of emotion, sociability, and work competency. *Journal of Social Behavior and Personality, 9*(1), 129–39.

Kwon, Y.-H. (1994b). The influence of appropriateness of dress and gender on the self-perception of occupational attributes. *Clothing and Textiles Research Journal, 12*(3), 33–9.

Kwon, Y.-H., & Farber, A. (1992). Attitudes toward appropriate clothing in perception of occupational attributes. *Perceptual and Motor Skills, 74,* 163–8.

Maycumber, S. G. (1998, January 9). Young men's pants preference shifting. *Daily News Record, 28*(4), pp. 8–9.

McCracken, G. D. (1985). The trickle-down theory rehabilitated. In M. R. Solomon (Ed.) *The psychology of fashion* (pp. 39–54). Lexington, MA: D. C. Heath.

McLeod, H., & Damhorst, M. L. (1996). African-American male executive dress: Issues of aesthetics, conformity and ethnic identity. In J. A. Costa (Ed.) *Gender, marketing and consumer behavior: Proceedings of the third conference* (pp. 165–7). Salt Lake City, UT: University of Utah Printing Service.

Molloy, J. T. (1975). *Dress for success.* New York: David McKay Co.

Molloy, J. T. (1977). *The woman's dress for success book.* Chicago: Follett.

Roberts, H. E. (1977). The exquisite slave: The role of clothes in the making of the Victorian woman. *Signs, 2*(3), 554–69.

Rubinstein, R. P. (1995). *Dress codes.* Boulder, CO: Westview Press.

Rucker, M., Taber, D., & Harrison, A. (1981). The effect of clothing variation on first impressions of female job applicants: What to wear when. *Social Behavior and Personality, 9*(2), 124–9.

Scherbaum, C. J., & Shepherd, D. H. (1987). Dressing for success: Effects of color and layering on perceptions of women in business. *Sex Roles, 16*(7/8), 391–9.

Sherry, J. F., Jr., McGrath, M. A., & Levy, S. J. (1995). Monadic giving: Anatomy of gifts given to the self. In J. F. Sherry, Jr. (Ed.) *Contemporary marketing and consumer behavior: An anthropological sourcebook* (pp. 399–432). Thousand Oaks, CA: Sage.

Solomon, M. R. (1996). *Consumer behavior: Buying, having, and being.* Englewood Cliffs, NJ: Prentice Hall.

Solomon, M. R., & Douglas, S. P. (1985). The female clotheshorse: From aesthetics to tactics. In M. R. Solomon (Ed.) *The psychology of fashion* (pp. 387–401). Lexington, MA: D. C. Heath.

Thurston, J. L., Lennon, S. J., & Clayton, R. V. (1990). Influence of age, body type, fashion, and garment type on women's professional image. *Home Economics Research Journal, 19*(2), 139–150.

Workman, J. E., & Johnson, K. K. P. (1993). Cultural aesthetics and the social construction of gender. In S. J. Lennon & L. D. Burns (Eds) *Social science aspects of dress: New directions* (pp. 93–109). Monument, CO: International Textile and Apparel Association.

# 4

# Dress for Success in the Popular Press[1]

## Jennifer Paff Ogle and Mary Lynn Damhorst

The U.S. workforce is in the midst of social transformation; women are attaining middle and upper management positions in increasing numbers. According to the Statistical Abstract of the United States (Bureau of Census, 1992), women in 1990 comprised 30.6 per cent of the workforce category 'managers, marketing, advertising, and public relations' in comparison to 21.8 per cent in that job category in 1980. This job category includes a substantial proportion of management and executive positions in private industry. Futurists project continued and greater movement of women into leadership roles in business over the next few decades (Aburdene & Naisbitt, 1992). As gender representation among business managers and executives change, the gender of decision-makers and holders of superordinate power also changes.

The change in gender representation in business provides an opportunity to explore concomitant changes in role dress as women move in greater proportion into management and executive roles. As individuals take on new roles, dress symbols[2] employed in performance of those roles are likely to be adopted, adapted, and modified by the new role-takers in a process of meaning change (Blumer, 1969). In addition, the entrance of new types of individuals into a role arena will inevitably adjust societal and organizational expectations for those role players and meanings assigned to symbols used in execution of the role.

To examine one source of information about changing business dress, we explored magazine and newspaper articles offering business-dress advice to men and women during the 1980s and 1990s. The recommendations as a whole were analyzed for indications of social norms and expectations for men and women in business. Consideration was given to how these dress recommendations could be interpreted in terms of gendered power relations in the business arena.

We recognize that media reflections of social behaviors may not mirror exactly what real people do; media often exaggerate or over-simplify trends, emphasizing some behaviors and ignoring others. Men and women in business may not have actually worn all that was advised in the articles we studied. However, media content can give some insight, when interpreted cautiously, into how people thought about and interpreted their own and others' dress. Stereotypes and ideas projected in the media set a backdrop of archetypes that, in part, shape meanings assigned to behaviors displayed by people in real life contexts (e.g., Belk & Pollay, 1985; Gross & Sheth, 1989; Kaiser, Lennon, & Damhorst, 1991).

## Dressing for Work Roles

Dress helps individuals perform business roles (Rafaeli & Pratt, 1993). Role dress, such as the men's suit, has the familiarity and history to serve as a significant symbol for management and administrative roles in business. Men's business dress has undergone centuries of development since 1666, when Charles II of England proclaimed a simplified, 'useful' three-piece suit for men of the court, business, and commerce (Kuchta, 1990). Dress that is a significant symbol has high consensus in meaning to a group of people and consequently draws appropriate reactions from others (Davis, 1982). Human beings act toward an individual wearing business dress on the basis of the meanings that the dress symbols have for them (Blumer, 1969). Dress, therefore, helps the person in a management role learn the role and perform the role due to shared meanings. Work identity is managed and constructed, in part, through dress. Dress serves, then, as a visual metaphor for management identity (Davis, 1992).

Kanter (1977) proposed that similarity of appearances among management personnel in a large corporation helped to reduce uncertainty in the organization in that the standard management appearance signified commitment to professionalism and to organizational and business goals on the part of managers. The managerial business suit indicates value of the wearer to the organization and thereby helps to promote, support, and maintain the organization (Stone, 1962).

The men's business suit represents more than the individual role taker. The suit is the epitome of modernity and industrial capitalism in that it is rational in its simplicity, rule-abiding, functional for getting the job done, unequivocal in its body-structure relationship, clear and direct in meanings that suppress individual distinctions, and harmonious with the (aspired) objectivity of corporate environments (e.g., Morgado, 1996). Borrowing Foucault's (1977) perspective, the modern men's business suit is a form of drill that, through its restrictions, produces the 'disciplined body' that performs efficiently and maintains order while accomplishing the serious work of business for modern society. The men's business suit encodes the ideology of corporate America. Its uniformity and stability continually reproduces the dominant class (i.e., White male businessmen) to reaffirm the hegemony and legitimize the power of its wearers (Mannheim, 1960).

Up through the 1970s gender was a significant component of management dress. A male individual and a business suit were inseparably linked as a composite symbol for management identity. As women have moved into powerful positions in business, they have had to deal with the incongruity of a female gender identity and a business identity. This historical association of business identity with gender suggests that recent changes in business dress can lend insight into changing roles of women in business as well as changing definitions of what is male and female and therefore powerful and powerless within the business context.

In 1986 Saunders and Stead suggested that due in part to women's relatively recent influx into management arenas, a 'standard' of dress for the managerial business woman had not clearly emerged. While women were first beginning to enter management ranks in noticeable numbers, popular dress advisors such as John Molloy (1977) and Betty Harragan (1977) were recommending that women adopt the highly restricted dress styling of men's business dress, with limited and timid modifications to identify female gender of the wearer. Perhaps at the early stage of role acquisition, borrowing existing dress styles from men who predominated managerial ranks seemed a safe strategy for women so new to the corporate role. However, Kanter (1977) observed that few female executives in a large corporation dressed similarly to male executives in the firm.

Similarly, much of the scholarly research on business dress conducted during the early 1980s leads us to believe that a fairly limited range of variation was the ideal in women's business dress. A small degree of variety in color, style lines, and neckline depth (e.g., Cash, 1985; Damhorst & Reed, 1986; Forsythe, Drake, & Cox, 1984; Rucker, Taber, & Harrison, 1981; Sherbaum & Shepherd, 1987) were reported to increase perceptions of women's professional appropriateness and competence. Much of the research, however, examined interview dress, which may require extensive attention to professional symbolism for the interview situation. These research findings may specify more limited and formalized codes[3] than might be expected in dress that could be effective during an ordinary day on the job.

In addition, the nature of the research methods and analyses adopted in earlier studies limits the findings. The researchers used rigidly controlled experimental designs and a limited array of stimuli. While some caution about the small, relative difference in perceived effectiveness was occasionally reported (Damhorst & Reed, 1986; Sherbaum & Shepherd, 1987), the overall aim of the body of research seemed to be to identify the most effective business dress for women. When researchers presented a broader array of dress options as stimuli, a greater degree of diversity was found in dress deemed as appropriate and professional (Damhorst, Eckman, & Stout, 1986; Damhorst & Fiore, 1993; Solomon & Douglas, 1987). Solomon and Douglas (1987) proposed that norms for women's business dress consisted of a 'fuzzy set' of choices that are probably evaluated on proximity to an ideal set of characteristics, similar to Holbrook and Dixon's (1985) discussion of 'complementarity in aggregate patterns of revealed preferences' (p. 122) in current styles or looks. In the aggregate pattern of women's business dress, few specific criteria are always present in any member of the fuzzy set, but some relation to an archetype of the men's suit must be present. For example, Damhorst and Fiore (1993) found that for management interviews, personnel interviewers judged a surprising variety of collar styles, colors, fabrics, and jacket and skirt details as acceptable, as long as some degree of men's classic tailoring was present. Both uniformity and diversity were accommodated within the flexible code for women's interview dress.

This tolerance for variety in women's suits was striking in contrast to the relative uniformity of men's suits. Fuzziness in aggregate patterns of choices for men's business dress is present in the twentieth century, but the degree of variety in choices is highly restricted in comparison to women's business-dress choices (McCracken, 1985). Turner (1991) suggested that such looseness of rules and less predictable aesthetic choice in women's business dress could only send conflicting messages about executive power and question the legitimacy of male dominance in management and capitalist rationality in business. Without highly restrictive norms demanding similarity in dress, how can women be trusted to be businesslike (Kanter, 1977)?

**Theoretical Groundings**

Did dress advice articles recommend variety in women's business dress and uniformity in men's business dress? What does the match or mismatch reflect about gender roles and power relations in business? To answer these questions, we took a triangulation approach (Denzin & Lincoln, 1994) in which a variety of theories were employed to gain a multifaceted understanding of the phenomenon of business-dress advice and its relationship to (gendered) power relations in the workplace. These theories were useful in developing and exploring alternative propositions about what we might find within the recommendations. Theories were not deductively tested, but were examined for fit with patterns in the data.

## Postmodern Aesthetics

The current cultural condition, called 'postmodern' by some, has been character-ized as one of marked change (Featherstone, 1991; Gitlin, 1988; Lyotard, 1984). Postmodernism is 'indifferent to consistency and continuity, altogether' (Gitlin, 1988, p. 35). Kaiser, Nagasawa, and Hutton (1991, 1995) have proposed a theory that the postmodern condition produces a process of fashion change fueled by questioning of previous rules of aesthetics, morality, gender definitions, and power relationships. Objects and experiences are eclectically procured and assembled to aid in a constant construction and redefinition of self (Featherstone, 1991). In this cultural moment of fluidity and vagueness of boundaries of identities and meanings, ambiguity and ambivalence constantly fuel experimentation and reformulation of personal expression through dress (Kaiser et al., 1995). Fashion trends are fleeting and multivalent, producing many current looks which the consumer can choose to adapt in part or whole (Kaiser et al., 1991; Wilson, 1992).

If Kaiser et al.'s (1991) theoretical propositions about meanings in the postmodern condition hold true in the arena of business-dress recommenda-tions, we should find authors advising women, who have traditionally had freedom to explore elaborated and varied codes of dress (McCracken, 1985), to pursue playful *bricolage* and to push the restrictive limits of business dress codes. Similarly, if their proposition holds, we should see authors' recom-mendations for men reflecting a move from restrictive uniformity toward questioning of and play upon traditional codes.

## Trickle Down Theory

Classic theories addressing class emulation and the adoption of dress styles are also pertinent to the present study. McCracken (1985) proposed that as women entered upper ranks of the business arena, they adopted dress styles worn by men, their superordinates in business, in a 'trickle down' process of style diffusion. McCracken extended Simmel's (1904), Veblen's (1912), and Barber and Lobel's (1952) class-based theories of fashion change to explain how behavioral imitation in dress choices may have an instrumental goal such as career advancement. While attempting upward mobility in a social system (i.e., the U.S. business community), women purposefully appropriated parts of the men's business suit to make optimal use of its expressive qualities. McCracken (1985) contended that the business suit expresses 'ability, disci-pline, and reliability, the very qualities most useful to their [business men's and women's] occupational roles' (p. 47). Wearing dress that symbolizes positions of authority and power might help women to achieve those positions.

However, for the 'trickle down' theory to fully apply, we expect to find that men move away from the long standard business suit to a new form of business dress. As imitation among subordinates (i.e., women) becomes prevalent, the emulated upper strata tend to move on to new styles to maintain distinction from the lower strata. McCracken (1985) purported that a new style of 'heroic elegance' for men was promoted in the mid-1980s, a possible move to differentiate the ruling elite of men from women invading the boardroom.

**Symbolic Self Completion**

Symbolic self-completion theory (Wicklund & Gollwitzer, 1982) can also lend insight into the imitation of behaviors and adoption of group symbols in early stages of role taking. Solomon (1983; Solomon & Douglas, 1985) applied the theory to adoption of consumer products such as dress for enactment of occupational roles. When an individual takes on a new role, he or she is likely to conform to role norms to help in learning and gaining confidence in the role. The individual who is accomplished or experienced in a role may be confident enough to relax from strict norm adherence resulting in greater variety of self-expression in the role. The accomplished role taker is more likely to choose role props for self-actualization rather than instrumental accomplishment of the role.

For the present analysis, we stretch to adapt symbolic self-completion theory to businesswomen in the aggregate rather than to individual role enactments. Extending the theoretical tenets, we expect to find uniformity recommended in earlier dress advice articles, when women were newer to the business arena. We also expect to find slightly diversified or relaxed codes recommended in the 1990s articles, when the proportional representation of women in management ranks was increasing and women were becoming familiar as accomplished players in the business world.

If symbolic self-completion theory holds, however, men's business dress recommendations should be varied throughout the period studied, as men's predominance in business roles is long established. Further, advice reflective of this theory would encourage men to stray from established norms, particularly in articles focusing upon dress for men with institutional seniority or a record of marked career success.

**Assimilation Process**

Theory concerning the various ways that people adapt to new cultural environments also applies to the present research. Gans (1962) suggested that as individuals 'immigrate' into a new culture, just as women have moved into the men's culture of corporate America, they adopt behavioral practices of the new dominant culture. Individuals who acculturate adopt some new norms but do not fully become part of the new culture. Their social identity is still largely circumscribed by their native group, relegating the immigrants to marginal membership in the new culture. An acculturated immigrant's appearance to some extent will match or emulate that of dominant group members, but their appearance may also mark and underscore their marginal status. McCracken (1985) interpreted women's 'dress for success' suits as only partial adoption of the men's suit. For women entering business roles, their 'native' culture would be that of women and women's traditions in U.S. society within which aesthetic play and high involvement with dress was an acceptable and common engagement (McCracken, 1985; Sahlins, 1976).

Immigrants who assimilate become accepted into the new culture, sharing power and prestige, despite their differences with the dominant group (Hood & Koberg, 1994). Assimilated immigrants may appear highly similar to their adopted group (Arthur, 1997), or their differences in appearance may be integrated into evolving mainstream norms and evolving definitions of the hegemonous power group. If women are highly assimilated into executive ranks, we might find that women have adopted men's dress styles completely or that their differences in dress may be fully accepted and currently influencing men's business dress.

## Purpose

The purpose of this study was to explore popular press recommendations concerning business dress as a reflection of the development of men's and women's roles and power relations in business. Prior to this research, limited analyses (e.g., Forsythe, 1993) of popular press business dress advice for women had been undertaken. As such, in this study we conducted an exhaustive analysis, examining and comparing the content of popular press articles dispensing business-dress advice to both men and women. To help in understanding our findings, we examined the fit of predictions stemming from several theories to our data. In doing so, these theories, and our predictions stemming from them, became the lens through which we interpreted our findings.

## Method

An inductive content analysis approach was adopted to examine specific business dress recommendations in the popular press as well as the degree of variety or uncertainty reflected in these recommendations. Magazine and

**Table 4.1.** Source of articles

| Magazine/Newspaper Title | Number of Articles |
| --- | --- |
| Glamour | 28 |
| Working Woman | 14 |
| Madamoiselle | 5 |
| Essence | 4 |
| New York Times | 5 |
| Des Moines Register | 5 |
| Business Week | 3 |
| Vogue | 5 |
| Black Enterprise | 2 |
| Redbook | 2 |
| Ebony, Esquire, Forbes, Fortune, GQ, Harper's Bazaar, Ladies' Home Journal, McCall's, New York Times Magazine, Wall Street Journal, Washington Post | 1 each |
| Total Articles | 84 |

newspaper articles giving advice and description of business dress were collected through an exhaustive sampling of articles published from 1986 to 1994 and listed in the *The Reader's Guide to Periodical Literature*, *The New York Times Index*, and *The Wall Street Journal Index*. Supplementary articles were added from the *Washington Post* and the *Des Moines Register*, newspapers that were not exhaustively sampled for this study.

Using this process we located a total of 84 articles composed by 48 authors and located in 21 different city and national newspapers and general audience magazines. Table 4.1 contains a list of magazines and newspapers from which the articles were sampled. In twenty cases, no specific author was provided or an anonymous author was credited (e.g., 'editor'). No individual author wrote more than three articles.

Advice in each article was recorded if related to: makeup and grooming, hair, accessories, jewelry, clothing style characteristics, hosiery, shoes, the context in which styles would be appropriate, and other miscellaneous comments related to dress. Only the written text of the articles was analyzed; nontext images (e.g., photographs or drawings) featured with the articles were not analyzed. Article content was organized and analyzed according to recommendations for dress and context of use.

The number of articles in which a recommendation appeared was our unit of quantification rather than the number of authors who made a specific recommendation. This decision was based on two factors. First, we took a viewer perspective in our analysis, making the content and frequency of given messages that a reader would encounter the focus of analysis rather than the authors. We assumed that the frequency with which a piece of advice appeared in the media would provide a better indication of the composite or aggregated messages dispensed to media users. Similarly, we assumed that most readers would be unlikely to pay attention to or remember a given popular press author, but more likely to remember a piece of repeatedly encountered advice. Second, it was not always possible to ascertain author identity. As such, it was impossible to conduct an analysis with author as key variable. When possible, author gender and magazine source were considered for potential impact on advice content.

## Findings

Of the 84 articles analyzed, 80 included recommendations for women and 12 included recommendations for men. Advice dispensed did not vary by publication source or ethnicity of target audience. For example, *Glamour* magazine, representing 35 per cent of the articles, offered varied advice across articles. Five general patterns emerged from the recommendations: high-consensus recommendations, variety in recommendations, context-related recommendations, femininity and sexiness of recommended dress, and pervasive dress philosophies.

### Recommendations for Women

*High-consensus recommendations*   In a few cases, garment characteristics (e.g., fabrication, style, fit, etc.) were frequently recommended as appropriate or inappropriate for work attire. Instances in which nine or more articles (over 10 per cent) recommended a garment or accessory and were unopposed in other articles were interpreted as indicating clearly defined and widely accepted advice about appropriate women's work dress. (Agreement levels were rarely above 10 per cent.) Suggested as appropriate in nine or more unchallenged articles were: suits in bright 'fashionable' colors; slim, fitted, straight skirts; silk fabric; wool fabric; scarves; flat heels; low heels; and fine quality, 'real' jewelry.

*Variety in recommendations*   The advice was usually explicit in detail and quite varied across articles. Often, the variety was manifested in blatant contrasts across articles. In other cases, the articles did not include overt disagreement, but their recommendations were so diverse that a clear standard of what was considered appropriate women's business dress could not be delineated. A wide and varied group of alternatives for each garment style, garment length, and color were identified as appropriate. Hence, the data overall indicated approval of many, varied dress options for women in business rather than defining a single, 'correct' look.

The following style and length details were deemed inappropriate in at least two or more articles: sarong or wrap skirts, short or very short skirts, leggings, severely man-tailored jackets and suits, sleeveless garments, dangling earrings, bow ties, pumps, sandals, and sneakers. Adding to the confusion, however, was at least one other article suggesting that these same items were appropriate.

Complexity in and qualifications of recommendations abounded. For example, six articles recommended plaid, yet one qualified the recommendation, limiting the endorsement to plaids containing four or fewer colors. One other article contended that women should never wear plaids or tweeds to work.

*Context-related recommendations*   Thirty-four of the articles presented context-specific recommendations, perhaps the principal factor leading to the diversity in recommendations.

> Specifics will vary depending on where you live, who runs your business, and how informal your workplace is. ("Caution: Beauty at Work", 1992, p. 170)

Some of these context-specific recommendations pertained to dress for certain occupations, occupational rankings, or regions of the country (i.e., the South, the West, or New York City). Other recommendations described the dress expectations of unique firms. Across the articles, specific advice was given for twenty-two different job fields. Banking was frequently mentioned as the most conservative field; fashion and design fields were the least conservative.

The contextual recommendations contained suggestions that varied with stage of employment. Nine articles addressed interview attire, for which conservative looks were consistently recommended. Some articles recommended that interviewees match the formality of their interview dress to that which would be expected in their prospective job, while others suggested dress 'one notch above' the formality of role attire norms. In all cases, articles emphasized the importance of dress in the interview situation. Recommendations regarding dress for entry level positions were relatively consistent, but several articles supported the notion that women only need to wear 'success suits' to interviews or during the first few months on the job ("Breaking the Code", 1990; Hoffman, 1991; Stacey, 1992).

Advice pertaining to mid-level positions frequently suggested that women dress to emulate executives in their particular field. Tailored jackets were recommended for these women. Advice about executive dressing was somewhat varied; four articles recommended understated, conventional business attire, while four others suggested that established career women could stretch beyond conservative dress norms.

> Your dress codes come from your environment, and as you rise in the organization your environment changes. (Moody in "Breaking the Code", 1990, p. 56)

Differing advice was also given for younger and older women. For example, 'shorter' skirts were said to be appropriate for younger women with 'pretty' legs, but 'silly' and inappropriate for older women (Radziwill, 1988, p. 136).

*Femininity and sexiness of recommended dress* Perhaps the most fervent dispute played out in the recommendations dispensed to women concerned the issue of sexually suggestive dress. The advice reflected two divergent views: (a) that sexy dress is appropriate for work and (b) that sexy dress is inappropriate for work. The seven articles whose authors protested sexually attractive or suggestive dress denounced all revealing and provocative styles as 'unquestionably unfit,' and, in the words of one author, warned readers not to wear clothes that 'scream "come to bed with me"'(Stacey, 1992, p. 175). Three of these seven articles also condemned all overtly 'feminine' dress (no matter how modest); according to these articles, women's work dress should serve professional purposes only and should not attract the sexual attention of male colleagues. (In these articles, authors tended to blur the distinction between the words 'sexy' and 'feminine', in some cases using them synonymously.) These recommendations were consistently justified with four arguments: (a) that wearing blatantly feminine or suggestive dress undermines a woman's authority, (b) that wearing blatantly feminine or suggestive dress increases a woman's chances of sexual harassment, (c) that wearing suggestive dress increases the chance of rumors alleging that the wearer's success is based on something other than her job performance, and (d) that women should not rely upon their 'feminine wiles' to get ahead in the workplace as they have superior means by which to foster career development (i.e., intellect, creativity, competence).

Nine articles supported the opposite claim and asserted that suggestive (even seductive) dress does have a place at work. Several of these articles indicated that women have 'reclaimed their sexuality' at work (Hoschwender, 1991, p. 230), and that sexuality can (and should) be used to a woman's advantage. For example, in several articles authors insisted that women ought to employ their physical presence to underscore their professionalism. Boldly asserting one's sexiness was interpreted as assertive and therefore conducive to emphasizing professional power. According to recommendations in these articles, authority and credibility are assumed if a person successfully holds a position of responsibility. These articles often cited two reasons for this new-found embracement of sexuality in the office: (a) that women's new confidence in taking on business roles should enable them to depart from the male standards from which they previously sought reassurance, and (b) that in an uncertain economy a woman reaching for success must distinguish herself beyond other competent workers with a dynamic and impressive look that uses all of her resources. Articles suggested a tough but feminine, sexy but authoritative look as achieved through the use of soft lines, authoritative colors, and suggestive, but not showy, garments. The articles did not explain how women could be 'suggestive but not showy.'

*Two pervasive dress philosophies*   As noted, our analysis revealed substantial variety in the recommendations pertaining to women's dress. This diversity in recommendations seemed indicative of a general acceptance for multiple forms of women's business dress. The recommendations were not completely disparate, however. Common themes in the advice were identified that roughly distinguished two diverging dress standards: (a) the low-risk, conservative, business suit look (n = 32), and (b) the innovative, stylish, individualistic look (n = 29). Some articles offered mixed advice, especially those addressing the importance of context.

Articles that recommended a conservative, suited look generally suggested a feminized version of the men's suit, with a caveat that the 'male clone look' of the early 1980s was no longer appropriate. Here it was suggested that because the professional attire worn by men in positions of power is usually traditional and afashionable, the simplest way to emanate a powerful image is to dress conservatively and with limited fashion flair. In contrast, articles recommending against the conservative standard frequently suggested that extremely conservative dress is often boring and indistinguishable, undermining a woman's right to self-expression and enjoyment of gender identity. In these articles, women were encouraged to use fashion to develop a personal style that could underscore their independence and move them up the career ladder.

## Recommendations for Men

*High-consensus recommendations*   Unlike the advice provided to women, there was a great deal of consistency across suggestions made for businessmen.

Ten articles suggested that businessmen wear either a suit or sportscoat. The two articles not suggesting a jacket were describing 'Casual Day' dress. Eight articles recommended that the jacket or suit be dark in color, preferably gray or navy. Seven articles suggested that neckties are an essential element of the business look.

*Variety in recommendations*   With a few exceptions, variety among recommendations for men was relatively slight. Some variation in small details was included, but the basic pieces of the suit were highly agreed upon. In contrast to recommendations for women, there was an absence of endless details about fabric and color possibilities in jackets and pants, collar and neckline styling, and length of jackets and pants. When details were provided, they were often prescriptive and limiting as to choices.

> Where is it written that a man's belt must match the color of his shoes? Here. Belt must match shoes. After that, just make sure to avoid extremes: An inch to an inch and a quarter is a good width. Finer finishes (pebble graining, for example) are preferred, Western stitching isn't. And buckles should be sturdy but simple – no Harley logos or turquoise, please. (Omelianuk, 1994, p. 113)

One exception to the relative consistency among recommendations concerned colors and patterns of men's dress shirts. Here, a variety of options was deemed appropriate, even bold windowpane checks (Omelianuk, 1994). There was even greater variation in advice related to neckties, particularly in color and pattern recommendations. One author (Nusbaum, 1989) indicated that the necktie is the only part of a man's business dress that provides him with an opportunity to express his personality or individual tastes.

Of the twelve articles dispensing advice to men, three provided most of the variety in recommendations. Interestingly, all three of these articles concerned Casual Day dress. In these articles, men were advised to adopt trendy, relaxed dress for the office. Thus, barring variety associated with Casual Day and shirt and tie recommendations, men's business dress advice was remarkably consistent.

*Context-related recommendations*   The issue of context was addressed in seven of the twelve articles, suggesting that what is considered appropriate dress for men may vary by office and occupation. However, in contrast to women, neither age nor geographical region was addressed as a factor that might influence men's dress options.

*Sexiness and the businessman*   In the twelve articles about menswear, sexual expression was simply not addressed. The only mention of display related to the recommendation to wear socks that were long enough to prevent exposure of a bare calf when legs were crossed. Decorum, rather than sexual display, was the reasoning behind the issue.

*One pervasive dress philosophy*  In contrast to the great variety characterizing the recommendations for women, advice dispensed to men was notably consistent and revealed one pervasive philosophy – conservatism. Prior to 1994 the casual look had yet to be widely recommended as acceptable business dress, and the tailored suit was consistently suggested as most appropriate for men in the workplace.

## Discussion

As is evident from the great variety in the recommendations for women, the advice dispensed in the articles, as a whole did not delineate a clear standard for women's business dress. This finding is consistent with those from Forsythe's (1993) review of business-dress advice. Very few recommendations were found for which there was complete consensus across articles. A female consumer attempting to glean clear advice from popular-press sources about business dress probably experiences great confusion if she reads more than one article.

For men, advice reflected relative consensus in recommendations for formal days at work, with only small room for variety in choice of shirt and colors and patterns of ties. Social expectations for men's business dress, as reflected in popular media, offer men few, relatively inflexible options. One author, Schiro (1989), contended that, due to limited range of choices to be made, men's professional dressing is easier than women's. Perhaps this is why so few articles were written that focused on advice for men's business dress during this time period.

### Support of Theories

The contextual advice and apparent questioning of restrictive dress codes for women fits with theoretical propositions (Kaiser et al., 1991, 1995) about dress in the postmodern era. The recommendations in advice articles reflected unease with whole-scale adoption of traditional men's suit styles on the part of women in business. Overall, it seems that the advice encouraged women, who traditionally have had the perquisite of fashion and elaborated codes of dress, to borrow some of traditional men's business dress (in particular, wearing a tailored or semi-tailored jacket) and to play with colors, patterns, fabrics, and style lines in these symbols. Eclectic borrowing from men's and women's dress results in a process of *bricolage* in which women take agency in putting portions of available dress styles together to formulate a distinctive and personalized visible identity in the workplace (e.g., Gubrium & Holstein, 1995). Bits of traditional women's culture (i.e., concern with fashion) and bits of men's dress symbols of business professionalism are constructed into an expression of competence at business, fashion, aesthetics, and being female, all in one multi-faceted identity.

Lyotard (1984) in *The Postmodern Condition* described how the self 'exists in a fabric of relations that is now more complex and mobile than ever before' (p.15). We can here take that almost literally as we look at recommendations for the dress with which a businesswoman expresses her identities in the workplace. Rather than emphasizing one role identity as business person, as the often recommended men's suit does (e.g., Joseph & Alex, 1972), the postmodern recommendations concerning businesswoman's dress present simultaneous nonverbal language games of multiplex identity (Lyotard, 1984). This identity comprises business acumen, personal taste and character, up-to-date savvy, aesthetic skill, sexual savvy (depending upon whose advice is acknowledged), and an array of contextual and situational adjustments. This interpretation is supported by Kimle and Damhorst (1997) who, in their interviews of businesswomen, found that each woman reported juggling just such an array of meanings while dressing for work each day.

In contrast, recommendations for men's business dress allow little room for expression of a multifaceted self. Only a few contextual adjustments and a small personal statement in the tie and shirt are allowed, if the wearer is brave enough. Recommendations concerning men's suits are clearly not of the postmodern era and have been little adjusted to the times. If suits have functioned well since 1666, however, it is probably threatening to modify them much. To engage in the hedonic of aesthetic variety would question traditional codes of 'rational' business dress and appear feminine – two violations that might signify lack of power. Men, who have long held power in the business arena, will probably be slow to give up their long-effective, instrumental symbols. It seems to take an organizational proclamation of 'Casual Day' to condone relaxation from rigid norms. Indeed, the 'staying power' of the male business suit, despite some relaxation with casual business-wear, may attest to the fact that modernity is not entirely behind us.

The endurance and seeming modernity of the men's business suit may indicate its status as a highly developed symbol in the U.S. or an example of what Crawley (1965) has referred to as 'sacred dress.' The suit and tie symbolizes the ideal role for men in industrial society. Altering the role would question the basis of the capitalistic, laissez- faire economy that is still, at least mythically, the root and guarantee of U.S. corporate society. The suit and tie for men of business, commerce, and administration is a sacrosanct symbol that survives even into the tradition-questioning, post-industrial society characterizing the end of the twentieth century (Baudrillard, 1983).

Perhaps least successful as an explanatory theory, the trickle down effect was not clearly evident in the dress advice for women. Some semblance to or partial adoption of menswear was present in the conservative look recommended for women. However, the recommendations for elaborate variations to downplay too masculine a look very much weaken the support for this theory. In addition, a consequent abandoning by superordinate men of the emulated business suit style is not yet evident despite McCracken's (1985) projections. Women are encouraged to incorporate such variety in their adoptions that they are the ones who are told to move beyond the trickled-down style.

Expansion of symbolic self-completion theory (Wicklund & Gollwitzer, 1982) to the collective of women in business could add to understanding of the high degree of variety recommended. The variety may reflect that the authors believe that women have entered business in sufficient numbers to lend confidence to stray from rigid norms of dress. We did not find, however, that the earliest years of recommendations analyzed (1986 and 1987) gave any less variety in recommendations than later years. We can only assume that borrowing of a restricted code (indicative of masculinity) occurred earlier than our data sample, when women were even scarcer in numbers in business. But if symbolic self-completion theory fits, why have we not found greater variety in recommendations for menswear? Men's domination in upper ranks of business should afford some relaxation of dress norms among men in the top ranks at least. The only room for variety seems to be in ties, shirts, and maybe suspenders carefully hidden under jackets. Perhaps these small variations are substantial changes for men who have not been socialized to manipulate an elaborated code in dress.

We might also conclude from the dress recommendations that women have only acculturated to the men's world of business rather than moved to full assimilation. Women are still largely defining themselves through dress as role takers in business who have not fully internalized business norms created by men. Rather than remaining as marginal players, however, the advisors imply that women's acculturated appearances are redefining what is professional in dress. We have yet to see women's dress norms reflected clearly in men's business dress, though variety in tie and shirt fabrics may be evidence of a small shift toward variety for men. If women continue to 'infiltrate' middle and upper ranks of businesses in increasing numbers and redefine, to some extent, the culture of business, we may see greater evidence of their assimilation into that culture.

The dress advice media could be accused of presenting ambiguity about women's identities. Douglas has noted (1994):

> The media, of course, urged [women] to be pliant, cute, sexually available, thin, blond, poreless, wrinkle-free, and deferential to men. But it is easy to forget that the media also suggested [women] could be rebellious, tough, enterprising, and shrewd (Douglas, 1994, p. 9).

In the advice articles, women were told to look sexy and feminine while also being powerful and competent (but not boring). The conflicting nature of these messages could be said to create what Frye (1983) has referred to as a 'double bind' situation, in which each available option carries with it some penalty:

> If one dresses one way, one is subject to the assumption that one is advertising one's sexual availability; if one dresses another way, one appears 'not to care about oneself' or to be 'unfeminine' (Frye, 1983, p. 3).

It seems to us that society is moving unevenly in an advance-and-retreat pattern to accept women into positions of business power. For women to take full share of power at the helms of business corporations may be too frightening for some. Women, power, and rationality in business are not congruent concepts for many in U.S. society. A partial adoption of men's business dress may help to soften the move of women into business positions of authority and control. Oddly enough, in other role arenas, women have been allowed to wear the same dress as men (e.g., as police, some facets of military roles, in school bands). The role of business leader may be too close to the roots of real power in capitalistic U.S. society to let women in readily. Underscoring her appearance as immigrant may soften the threat, but also slow assimilation by lending questions about women's fitness for the role.

Is this ambiguity of dress advice a latent plot to keep women from top ranks in business by encouraging inappropriate dress? Of course, some readers could come to the conclusion that there is a devious mission apparent in the variety and endless detail of advice given; in effect, this could keep women obsessed with appearance and too busy to get important work done (Faludi, 1991). Indeed, Naomi Wolf (1991) contended that women's business appearances, as promoted in the media, marginalized women. Wolf felt that society's encouragement of women to look fashionable and even sexy in the workplace represented a plot to support the fashion industry and a strategy that ultimately keeps women from leadership roles in business for which fashionable attire is inappropriate.

However, the variety of recommendations can also be interpreted as diversity of opinion as to what women can be in business and how they can go about manifesting their career identities. Overall, the diversity of recommendations does afford proactivity in choices. The ambiguity characterizing the recommendations comes across articles more than within any one article. Rather than simply creating a no-win, double-bind situation, the dress-advice articles may be serving as a platform for negotiation of women's business dress. Dress-advice articles may be part of an ongoing societal negotiation of meanings of women's appearances and their legitimacy in business leadership roles.

Returning to Turner's (1991) notion that a varied business-dress aesthetic could question the legitimacy of male domination, women's varied dress could serve as a form of resistance to corporate echelons and as a challenge to male hegemony. In essence, women in business may be proposing through dress what some feminists have long contended, that it is important to acknowledge feminine experience and knowledge as valid and equally valuable as masculine experience and ways of thinking (Fischer, Reuber, & Dyke, 1993; Jagger, 1983). Varied aesthetics and other feminine qualities can be valuable in a corporate environment, too. Women may mix masculine and feminine style components in their dress as they attempt to bring an androgynous mix of characteristics to the business arena.

## Conclusion

The advice in popular press articles on women's business dress tells us much about women's roles at the end of the twentieth century. The degree of variety in recommendations indicates both contextual specificity of women's work-role norms and a general degree of disagreement about what is appropriate. Some writers cling cautiously to older and once safer traditions of business-suit styling not originally created for or by women. Other authors seem anxious to leap away from men's traditions and recommend adoption of dress that, to some extent, celebrates the multiform and polychromatic appearances of traditional women's non-business dress.

In contrast, the advice for men does not indicate that sweeping changes are occurring in men's business dress. However, the encouragement of limited experimentation with ties and shirts and the possible trend toward greater casualness in business dress possibly foretell an emerging change. A redefinition of what is 'businesslike' behavior may be coming in the near future.

Futurists predict that we are moving to a new age of diversity and situation specificity (Aburdene & Naisbitt, 1992; Toffler, 1980). It is possible that the twenty-first century may include an era of strategic use of variety to customize norms to endless diversity in business situations. Women's less restricted (in comparison to men's) and elaborated dress code may be inherently adaptive to highly contextualized and customized business environments. Oddly enough, it may be that women's current experimentation with varied styles may lead the way to new flexibility of norms of business dress for both men and women.

Gherardi (1994) stated:

> Doing gender involves symbols, using them, playing with them and transforming them; it entails managing the dual presence: shuttling between a symbolic universe coherent with one gender identity and the symbolic realm of the 'other' gender. (pp. 598–9)

Women in business today are shuttling between female and male symbolic universes simultaneously and inhabiting the dual presence perhaps to a degree never before seen in history. Their androgynous incorporations (or recommendations to do so) of men's and women's dress symbols into a single appearance may reflect a general consensus that women in business can successfully combine characteristics and behaviors previously relegated to the domain of one or the other gender. Is this confidence in adoption of symbolic duality a resistance against the hegemonous power structure, a co-optation that mimics but also challenges the status quo? Is this duality problematic, as Douglas (1994) seems to frame it? Or does women's success at inhabiting a dual identity reflect or foretell a growing openness in U.S. businesses in general to accept and value women – bringing with them a portion of behaviors traditionally regarded as feminine – as adaptive and flexible players in the organization? As women in business frame their dress to fit their new roles, they may be shaping a new role. Certainly, only time will tell.

## Notes

1. This research was funded in part by the Family and Consumer Sciences Research Institute, College of Family and Consumer Sciences, Iowa State University, Ames, IA 50011.

2. We employ the term 'symbol' in congruence with definitions from the fields of communication and symbolic interaction. Symbols are objects and behaviors that represent 'something more than what is immediately perceived' (Charon, 1985, p. 39). Because symbols are used to communicate abstract qualities and ideas beyond the physical features of the object or behavior, symbols are meaningful in social interaction. Indeed, meanings are a result of social interaction surrounding objects

and behaviors. The business dress advice we studied recommended objects to wear and arrangements of those objects on the body in order to give impressions of management or professional role, professionalism, competence, and social power. These ideas are not present in the body modifications themselves; the symbolic dress styles carry meanings (according to the popular press advisors) that imply qualities of the wearer. In the symbolic interactionist tradition, we emphasize the word 'symbol' and do not distinguish among the terms 'symbol,' 'sign,' or 'icon,' due to the lack of clarity in definitions of these terms across scholars and fields (see Lyons, 1979).

3. We use the term 'code' in the general sense of the term, not as a reference to specific written dress codes in business organizations. Codes are the rules of combination of signs (or symbols) in communicative intercourse (Eco, 1976). The symbols and ordering of symbols used to produce and exchange meanings are defined by codes.

# References

Aburdene, P., & Naisbitt, J. (1992). *Megatrends for women*. New York: Villard Books.

Altheide, D. L., & Johnson, J. M. (1994). Criteria for assessing interpretive validity in qualitative research. In N. K. Denzin & Y. S. Lincoln (Eds), *Handbook of qualitative research* (pp. 485–99). London: Sage.

Arthur, L. B. (1997). Role salience, role embracement, and the symbolic self-completion of sorority pledges. *Sociological Inquiry, 67*(3), 364–79.

Barber, B., & Lobel, L. S. (1952, December). "Fashion" in women's clothes and the American social system. *Social Forces, 31*, 124–31.

Baudrillard, J. (1983). *Simulations* (P. Foss, P. Patton, & P. Beitchman, Trans.). New York: Semiotext(e), Inc.

Belk, R. W., & Pollay, R. W. (1985). Images of ourselves: The good life in twentieth century advertising. *Journal of Consumer Research, 11*, 887–97.

Blumer, H. (1969). *Symbolic interactionism, perspective and method*. Englewood Cliffs, NJ: Prentice Hall.

Breaking the Code. (1990, January). *Glamour*, p. 56.

Bureau of the Census. (1992). *Statistical abstract of the United States* (112th Ed.). Washington, D.C.: United States Department of Commerce, Economics and Statistics Administration.

Cash, T. F. (1985). The impact of grooming style on the evaluation of women in management. In M. R. Solomon (Ed.), *The psychology of fashion* (pp. 343–55). Lexington, MA: Lexington Books.

Caution: Beauty at work. (1992, April). *Mademoiselle*, 170–1.

Charon, J. M. (1985). *Symbolic interactionism* (2nd ed.). Englewood Cliffs, NJ: Prentice-Hall.

Crawley, E. (1965). Sacred dress. In M. E. Roach & J. B. Eicher (Eds), *Dress, adornment, and the social order* (pp. 138–41). New York: John Wiley and Sons.

Damhorst, M. L., Eckman, M., & Stout, S. (1986). Cluster analysis of women's business suits [Abstract]. *ACPTC Proceedings: National Meeting* (p. 65). Monument, CO: Association of College Professors of Textiles and Clothing.

Damhorst, M. L., & Fiore, A. M. (1993). Evaluations of women's suits by male and female personnel interviewers. In J. A. Costa (Ed.), *Gender and Consumer Behavior Second Conference Proceedings* (pp. 58–60). Salt Lake City, UT: University of Utah Printing Service.

Damhorst, M. L., & Reed, J. A. (1986). Clothing color value and facial expression: Effects on evaluations of female job applicants. *Social Behavior and Personality, 14*(1), 88–98.

Davis, F. (1982). On the "symbolic" in symbolic interaction. *Symbolic Interaction, 5*, 111–26.

Denzin, N. K., & Lincoln, Y. S. (1994). *Handbook of qualitative research*. Thousand Oaks, CA: Sage Publications.

Douglas, S. (1994). *Where the girls are: Growing up with the mass media*. New York: Times Books.

Eco, U. (1976). *A theory of semiotics*. Bloomington, IN: Indiana University Press.

Faludi, S. (1991). *Backlash: The undeclared war against American women*. New York: Crown Publishers.

Featherstone, M. (1991). *Consumer culture and postmodernism*. London: Sage Publications.

Fischer, E. M., Reuber, A. R., & Dyke, L. S. (1993). A theoretical overview and extension of research on sex, gender, and entrepreneurship. *Journal of Business Venturing, 8*, 151–68.

Forsythe, S. M. (1993). Dressing for success: The myth and the reality. *Journal of Home Economics, 85*(4), 49–53.

Forsythe, S. M., Drake, M. F., & Cox, C. A. (1984). Dress as an influence on the perceptions of management characteristics in women. *Home Economics Research Journal, 13*(2), 112–21.

Foucault, M. (1977). *Discipline and punish: The birth of the prison*. New York: Pantheon Books.

Frye, M. (1983). *The politics of reality: Essays in feminist theory*. Freedom, CA: The Crossing Press.

Gans, H. J. (1962). *The urban villagers: Group and class life of Italian-Americans*. New York: The Free Press.

Gherardi, S. (1994). The gender we think, the gender we do in our everyday organizational lives. *Human Relations, 47*, 591–610.

Gitlin, T. (1988, November 6). Hip deep in postmodernism. *The New York Times Book Review*, pp. 1, 35–6.

Gross, B. L., & Sheth, J. N. (1989). Time-oriented advertising: A content analysis of United States magazine advertising, 1890–1988. *Journal of Marketing, 53*, 76–83.

Gubrium, J. F., & Holstein, J. A. (1995). Individual agency, the ordinary, and postmodern life. *The Sociological Quarterly, 36*, 555–70.

Harragan, B. L. (1977). *Games mother never taught you: Corporate gameship for women*. New York: Warner Books.

Hoffman, D. (1991, June 2). Work clothes 101: Suits are still best. *The New York Times*, p. 56.

Hood, J. N., & Koberg, C. S. (1994). Patterns of differential assimilation and acculuration for women in business organizations. *Human Relations, 47*(2), 159–81.

Hoschwender, W. (1991, October). Vogue beauty: Appearance at work. *Vogue*, 230–6.

Holbrook, M. B., & Dixon, G. (1985). Mapping the market for fashion: Complementarity in consumer preferences. In M. R. Solomon (Ed.), *The psychology of fashion* (pp.109–26). Lexington, MA: Lexington Books.

Jaggar, A. (1983). *Feminist politics and human nature*. NJ: Rowman and Allenheld.

Joseph, N., & Alex, N. (1972). The uniform: A sociological perspective. *American Journal of Sociology, 77*, 719–30.

Kaiser, S. B., Lennon, S. J., & Damhorst, M. L. (1991). Forum: Gendered appearances in twentieth century popular media. *Dress, 18*, 49–77.

Kaiser, S. B., Nagasawa, R. H., & Hutton, S. S. (1991). Fashion, postmodernity and personal appearance: A symbolic interactionist formulation. *Symbolic Interaction, 14*(2), 165–85.

Kaiser, S. B., Nagasawa, R. H., & Hutton, S. S. (1995). Construction of an SI theory of fashion: Part 1. Ambivalence and change. *Clothing and Textiles Research Journal, 13*(3), 172–83.

Kanter, R. M. (1977). *Men and women of the corporation*. New York: Basic Books, Inc., Publishers.

Kimle, P. A., & Damhorst, M. L. (1997). A grounded theory model of the ideal business image for women. *Symbolic Interaction, 20*, 45–68.

Kuchta, D. M. (1990). Graceful, virile, and useful: The origins of the three-piece suit. *Dress, 17*, 118–26.

Lyons, J. (1977). *Semantics (Vol. 1)*. Cambridge, England: Cambridge University Press.

Lyotard, J. F. (1984). *The postmodern condition: A report on knowledge* (G. Bennington & B. Messumi, Trans.). Minneapolis: University of Minnesota Press. (Original work published 1979)

Mannheim, K. (1960). *Ideology and utopia*. London: Routledge & Kegan Paul.

McCracken, G. D. (1985). The trickle-down theory rehabilitated. In M. R. Solomon (Ed.), *The psychology of fashion* (pp. 40–54). Lexington, MA: Lexington Books.

Molloy, J. T. (1977). *Women's dress for success book*. Chicago: Follett.

Morgado, M. A. (1996). Coming to terms with postmodern: Theories and concepts of contemporary culture and their implications for apparel scholars. *Clothing and Textiles Research Journal, 14*(1), 41-53.

Nusbaum, E. (1989, January). Suitable attire: Guys, make the fashion grade on first job hunt. The *Des Moines Register*, pp. 1E–2E.

Omelianuk, S. (1994, August). All about suits. *Gentlemen's Quarterly*, 104–17.

Radziwill, L. (1988, April). Fashion: Less is more. *McCalls*, 136.

Rafaeli, A., & Pratt, M. G. (1993). Tailored meanings: On the meaning and impact of organizational dress. *Academy of Management Review, 18*, 32–55.

Rucker, M., Taber, D., & Harrison, A. (1981). The effect of clothing variation on first impressions of female job applicants: What to wear when. *Social Behavior and Personality, 9*(1), 53–64.

Sahlins, M. D. (1976). *Culture and practical reason*. Chicago: University of Chicago Press.

Saunders, C., & Stead, B. (1986). Women's adoption of a business uniform: A content analysis of magazine advertisements. *Sex Roles, 15*(3/4), 197–205.

Scherbaum, C., & Shepherd, D. (1987). Dressing for success: Effects of color and layering on perceptions of women in business. *Sex Roles, 16*(7/8), 391–9.

Schiro, A. M. (1989, March 2). For men, clothes that make the character. The *New York Times*, p. 62.

Simmel, G. (1904). Fashion. *International Quarterly, 10*, 130–55.

Solomon, M. R. (1983). The role of products as social stimuli: A symbolic inter-actionism perspective. *Journal of Consumer Research, 10*, 319–29.

Solomon, M. R., & Douglas, S. P. (1987). Diversity in product symbolism: The case of female executive clothing. *Psychology & Marketing, 4*(3), 189–212.

Solomon, M. R., & Douglas, S. P. (1985). The female clothes horse: From aesthetics to tactics. In M. R. Solomon (Ed.), *The psychology of fashion* (pp. 387–401). Lexington, MA: Lexington Books.

Stacey, M. (1992, June). Risqué business: How sexy is too sexy? *Mademoiselle*, 173–175.

Stone, G. (1962). Appearance and the self. In A. M. Rose (Ed.), *Human behavior and social processes: An interactionist approach* (pp. 86–118). New York: Houghton Mifflin.

Toffler, A. (1980). *The third wave*. New York: Bantam Books.

Turner, B. S. (1991). Recent developments in the theory of the body. In M. Feather-stone, M. Hepworth, & B. S. Turner (Eds), *The body: Social process and cultural theory* (pp. 1–35). London: Sage Publications.

Veblen, T. (1912). *The theory of the leisure class*. New York: Macmillan.

Wicklund, R. A., & Gollwitzer, P. M. (1982). *Symbolic self completion*. Hillsdale, NJ: Erlbaum.

Wilson, E. (1992). Fashion and the postmodern body. In J. Ash & E. Wilson (Eds.), *Chic thrills*. Berkeley: University of California Press.

Wolf, N. (1991). *The beauty myth*. New York: William Morrow.

# 5

# *Sex, Dress, and Power in the Workplace: 'Star Trek, The Next Generation'*

## Sharron J. Lennon

As women have entered the workforce in ever-increasing numbers, dress and human behavior researchers (Damhorst, 1984–5; Easterling, Leslie, & Jones, 1992; Forsythe, Drake, & Cox, 1984; Johnson & Roach-Higgins, 1987a, 1987b; Kimle & Damhorst, 1997; Thurston, Lennon, & Clayton, 1990) have shown an interest in the study of workplace dress. The workplace is an ideal site to examine relationships between dress and power due to its hierarchical nature and the typical formality of the workplace, both of which can be reflected in dress. Workplace dress has been studied using a variety of approaches; (1) by developing stimuli depicting individuals and measuring the impressions conveyed by the stimuli (Damhorst, 1984–5; Forsythe, Drake, & Cox, 1984), (2) by interviewing (Kimle & Damhorst, 1997) or surveying (Easterling, Leslie, & Jones, 1992) employed individuals about workplace dress, and (3) by analyzing how workplace dress is depicted on television (Lennon, 1990a, 1990b, 1992).

Television and other media, in addition to dress and other artifacts (Weibel, 1977), are cultural products or cultural forms and represent abstract ideas within a culture or society (Johnson, 1986–7). Studies of media are important to undertake because media and society reflect each other (Belk & Pollay, 1985). As a result, in a television series the use of dress will reflect how society uses and interprets dress. While media does not accurately mirror life, media does provide information regarding the society that produced it.

The focus of this chapter is to analyze and discuss how power is conveyed on television using 'Star Trek, The Next Generation' as an example. Since biological sex is often related to power in many cultures, the extent to which men and women play equally influential roles and participate equally in decision-making are of interest in the analysis. Dress is often used by authors, playwrights, and certainly costume designers to convey information about the characters they create (Anderson & Anderson, 1985; Corbett, 1977; Cunningham, 1989; Russell, 1973); thus characters' dress is also examined. Power is defined and the various bases of interpersonal power are discussed. To set the stage for the analysis, a theoretical framework for the research and background information on the television series 'Star Trek, The Next Generation' is introduced.

## Power

French and Raven (1959) present a typology of the bases of social power in interpersonal influence which has been subsequently revised and updated several times (Raven, 1965, 1983, 1992, 1993). Raven (1992) defined social influence as 'a change in the belief, attitude or behavior of a person, the target of influence, which results from the action, or presence, of another person or group of persons, the influencing agent' (p. 218). Given this definition of social influence, social power is then defined as the potential to have such influence (Raven, 1992). Raven identified six bases of social power that are called coercion, reward, legitimacy, expert, reference, and information. Coercive power is based on threats of punishment, rejection, or disapproval. Reward power is based on the ability to provide tangible rewards or personal approval. Legitimate power is based on position, reciprocity, equity (e.g., I worked hard so I deserve something), or dependence (e.g., an obligation exists to help those who cannot help themselves). Expert power is based on expertise (e.g., we comply because we assume the advice is correct). Referent power is based on the desire to identify with someone. Informational power is based on a logical presentation of information by the influencing agent, which persuades the target to comply. With each of these six bases of power, the target exercises control and can decide whether to comply or not.

There are two other ways to influence outlined by Raven (1993), force and manipulation. Force is a change that occurs without the target's volition. Manipulation occurs when a target is influenced because some aspect of the target or the target's environment has been affected. An example of this would be when a driver is influenced to use a seat belt because the car will not start otherwise (Raven, 1993).

Based on these definitions, it is possible to see how different types of dress cues could represent and convey different types of social power. For example, police uniforms represent coercive power because police can arrest or detain citizens. A doctor's white lab coat represents expert power; physicians' advice is followed because patients have faith in their expertise. Because legitimate power is sometimes based on position in relationships, military rank signifies legitimate power to influence those of lower ranks. In this way, military uniforms represent legitimate power. A woman's extraordinary beauty might represent reward power. Finally, to Catholics the white clerical garb of the pope might represent informational power as a result of the belief that the pope has direct communication with God.

## Theoretical Framework

Perspectives based on the processes of social perception, symbolic interaction, and socially-shared cognition (Resnick, 1991) can be used to understand how dress and other appearance characteristics are used to convey power on 'Star Trek, The Next Generation'. Social perception is concerned with cognitive processes as they relate to people or information about people as the objects of perceptions. Impression formation refers to impressions formed of people during first encounters. Although impression formation is an individual process, there is fairly strong agreement among people regarding the kind of impression conveyed by a particular stimulus person (e.g., Damhorst, 1990; Davis, 1984). Although this agreement suggests an objective reality with respect to impressions associated with a given stimulus person, over thirty years ago psychologists began to question the existence of such an objective reality in impression formation (Dornbusch, Hastorf, Richardson, Muzzy, & Vreeland, 1965). Individuals seem to have unique ways of describing or categorizing others. These ways of describing or categorizing differ between people. Yet researchers have demonstrated that person schemata (e.g., Wyer, 1980; Wyer & Martin, 1986), or expectations for types of personality traits thought to co-occur together, are shared by people of the same culture and differ across cultures (Hoffman, Lau, & Johnson, 1986). The dilemma raised is 'how can people know the same thing if they are each constructing their knowledge separately?' (Resnick, 1991, p. 2).

What is known or perceived is not simply built on personal experience, but is influenced by information received from others whether in the form of writing, speech, pictures, or gestures (Resnick, 1991). Dialogue and inter-action are other such sources of information. Not only is knowledge influenced by personal and social sources of information, social experiences shape the very processes by which information is interpreted (Mead, 1934) and constructed (Alba & Hasher, 1983). By putting the *social* back in social cognition in this way, social cognition may be seen as the way in which people jointly construct knowledge about people (Morgan & Schwalbe, 1990; Resnick, 1991). To distinguish jointly constructed knowledge from individually con-structed knowledge, Resnick coined the term *socially shared* [sic] *cognition*. Because of socially-shared cognitions it is possible for a costume designer to convey information about a particular character visually such that the inform-ation is widely understood by audiences. In the context of visual information, socially-shared cognition occurs when a group of people recognizes and understands the meaning of a visual cultural icon (e.g., Santa Claus).

The portrayal of television characters is affected by the writers' perceptions of what the audience wants, the writers' perceptions of what the audience needs, and the stereotypes held by the writers (Lennon, 1990a). As they create characters, screenwriters, playwrights, and authors select symbols, such as dress cues, whose meanings are shared by audience members, and use them with their characters in order to facilitate socially-shared cognition. Characterization analysis, the analysis of characters in some form of media, often depends on dress cues associated with characters, especially when the form of the media is visual. Theater costume designers identify the primary function of stage costume to be the enhancement of characterization (e.g., Anderson & Anderson, 1985). Through characterization an author can attempt to manage or control the impression (Schlenker, 1986) of an individual's personality that is conveyed to an audience. This can be achieved by manipulating (a) visual characteristics of the actor and the salience of those characteristics, and by manipulating (b) the set or context (including interactions) of the play, novel, or television show within which the clothing and appearance of the actor is perceived (Corbett, 1977). Thus, socially-shared cognition is facilitated by a judicious selection of appearance characteristics.

Socially-shared cognition may arise from human interaction, since it is through everyday activities that humans learn symbolic meanings and act and interpret information on the basis of those meanings (Mead, 1934). A focus on interaction is appropriate for a study of social power because much of the potential for influence is likely to arise within interaction. Two types of interaction arise in television programs: interaction between actors and para-social interaction between audience members and cast members (Horton & Wohl, 1956). The term para-social interaction describes the imaginary face-to-face interaction that a viewer has with a television performer such as a newscaster or character in a television program (Perse & Rubin, 1989). In research focusing on soap opera characters, viewers reported affective program involvement and a physical attraction to the characters (Rubin & Perse, 1987). Thus, by focusing on interaction, power can be studied and through the use of shared symbols, such as clothing, meanings can be manipulated and conveyed to an audience.

In earlier research, Leslie Burns and I (Lennon & Burns, 1993) developed a means of analyzing information about dress in media, although our focus was on literature. Using implicit personality theory (Schneider, 1973), we assumed that authors use dress to convey characters and that readers form impressions of those characters partly on the basis of information associated with specific dress cues. We demonstrated how inconsistencies (a) in dress cues and contexts, or (b) between dress cues and social roles convey information about characters in literature. We found that situational cues are used in conjunction with dress cues to achieve a desired meaning. We suggested locating dress cues in a story, for example, relating those cues to research findings, and, within the context of the story, interpreting the dress cues based on research. Although our original focus was on written media, we suggested using the same approach with visual media, such as television. This is one approach I am using in this chapter.

Within the context of a television show or play a character's clothing is called a costume. An effective costume visually defines a character by establishing, among other things, age, sex, social class, rank, occupation, and personality (Anderson & Anderson, 1985, pp. 30–6; Cunningham, 1989, pp. 1–2; Russell, 1973, pp. 9–10).

> A costume is a 'magic' garment – a garment that enables an actor to become, for a time, someone else. . . . Sometimes the magic works subtly . . . touching the store of cultural information in the collective memory of [an] audience. Other costume images are so well-known within a culture that the appearance of an actor in that costume immediately identifies that character (Cunningham, 1989, pp. 1–2).

Some of these characteristics such as age,[1] sex, and in some instances, occupation may be relatively easy to establish in some contexts. However, designing clothing for science fiction may be difficult because the designer is creating looks that have not been seen before (Warren, 1991). Thus the clothing has to communicate in the present context and yet look realistic for what the audience might imagine the future to be.

'Star Trek, The Next Generation' was selected for analysis for three reasons. First, because costume designers for science fiction are creating looks for the future, they are not as limited in possibilities for characters' appearances as they might be if designing for the here-and-now; as such they may be even more likely than other costume designers to rely on dress cues to convey information about characters. Second, most of the action on 'Star Trek, The Next Generation' occurs in the workplace, where status hierarchies exist and are likely to (a) reflect power and (b) be reflected in dress. Third, the series focuses on the mission of a military vessel and its crew; thus, (a) military rank is likely to be visually apparent in dress and (b) power is likely to be evident in interpersonal on-the-job interactions.

## 'Star Trek, The Next Generation' and Power

In many ways, 'Star Trek, The Next Generation' is the ideal television series on which to focus a study in power. First, the 'Star Trek' universe is a universe 'ruled by the dictates of the balance of power' (Richards, 1997, p. 28). Maintaining equilibrium with other planetary governments is the focus of many episodes. Three such planetary governments, the Romulan Empire, the Klingon Empire, and the Cardassian Union, seek to extend their power through expansion, colonization, and war. Such means of extending power represent examples of both force and manipulation in Raven's (1992) terms.

Second, the series itself had referent power in the sense of its profound influence[2] on fans and on consumption. For example, a linguist (Gorman, 1993; Tell Scotty, 1992) invented the Klingon language in 1985. Since then more than 250,000 copies of *The Klingon Dictionary* have been sold. In addition, over 50,000 copies of an audiotape entitled 'Conversational Klingon' have sold (Gorman, 1993). Dr Mae Jemison is additional proof of the influence of 'Star Trek' on society. Jemison, who was the first African American woman in space, reports that she was inspired to be an astronaut by the Uhura character from the original series (Nemecek, 1995). Since fans and consumers identify with the 'Star Trek' universe and its characters (Davis, 1995), they have consumed nine feature-length movies, an animated television series, fan magazines, conventions, museum exhibits, and a variety of other memorabilia.[3] Consequently, although 'Star Trek, The Next Generation' finished seven years of production in 1994, two spin-off series were created for television, 'Star Trek, Deep Space Nine', and 'Star Trek Voyager'.

**The 'Star Trek' Universe**

The original 'Star Trek' was a science fiction television series that aired from 1966 to 1969. It portrayed life and the workplace aboard a starship, a ship with intergalactic capabilities, from the United Federation of Planets in the twenty-third century. The original series, although canceled after only three years, became one of the few television series to become more popular in syndication than when it was originally aired (Blair, 1983).

The second television series, 'Star Trek, The Next Generation', is the focus of this research. This series, set in the twenty-fourth century, was broadcast from 1987 to 1994 and became more popular than the original series (Turque, 1990). The meaning of the series and perhaps at least part of its popularity and social influence can be explained by its success at creating a coherent universe (Richards, 1997). For example, the 'Star Trek' universe is equipped with social structure and institutions, ideologies, attitudes and belief systems.

Many useful technologies exist in the 'Star Trek' universe. For example, large starships are equipped with holodecks, or Holographic Environment Simulators, which allow the extremely realistic simulation of virtually any environment. Holodecks rely on three-dimensional projections, which are programmable according to user preferences (Okuda, Okuda, & Mirek, 1994,

p. 128). It is also possible to travel faster than the speed of light due to warp technology (p. 371). Matter, even people, can be converted into energy and transported hundreds of kilometers, even through solid rock using such technology (p. 349). In addition, the matter-energy converter makes possible the replication of food (p. 274) and other types of artifacts.

Using replication technology to create material goods, crew members can 'shop' at the ship's replication center (Nemecek, 1995, p. 152). Because of such technology, currency, gems, and precious metals have little value within the Federation. Instead of accumulating wealth, people may have a collection of rare (p. 125) or ancient items, such as works of art (p. 243) or even books (e.g., Okuda et al., 1994, pp. 53, 333), which are highly valued. People and individuals are valued for the ways in which they are different and unique (Davis, 1995), which might include their ethnic heritage, talents, abilities, and expertise. In the original series and each one thereafter, 'Star Trek' promoted the ideals of tolerance for differing cultures and respect for life in all forms. This value is codified in the prime directive, which prohibits interference in the normal development of any society.

*Dress on 'Star Trek, The Next Generation'*   Throughout the seven years of the series, the primary color of one's uniform carried specific meaning. Blue uniforms were worn by individuals with knowledge of the sciences such as astrophysics or medicine. Red uniforms symbolized that the wearer, such as the captain or others who were training for such a position, performed command functions. Gold uniforms were worn by those in support positions such as security and engineering. In this way the color of a character's uniform indicated type of occupational role and, thus, expertise. In the first two years of the series, most uniforms were unisex jumpsuits, zipped up the front and collarless, with long sleeves. The pant half of the jumpsuit was always black and the top half was red, gold, or blue with black. Because these uniforms were snug-fitting and made from spandex (Warren, 1991), they were uncomfortable for the actors to wear for their ten-hour or longer days. For a few episodes one of the main characters and some of the extras (including at least one man in the series premiere) wore the 'skant' (Nemecek, 1995) a short-sleeved mini-dress with princess-seam lines, which was accessorized with knee-high black boots.

For the third season a new costume designer was hired, Robert Blackman (McLaughlin, 1996; Snead, 1995), who designed a new 'Starfleet' standard uniform and instituted significant changes in characters' appearances. New uniforms were designed for all characters above the rank of ensign (Nemecek, 1995). The men wore two-piece uniforms (Warren, 1991); the top was a short jacket which zipped in the back, had a banded bottom (Okuda et al.,

1994, pp. 358, 360) and a two-piece band collar, and was made from wool crepe[4] (Warren, 1991). The male characters wore t-shirts made of a light-weight girdle fabric under their uniforms with a few extra layers around the waist (Snead, 1995). The colors of the uniforms remained the same, as did the design lines. However, the new uniforms were much more comfortable to wear than the old ones. For the female officers, the uniforms were still one-piece (Nemecek, 1995), and made of spandex, but they were cut so that the stretch was horizontal rather than vertical (Snead, 1995). In addition, a two-piece band collar was added and a zipper was placed in the back. The female characters' uniforms were also equipped with padded bras (Snead, 1995). All non-human crew members on the 'Enterprise' were members of bipedal species[5] and wore the standard 'Starfleet' uniforms, except in the case of the ship's counselor.

*Characters and context*   'Star Trek, The Next Generation' was noted for its philosophical messages, creative storylines, and ensemble cast (Stark, 1991). The pre-season publicity described the following regular cast: a balding captain, a handsome first officer, an android second officer, a female security chief, the alien counselor, the chief medical officer, her brilliant teenage son, and a blind navigator who later became the chief engineer (Merrill, 1995). However, prior to the premiere episode, a Klingon tactical officer was added to the cast.[6] Besides these regulars who were commonly featured in episodes,[7] there were also some recurring characters including an omnipotent being, a very wise and long-lived bartender, an alien ensign with *attitude*, an alien ambassador, and a neurotic engineer.

Story lines focused on the officers and crew of the starship 'Enterprise', the flagship of the Federation. In 'Star Trek, The Next Generation' the starship was on a ten-year mission of exploration and carried over 1,000 crewmembers (Merrill, 1995) and their families (Nemecek, 1995, p. 5). The 'Enterprise' had schools, nurseries, an infirmary, recreational facilities, an arboretum, many types of laboratories including an astrophysics laboratory, and generally any facility necessary to sustain a high quality of life. Crew members, both 'Starfleet' and civilian, represented a variety of ethnicities, species, and sexes. For example, the original 'Star Trek' was groundbreaking in its day for including cast members of both sexes representing Caucasian, Asian, and African ethnicities (Casper & Moore, 1995; Logan, 1991).

However, although women were represented, the original series was criticized for its sexism and lack of any substantive roles for women (Cranny-Francis, 1985; Deegan, 1986; Littleton, 1989; Logan, 1991; Reid-Jeffery, 1982). For example, female crew members were often depicted as weak, irrational, emotional, subservient, disposable, and manipulated easily with sex (Reid-Jeffery, 1982). Female guest characters, both human and alien, played sexual providers, mothers, controlled daughters, or dominated wives (Reid-Jeffery, 1982). Henderson (1994) noted that the women in 'Star Trek' with outright power were aliens. Whether the role of women has improved on 'Star Trek, The Next Generation' is questionable and remains a topic of discussion (Joyrich, 1996; Wilcox, 1992). Wilcox, for example, holds that women frequently exercise power on the series and that women's roles have evolved considerably as compared to women's roles on the original series.

*Decision-making on 'Star Trek, The Next Generation'*   In 'Star Trek, The Next Generation' episodes there are three primary contexts in which decision-making occurs: on the bridge or command center of the ship, during away missions, and during staff briefings. As with seafaring vessels, on the 'Enterprise' the commanding officer controls the ship from the bridge. Only important characters have bridge assignments or business on the bridge; in times of battle, non-essential personnel are ordered to leave the bridge. In order to visit other ships or planets which often send out distress calls in the series, crew members are sent on away missions or away teams; only characters with valuable skills are sent on away teams. During the course of an episode, staff briefings are held to discuss strategies for solving problems; only crew members or featured guests whose expertise, advice, or skills bear on the issue under discussion attend the staff briefings. Characters in each of these three key settings have some type of social power, primarily expert power, legitimate power, informational power, or some combination thereof.

*Research questions*   To analyze social power, biological sex, and dress the following research questions were formulated. $R_1$: Are men more likely to be depicted in decision-making activities (e.g., exercising power) than women? $R_2$: Are dress cues associated with power? $R_3$: Do inconsistencies between dress cues and contexts convey power? $R_4$: Do dress cues and roles convey information about power?

## Part 1: Quantitative Analyses

To address $R_1$: Are men more likely to be depicted in decision-making activities (e.g., exercising power) than women? I considered interactions in which characters have bridge duty, are sent on away missions, and are present for meetings in the briefing room. Each of these interaction contexts represents an instance in which decision-making generally occurs and is directly related to social power; individuals present within each of these contexts has the potential to influence. Therefore, these contexts of decision-making were the focus of my content analysis.

## Method

To address the first research question, videotaped episodes from television were used. A complete set of episodes from all seven years of the series was not available on videotape; however, a complete set was available for the first five years of the series. Therefore, for purposes of random selection the 126 episodes broadcast during the first five years of the series were used as the population for the content analysis; thirty-five (28 per cent) of those episodes were viewed. The decision was made to analyze seven episodes per season because seven represented more than 25 per cent of all episodes in any given season and because some variety would be represented therein. Episodes were randomly selected from each of the five seasons: 1987–88, 1988–89, 1989–90, 1990–91, and 1991–92. The episodes were viewed five times at a minimum and characters from the series were categorized as recurring or as guest characters; their roles and appearances were also classified. A second coder also coded a subset of the episodes to insure inter-coder reliability ($rs > .75$) for the frequency counts. For the frequency counts, all crew members were included. Any discrepancies in information were resolved by re-watching the episodes in question until agreement between coders was reached.

To determine if women and men shared equally in decision-making on the 'Enterprise', the frequencies with which men and women were part of the bridge crew, were sent on away teams, and were part of staff briefings were recorded. When the action switched from the bridge of the 'Enterprise' to a planet, for example, only one or two people might be seen on the ship's bridge. Therefore, bridge crew members were counted only in scenes in which at least six people could be seen on screen. In addition, the frequencies with which guest characters appeared were also noted. Information regarding sex, appearances, and the guest characters' occupations was noted.

## Results and discussion

In the 35 coded episodes there were 113 bridge scenes, 49 staff briefings, and 33 away teams sent to a planet's surface or another ship. There were eight regularly-featured women (a year or longer) and nine regularly-featured men. These individuals did not all appear in any one year of the series due to attrition of some characters and addition of new characters. However, on average there were eight regular male characters in each episode and three regular female characters in each episode. In accord with Raven's (1992) definition of power, guest characters were categorized as powerful or not powerful as a function of their occupations and whether they (the occupations) were potentially influential. For example, ambassadors, world leaders, and military officers were attributed legitimate power, whereas terrorists and police officers were attributed coercive power.

Data were analyzed using the binomial test which is appropriate for populations consisting of only two classes (Siegal, 1956), such as men and women. The binomial test is a goodness-of-fit type of test that is used to determine whether it is reasonable in this case to expect the observed frequencies from a population to be made up of equal numbers of men and women. Since the binomial distribution approximates a normal distribution when applied to these data, the appropriate test statistic is $z$ ($\mu = 0$, $s = 1$).

Based on the binomial test, it is unlikely that the observed numbers of men and women in the bridge crew occurred by chance, $z$ (N = 399) = 7.97, $p < .0001$ (2-tailed). When averaging over all bridge scenes for all episodes and across all years, the bridge crew was made up of 5.6 men and 2.3 women. Men were more likely than women to be portrayed in the bridge scenes. It is also unlikely that the observed numbers of men and women sent on away teams occurred by chance, $z$ (N = 163) = 6.66, $p < .0001$ (2-tailed). On average the away teams consisted of 1.9 men and 1.1 women. Thus men were more likely than women to be portrayed on away team missions. Another measure of one's power is the extent to which one participates in staff meetings. The observed numbers of men and women 'at the table' for important decisions is unlikely to have occurred by chance, $z$ (N = 260) = 7.82, $p < .0001$ (2-tailed). When averaging over all briefing room scenes for all episodes and across all years, 3.9 men and 1.3 women attended each staff briefing. More men than women were portrayed participating in staff meetings. Although Wilcox (1992) proclaimed a significant revolution in women's roles on 'Star Trek, The Next Generation', these results do not support that assertion. In fact, with two to three times as many men as women involved in decision-making on the program, it would be difficult for the male characters *not* to exert more power than the female characters.

Another measure of the power of the characters is their occupational status. In the case of guest characters, occupation was used as a proxy of power in interactions. The primary types of power that could be easily discerned in this manner were legitimate power and expert power, both of which relate to occupational status. To a lesser extent, coercive power could sometimes be assessed (e.g., terrorist). However, it was not always possible to establish type of power evident in interactions involving guest characters, because the interaction may have been short or unrevealing for an assessment of the basis for influence. For example, it was not possible to unambiguously assess reward power, informational power, and referent power. Two coders independently coded the occupations of the guest characters and generally agreed on assessments of power ($rs > .70$). Only those occupations on which the coders agreed were used in the following analysis.

Although Wilcox (1992) states that women are frequently shown in positions of power on 'Star Trek, The Next Generation', there were eighteen powerful female guest characters (e.g., scientists, world leaders, admirals, captains, terrorists) as compared to forty-six powerful male guest characters. A binomial test was calculated from these data; results suggest that the observed numbers of powerful male and female guest characters were unlikely to have occurred by chance, $z$ (N = 64) = 3.50, $p < .001$ (2-tailed). Men were more likely to be depicted as powerful guest characters than women. In all, there were 81 guest characters featured in the 35 episodes, 55 were men and 26 were women. These frequencies were unlikely to have occurred by chance, $z$ (N = 81) = 3.22, $p < .002$ (2-tailed). Men were much more likely than women to be depicted as guest characters on 'Star Trek, The Next Generation'.

All the recurring characters, even the bartender and the doctor's son, were portrayed as either highly skilled or highly talented. Thus, all had expert power. In the thirty-five coded episodes there were eight recurring female characters: a female security chief, a helm officer, a waitress/bartender, a botanist, an ambassador, a counselor, and two physicians. During the same five-year period there were nine recurring men's roles; these roles include captain, first officer, science officer, chief engineer, security chief, engineer, omnipotent being, transporter chief, and the doctor's son. It should be noted that the three recurring female characters were members of nurturing/helping professions (Wilcox, 1992), long considered appropriate for women. In comparison, none of the men's recurring roles included care taking or other helping professions. Thus, the most important recurring roles for women were traditional helping roles in contrast to the men's roles. Furthermore, at least some of the men were in high-ranking command positions, but only one recurring female character was in a command position and it was low-ranking (i.e., ensign). The nine recurring male characters appeared a total of 197 times, yet the eight recurring female characters appeared only eighty-four times. These frequencies were unlikely to have occurred by chance, $z$ (N = 281) = 6.69, $p < .0001$ (2-tailed). Thus, on the 'Enterprise' men were featured more often as regular characters than women.

To summarize from the statistical results, men were more likely than women to be depicted (a) on the bridge, (b) on away teams, (c) in briefing room meetings, (d) as powerful guest characters, (e) as guest characters, or (f) as recurring characters. Male characters were depicted more often overall and were depicted more often in decision-making activities than female characters.

## Part 2: Qualitative Analyses

To address the remaining research questions the set of videotaped episodes used for the content analysis was supplemented with other available episodes from all seven years of the series. Although these videotapes were not systematically selected, they were viewed and analyzed visually. Copious notes were taken regarding appearance characteristics of the recurring and guest characters including hair styles, makeup, and clothing; notes were added over multiple viewings of the same episode. Characters' appearances were sketched to aid the analysis. In viewing the tapes, sometimes appearance information was overlooked; such discrepancies in appearance information were resolved by rewatching the episodes in question. In this analysis my purpose was to explore relationships between power, appearance, and biological sex of characters. To illustrate the relationship between power and appearance I offer the following interpretations of appearance in interaction contexts.

In addressing $R_2$: Are dress cues associated with power? I found legitimate power to be related to dress cues. Legitimate power is evident in the contrast between the official cadet uniforms and the regulation uniforms. Cadet uniforms, featured in two episodes (i.e., 'Allegiance, The First Duty'), appear identical to standard regulation uniforms with color reversals. Whereas the regulation uniforms have colored bodices (i.e., red, gold, or blue) with black yokes, the cadets' uniforms have black bodices with colored yokes (i.e., red, gold, or blue). These differences provide a strong visual distinction between officers and cadets that can be seen immediately.

Additionally, legitimate power differences in dress are evident in 'Star Trek, The Next Generation' when admirals and vice admirals are featured. The rank of admiral is differentiated from the rank of captain by a different style of uniform and decoration on the uniform. Several variations of admirals' uniforms were used in the series (Okuda et al., 1994, p. 360). As compared to lower-ranking officers, admirals wore uniforms which were highly decorated with metallic braid and which had elaborate design lines. These uniforms can be seen in 'Conspiracy, Best of Both Worlds', and 'Suddenly Human'. Because starship captains were often required to follow orders with which they disagreed (e.g., 'Ensign Ro'), it is clear that captains exercise less legitimate power than admirals or vice admirals.

Legitimate power associated with differences in status is also illustrated by the dress of non-military characters in the series. For example, one of the regular male characters was the doctor's early-adolescent son who was portrayed as a prodigy aspiring to a 'Starfleet' career. Beginning in the second year of the series and continuing in nearly every episode until his character left the series, he wore a gray West Point-inspired non-regulation 'uniform' (Nemecek, 1995, p. 64). It had the appearance of a one-piece jumpsuit, the top of which featured much the same design lines as the regulation 'Starfleet' uniforms. It was a uniform in the sense that it was worn all the time. However, since it was not a regulation uniform, nor for that matter a regulation color, it is clear that the wearer had lower status than the crew.

Age was also associated with legitimate power in numerous episodes. Age is not typically thought of as a dress cue in terms of purposeful manipulations of appearance. However, in the context of visual media age can and is manipulated. For example, makeup, hair color, posture, body movement, and clothing can all be used to convey age of a character. On the 'Enterprise' the captain was visibly the oldest of the regular characters and he was clearly in command of his crew. Admirals, vice admirals, ambassadors, world leaders, and many of the scientists who were featured as guest characters also appeared to be visibly older than the 'Enterprise' crew. Such individuals also have legitimate power and expert power.

Thus, some specific dress cues were associated with differences in power. In general, as might be expected, differences in uniforms (official and unofficial) did relate to differences in legitimate power. Specifically, color reversals, metallic braid, elaborate design lines, and regulation colors are all specific dress cues that indicated power on 'Star Trek: The Next Generation'. However, in terms of specific *items* of dress only the uniform was associated with power. That is, no specific shoes, hats, belts, cosmetics, or hairstyles were associated with power. Physical characteristics of characters, which could possibly be manipulated by a creative staff, such as height, weight, muscle tone and definition, and ethnicity did not necessarily convey power. However, age was associated with legitimate power; the captain, ambassadors, and world leaders appeared older than other less-powerful guest characters.

The third research question ($R_3$: Do inconsistencies between dress cues and contexts convey power?) was developed based on the analysis I noted earlier that I developed with Leslie Burns (Lennon & Burns, 1993). Recall that we found authors used inconsistencies between clothing and context to provide information to readers. In the context of 'Star Trek: The Next Generation' I was interested in the possibility that inconsistent cues might be associated with information about power. I did find that the appearance of regular characters combined with a context in which the appearance was inconsistent, sometimes conveyed a subtle form of power. Period clothing was used to demonstrate the fantastic powers of a race of omnipotent beings, the members of the Q Continuum, who often whisked the captain or first officer[8] to other time periods. In nearly every episode featuring these omnipotent beings, one of the characters was portrayed wearing period clothing which was clearly inappropriate for the 'Star Trek' universe, but which did situate the action in another time period. Since these episodes included segments created by the Q, containing historic simulations unrelated to holodeck use, the audience was led to the conclusion that the Q were incredibly powerful. This type of power was called force by Raven (1992; 1993).

In 'Tapestry' the out-dated cranberry uniforms from an earlier time period were used to convey to the audience both a sense of backward movement through time and fantastic power. In the preview of the episode, the captain died of a chest wound and met Q in the afterlife. As the episode unfolded, Q not only revived him, but also allowed him to relive his youth. Although much of the action took place in the captain's past with his young friends, the captain did not become younger. However, the audience was able to follow this movement back in time, and hence the power of Q in sending him there, because (a) the captain was seen with youthful associates, and (b) both he and his associates were dressed in regulation cranberry uniforms from an earlier era.[9] Had the uniforms used in the 'past' scenes been of the current style, it would have been difficult, perhaps impossible, for the audience to comprehend the backward movement through time. The perception of the power of the Q depends on the audience's understanding of the movement through time. Without the out-of-date uniforms, power would not have been conveyed as effectively, if at all.

To understand the legitimate power of the uniform, it is useful to consider the powerlessness that occurs when an officer is suddenly without the uniform. In 'Devil's Due', the captain is transported by an alien from his quarters to a science station on a nearby planet. There he materializes wearing only his pajamas among members of his crew and the planet's science team. Given his appearance, it is apparent he had arrived by means of which he had no control. Related dialogue with a crew member aboard the 'Enterprise' confirms this, 'Will you beam me directly to my quarters?' And when that option failed, 'fetch me in a shuttle and . . . bring along a uniform.' Clearly, pajamas are inappropriate for the workplace and, for the captain, being transported without consent is not as bad as being transported sans uniform. Had the captain been transported wearing a uniform, the alien's power would have been less visually apparent than it was. Also important in conveying power in this situation is the context in which the captain materialized. In workplaces and other similar settings, it is the joint combination of clothing together with a context for which the clothing is inappropriate that facilitates the audience's perception of power. In 'Star Trek, The Next Generation' inconsistencies between dress cues and context do convey power.

Another way to study power in the 'Star Trek, The Next Generation' workplace is to focus on what the clothing and appearance of the characters convey to the audience. Such an analysis focuses on socially-shared cognition. Since clothing and appearance cues are under the control of the creative staff of 'Star Trek, The Next Generation', viewers can assume that those particular cues were purposely selected to convey certain information. Since viewers of 'Star Trek, The Next Generation' do not live in the twenty-fourth century, the information they infer from characters' appearances will be consistent with the present time-frame. The analysis of characters' appearances in this way is a form of characterization analysis. In earlier work, Leslie Burns and I (Lennon & Burns, 1993) suggested beginning with a character's portrayal and working backwards to locate specific symbols of dress which might have been selected by the creative team to convey the character and the character's personality. Specifically, we suggested focusing on appearance information (i.e., symbols of dress) in a character's portrayal, searching for empirical research related to the appearance in question, and then forming an associated composite impression based on those empirical results. To illustrate, suppose a character is featured who is tall, trim-built, and muscular. Using that image, we found related research and applied it as follows (p. 164):

> Tallness is associated with status (Wilson, 1968). Muscular individuals have been rated as stronger, more masculine, better-looking, younger, taller, more mature, more adventurous, and more self-reliant than people with other types of body build (Wells & Siegel, 1961; Strongman & Hart, 1968).

Given the description of the character as tall, trim-built, muscular, the audience might consequently infer from the related research findings that the character is strong, masculine, good-looking, mature, adventurous, self-reliant, and has high status. In this way, research findings can be applied to an appearance to suggest possible information that is conveyed by that appearance to audience members (Lennon & Burns, 1993). In addition to interpretation, I also used this method to address $R_3$: Do Inconsistencies between dress cues and contexts convey power?

Beginning with season three and continuing thereafter, the standard uniforms of the men and women differed in terms of fabric. The women's uniforms were made from spandex, while the men's were made from wool. Although the overall look was similar, the women's uniforms were much more body revealing than the men's. Television is not the only media in which women's clothing is more revealing than men's. Advertising researchers have found similar results; women in magazine ads are much more likely than men to be depicted (a) in 'sexy' dress (Soley & Reid, 1988), or (b) as suggestively clad or nude (Soley & Kurzbard, 1986).

Furthermore, clothing that is body revealing may be judged inappropriate for women in certain occupations (Damhorst, Eckman, & Stout, 1986). Damhorst et al. concluded that workplace dress is considered inappropriate if it contains certain extreme components such as a body-dominant silhouette, an unconventional combination of colors or textures, or trendy elements. When professional female characters are depicted in sexy or other inappropriate dress, viewers may attribute negative characteristics to them. Kimle and Damhorst (1997) interviewed professional women, eliciting their opinions about their career appearances. Interviewees expressed the opinion that women should avoid sexy, flashy, and even feminine styles in order to maintain a businesslike appearance. In particular, the avoidance of blatant sexuality in workplace dress was endorsed. Thus sexy clothing or clothing with a body-dominant silhouette is likely to be evaluated as inappropriate for women in the workplace, because body-revealing clothing tends to be inconsistent with a workplace role.

To the extent that these perceptions are socially shared (Resnick, 1991), viewers of 'Star Trek, The Next Generation' are likely to infer that the female characters who wear body-revealing clothing in the workplace are not only immodest, sexy, sexually exciting, or seductive, but also are inappropriately dressed and unprofessional. Indeed, the case can be made that the women's tight-fitting uniforms serve to objectify them. According to Hall and Crum (1994) when media images focus on women's bodies, the women are less likely to be perceived as persons. Such a perspective suggests that the women's uniforms, and therefore, the women wearing them, are associated with a lack of power (i.e., legitimate, expert, referent, coercive, informational). This interpretation is consistent with the finding that women are much less likely than men to be part of decision-making processes aboard the 'Enterprise'.

To summarize, inconsistencies between dress cues and context convey power albeit in a subtle way. That is, neither the dress alone nor the context alone is responsible for the illusion of power conveyed to the audience. Rather they work in combination when they are inconsistent with each other. The power of various aliens over crew members was conveyed in this way. In addition, the body-revealing nature of women's uniforms is inconsistent with workplace requirements and effectively robs the women wearing them of power in their workplace.

To address $R_4$: Do dress cues and roles convey information about power? I used the method developed with Leslie Burns (1993) and found relationships between biological sex and power. Not only were women less likely to be featured as powerful characters than men were, fewer women had access to decision-making, and their physical appearances underscored their lack of power. For example, the female recurring characters infrequently wore standard Federation uniforms, although all adult male recurring characters always wore the standard Federation uniform. The contrast between men's regulation dress and the women's non-regulation dress serves to illustrate the differences in power. Power was represented visually by the clear association of the regulation uniform with recurring male characters more than with recurring female characters. Researchers interested in uniforms associated with protective organizations (e.g., police, military) have found that uniforms convey authority (Volpp & Lennon, 1988), legitimacy (Bickman, 1974; Geffner & Gross, 1984), professionalism (Gundersen, 1987), and competency (Mauro, 1984). Thus, viewers of 'Star Trek, The Next Generation' are likely to infer that the male characters possess more authority and legitimacy and that they are more professional and competent than the female characters.

$R_4$ can also be addressed by applying an interpretive approach to the appearances of the female characters. While the limited roles of the female characters, their activities, and their appearances suggest lack of power, there is yet another perspective. Socially-shared cognition arises in human interaction, thus it is important to both (a) consider interactions between characters, and (b) consider para-social interactions between audience members and the television show cast. Television viewers do engage in para-social (imaginary face-to-face) interactions (Horton & Wohl, 1956) with television characters. Rubin and Perse (1987) found that viewers involved in para-social interactions are affectively involved with and physically attracted to characters. Given this, especially because the prime audience for 'Star Trek, The Next Generation' was men between the ages of 18 to 49 (Nemecek, 1995), it is also possible that the women's appearances might be associated with reward power. In other words, the body-revealing nature of the women's appearances may be rewarding for male viewers. This perspective is reasonable since the way a television character is portrayed is affected by the writers' perceptions of what the audience wants. Such a perspective also privileges the male gaze. Ironically, reward power achieved in this way through attraction may strip female characters of other direct sources of power (Freedman, 1986).

I also addressed $R_4$ through an interpretation of father-son interactions. Referent power is sometimes reflected in the clothing of fathers and sons on 'Star Trek, The Next Generation' and father-son relationships are explored in several episodes. In 'New Ground', the five-year-old son of the Klingon tactical officer looks physically very much like his father, even to the point of his hair arrangement and exercise garb. Whereas the two Klingons are visibly similar, in 'Suddenly Human' a human boy and his adoptive father, who is not human, are physically dissimilar. However, their clothing is quite similar. Both ensembles featured short boots, gloves, and what appeared to be a long-sleeved shirt with a standing collar. Both costumes also featured short jackets made from similar fabric. The story line of this episode focused on the adoptive youth's struggle with conflicting loyalties to his adoptive family and his newly-found birth family. At the episode's end the youth made the decision to maintain the existing relationship and remain with his adoptive father. Referent power of the father is reflected by both (a) the father-son similarity in dress, and also (b) the son's loyalty to his adoptive father.

## Summary

Social power on 'Star Trek, The Next Generation' is related to dress. Uniform color is associated with expert power as is the generic uniform; the decorative trim and elaborate design lines of admirals' uniforms are associated with legitimate power. Also associated with legitimate power are uniform color reversals on cadet uniforms and one character's non-uniform 'uniform' that is similar in design, but different in color from crew uniforms. Referent power is associated with similarities in appearance of father-son pairs. Movement through time and space associated with force is attributed to characters when inconsistencies occur between context and specific items of dress (pajamas, period clothing). Social power is clearly associated with biological sex. As compared to male characters, female characters are depicted less often in powerful roles, in decision-making activities, and in regulation 'Federation' uniforms. Types of social power evident in the series that are related to dress or biological sex include legitimate power, reward power, expert power, referent power, and force.

Research results can be used to determine the types of information conveyed by an appearance to audience members (Lennon & Burns, 1993). As a result, 'Star Trek, The Next Generation' viewers are likely to attribute more authority, legitimacy, professionalism, and competency to the male characters than female characters. In addition, female characters wear body-revealing clothing in the workplace. This suggests that female characters are immodest, sexy, sexually exciting, or seductive (perhaps relating to reward power) and are inappropriately dressed for the workplace and unprofessional. In conclusion, men in the 'Star Trek' universe have more legitimate, referent, and expert power in the workplace, while the women may have reward power within para-social audience interactions.

## Implications

Perennial questions in media analyses (Belk & Pollay, 1985) are: Does media influence society? Or does society influence media? I have presented some evidence that the 'Star Trek' series have been powerful in their effects on consumers. Some of those effects include highly successful movies, conventions, development of a language for a group that only exists in the 'Star Trek' series, and inspiration to become an astronaut. Thus, in several different ways, 'Star Trek' has had a profound effect on viewers. Clearly, this is one series that has influenced the society that produced it.

However, throughout the 'Star Trek' series, the content of the stories also reflected the society that produced it. In the original 'Star Trek' series, episodes focused on birth control, individual freedom, the Cold War, and racism; all important social issues in the U.S. in the sixties. In 'Star Trek: The Next Generation', episodes focused on terrorism and drug addiction; important social issues in the U.S. in the late eighties and early nineties. U.S. society is also reflected in the series through the social power of its characters and how they are portrayed. If men and women in 'Star Trek': *The Next Generation* are portrayed as exercising differing amounts of social power in the idealistic future workplace, then certainly this suggests that such discrepancies exist in the realistic workplace of the here-and-now. If primarily men are depicted in decision-making activities on television, then it is possible that the writers of the episodes, at least, perceive this to be the natural order of things, even for the future. If dress cues are associated with power on television, then in real-life situations it is likely that dress cues are associated with power (i.e., it is unlikely that a creative staff would select such cues otherwise). Likewise since dress cues and roles convey information about power on television and since inconsistencies between dress cues and context convey power on television, it is likely that power is conveyed in much the same way in realistic settings. In this way, media analyses such as this one tell us much about the society that produced the media.

## Notes

1. Youth may be established through the use of white and pastel colors according to Cunningham (1989).
2. The series was influential because episodes focus on issues of concern to viewers such as questions about the nature of humanity or of individual rights (Richards, 1997).
3. MasterCard offers a 'Star Trek' credit card.

4. According to Nemecek (1995, p. 99) the uniforms were made from wool gabardine.

5. This is not the case in the series of 'Star Trek' novels published by Pocket Books.

6. He became security chief after the original one was killed in the first season.

7. Except for the original security chief.

8. In these instances, the fact that the captain and first officer are often so affected serves to underscore the power of the guest character.

9. In the 'Star Trek' universe the cranberry uniforms were worn by 'Starfleet' officers eighty years prior to the time in which 'Star Trek, The Next Generation' is set.

# References

Alba, J. W., & Hasher, L. (1983). Is memory schematic? *Psychological Bulletin, 93*, 203–31.

Anderson, B., & Anderson, C. (1985). *Costume design*. New York: Holt, Rinehart and Winston.

Belk, R. & Pollay, R. (1985). Images of ourselves: The good life in Twentieth Century advertising. *Journal of Consumer Research, 11*, 887–97.

Bickman, L. (1974). The social power of a uniform. *Journal of Applied Social Psychology, 4*, 47–61.

Blair, K. (1983). Sex and 'Star Trek'. *Science-Fiction Studies, 10*, 292–7.

Casper, M. J., & Moore, L. J. (1995). Inscribing bodies, inscribing the future: Gender, sex, and reproduction in outer space. *Sociological Perspectives, 38*(2), 311–33.

Corbett, E. P. (1977). *The little rhetoric and handbook*. New York: John Wiley & Sons, Inc.

Cranny-Francis, A. (1985). Sexuality and sex-role stereotyping in 'Star Trek'. *Science Fiction Studies, 12*, 274–84.

Cunningham, R. (1989). *The magic garment: Principles of costume design*. New York: Longman, Inc.

Damhorst, M. L. (1984–5). Meanings of clothing cues in social context. *Clothing and Textiles Research Journal, 3*(2), 39–48.

Damhorst, M. L. (1990). In search of a common thread: Classification of information communicated through dress. *Clothing and Textiles Research Journal, 8*(2), 1–12.

Damhorst, M. L., Eckman, M., & Stout, S. (1986). Cluster analysis of women's business suits (Abstract). *ACPTC Proceedings: National Meeting 1986, 65*.

Davis, E. (1995). True believers. 'Star Trek': *Four generations of stars, stories, and strange new worlds*, pp. 78–82.

Davis, L. L. (1984). Clothing and human behavior: A review. *Home Economics Research Journal, 12*(3), 325–339.

Deegan, M. J. (1986). Sexism in space: The Freudian formula in 'Star Trek'. In D.

Palumbo (Ed.), *Eros in the mind's eye* (pp. 209–24). New York, NY: Greenwood.

Dornbusch, S. M., Hastorf, A. H., Richardson, S. A., Muzzy, R. E., & Vreeland, R. S. (1965). The perceiver and the perceived: The relative influences on the categories of interpersonal cognition. *Journal of Personality and Social Psychology, 1*(5), 434–40.

Easterling, C. R., Leslie, J. E., & Jones, M. A. (1992). Perceived importance and usage of dress codes among organizations that market professional services. *Public Personnel Management, 21*(2), 211–19.

Forsythe, S., Drake, M. F., & Cox, C. (1984). Dress as an influence on the perceptions of management characteristics in women. *Home Economics Research Journal, 13*, 112–21.

Freedman, R. J. (1986). *Beauty bound.* Lexington, MA: Lexington Books.

French, J. R. P., & Raven, B. H. (1958). The bases of social power. In D. Cartwright (Ed.), *Studies in social power* (pp. 150–67). Ann Arbor, MI: Institute for Social Research.

Geffner, R., & Gross, M. M. (1984). Sex-role behavior and obedience to authority: A field study. *Sex Roles, 10*(11/12), 973–85.

Gorman, J. (1993, April 5). Klingon: The final frontier. *Time,* 57.

Gundersen, D. F. (1987). Credibility and the police uniform. *Journal of Police Science and Administration, 15*(3), 192–5.

Hall, C. C. I., & Crum, M. J. (1994). Women and "body-isms" in television beer commercials. *Sex Roles, 31*(5/6), 329–37.

Henderson, M. (1994). Professional women in 'Star Trek', 1964–1969. *Film and History, 24*(1–2), 48–59.

Hoffman, C., Lau, I., & Johnson, D. R. (1986). The linguistic relativity of person cognition: An English-Chinese comparison. *Journal of Personality and Social Psychology, 51*, 1097–105.

Horton, D., & Wohl, R. R. (1956). Mass communication and para-social interaction. *Psychiatry, 19*, 215–29.

Johnson, K. K. P., & Roach-Higgins, M. E. (1987a). Dress and physical attractiveness of women in job interviews. *Clothing and Textiles Research Journal, 5*(3), 1–8.

Johnson, K. K. P., & Roach-Higgins, M. E. (1987b). The influence of physical attractiveness and dress on campus recruiters' impressions of female job applicants. *Home Economics Research Journal, 16*, 87–95.

Johnson, R. (1986–7). What is cultural studies anyway? *Social Text, 16*, 38–80.

Joyrich, L. (1996). Feminist Enterprise? 'Star Trek: The Next Generation' and the occupation of femininity. *Cinema Journal, 35*(2), 61–84.

Kimle, P. A., & Damhorst, M. L. (1997). A grounded theory model of the ideal business image for women. *Symbolic Interaction, 20*(1), 45–68.

Lennon, S. J. (1990a). Bondage in women's clothing and changing sex roles: Evidence from sitcoms. *Empirical Studies in the Arts, 8*, 77–84.

Lennon, S. J. (1990b). Clothing and changing sex roles: Comparison of qualitative and quantitative analyses. *Home Economics Research Journal, 18*, 245–54.

Lennon, S. J. (1992, March). *Appearance themes in L. A. Law.* Paper presented at the Popular/American Culture Association meeting, Lexington, KY.

Lennon, S. J., & Burns, L. D. (1993). Analysis of symbols of dress in characterization. In S. J. Lennon & L. D. Burns (Eds), *Social science aspects of dress: New directions* (pp. 160–71). Monument, CO: International Textiles and Apparel Association.

Littleton, C. S. (1989). Some implications of the mythology in 'Star Trek'. *Keystone Folklore, 4*(1), 33–42.

Logan, M. (1991, August 31). 'Star Trek XXV': The craze continues. *TV Guide,* 4–7, 10–12.

Mauro, R. (1984). The constable's new clothes: Effects of uniforms on perceptions and problems of police officers. *Journal of Applied Social Psychology, 14,* 42–56.

McLaughlin, E. (1996). Clothes encounters. 'Star Trek': 30 Years, pp. 54–7.

Mead, G. H. (1934). *Mind, self, and society.* Chicago: University of Chicago Press.

Merrill, D. (1995, Spring). 'Star Trek': Four generations of stars, stories, and strange new worlds. 'Star Trek, The Next Generation', p. 112.

Morgan, D. L., & Schwalbe, M. L. (1990). Mind and self in society: Linking social structure and social cognition. *Social Psychology Quarterly, 53*(2), 148–64.

Nemecek, L. (1995). *The 'Star Trek, The Next Generation' companion.* New York: Pocket Books.

Okuda, M., Okuda, D., & Mirek, D. (1994). *The 'Star Trek' Encyclopedia: A reference guide to the future.* New York, NY: Pocket Books.

Perse, E. M., & Rubin, R. B. (1989). Attribution in social and parasocial relationships. *Communication Research, 16*(1), 59–77.

Raven, B. H. (1965). Social influence and power. In I. D. Steiner and M. Fishbein (Eds), *Current studies in social psychology* (pp. 371–81). New York, NY: Holt, Rinehart, and Winston.

Raven, B. H. (1983). Interpersonal influence and social power. In H. H. Raven and J. Z. Rubin (Eds), *Social psychology* (pp. 399–444). New York, NY: Wiley.

Raven, B. H. (1992). A power interaction model of interpersonal influence: French and Raven thirty years later. *Journal of Social Behavior and Personality, 7,* 217–44.

Raven, B. H. (1993). The bases of power: Origins and recent developments. *Journal of Social Issues, 49,* 227–54.

Reid-Jeffery, D. (1982). 'Star Trek': The last frontier in modern American myth. *Folklore and Mythology Studies, 6,* 34–41.

Resnick, L. B. (1991). Shared cognition: Thinking as social practice. In L. B. Resnick, J. M. Levine, & S. D. Teasley (Eds), *Perspectives on socially shared cognition* (pp. 1–20). Washington, DC: American Psychological Association.

Richards, T. (1997). *The meaning of 'Star Trek'.* New York, NY: Doubleday.

Rubin, R. B., & Perse, E. M. (1987). Audience activity and soap opera involvement: A uses and effects investigation. *Human Communication Research, 14,* 246–68.

Russell, D. A. (1973). *Stage costume design: Theory, technique, and style.* Englewood Cliffs, NJ: Prentice-Hall, Inc.

Schlenker, B. R. (1986). *Impression management* (2nd ed.). Monterey: Brooks/Cole.

Schneider, D. J. (1973). Implicit personality theory: A review. *Psychological Bulletin, 79,* 294–309.

Siegel, S. (1956). *Non-parametric statistics for the behavioral sciences.* New York, NY: McGraw-Hill Book Company, Inc.

Snead, E. (1995, Spring). Cosmic couture. *'Star Trek': Four generations of stars, stories, and strange new worlds*, pp. 70–6.

Soley, L., & Kurzbard, G. (1986). Sex in advertising: A comparison of 1964 and 1984 magazine advertisements. *Journal of Advertising, 15*(3), 46–54.

Soley, L., & Reid, L. (1988). Taking it off: Are models in magazine ads wearing less? *Journalism Quarterly, 65,* 960–6.

Stark, S. (1991, December 29). Viewers don't have to be Trekkers to appreciate longevity of TV show. *The Columbus Dispatch Televiewplus*, pp. 26.

Strongman, K., & Hart, C. (1968). Stereotyped reactions to body build. *Psychological Reports, 23,* 1175–8.

Tell Scotty to *Hljo!* (1992, April 20). *People*, 105.

Thurston, J. L., Lennon, S. J., & Clayton, R. V. (1990). Influence of age, body type, currency of fashion detail, and type of garment on the professional image of women. *Home Economics Research Journal, 19*(2), 139–50.

Turque, B. (1990, October 22). Still Klingon to a dream. *Newsweek*, 82.

Volpp, J., & Lennon, S. J. (1988). Perceived police authority as a function of uniform hat style and sex. *Perceptual and Motor Skills, 67,* 815–24.

Warren, B. (1991, September). Robert Blackman: Costume designer. *Star Trek: The Next Generation*, pp. 30–6.

Weibel, K. (1977). *Mirror mirror: Images of women reflected in popular culture.* New York, NY: Anchor Books.

Wells, W., & Siegel, B. (1961). Stereotyped somatotypes. *Psychological Reports, 8,* 77–8.

Wilcox, C. (1992). To boldly return where others have gone before: Cultural change and the old and new 'Star Trek's. *Extrapolation, 33*(1), 88–100.

Wilson, P. R. (1968). Perceptual distortion of height as a function of ascribed academic status. *Journal of Social Psychology, 74,* 97–102.

Wyer, R. S. (1980). The acquisition and use of social knowledge: Basic postulates and representative research. *Personality and Social Psychology Bulletin, 6*(4), 558–73.

Wyer, R. S., & Martin, L. L. (1986). Person memory: The role of traits, group stereotypes, and specific behaviors in the cognitive representation of persons. *Journal of Personality and Social Psychology, 50,* 661–75.

# 6

# *The Power of Style: On Rejection of the Accepted*[1]

## Gwendolyn S. O'Neal

Dress[2] is generally believed to communicate information about the wearer and to constitute external manifestations of the internal properties of the wearer (Craik, 1996; Davis, 1985; Kaiser, 1990). It is sometimes used to define and redefine the self in an attempt to influence, control, manipulate, or shape the interaction situation. Fashion, an ephemeral component of dress, is viewed by Fox-Genovese (1987) as a political instrument consisting of representations of social relations and values imposed by some. Items of fashion today, however, are more likely to be used by individuals to manage the personal milieu (O'Neal, 1996). When individuals engage in impression management through dress for the express purpose of controlling interaction, the act is political. In many instances, when the message in the presentation is misunderstood or considered as deviant, the propensity exists to intimidate or dominate (i.e., influence) the interaction. Thus, dress may serve as a political instrument for the purpose of influencing formal and informal relationships. As such, dress is power.

Generally, the struggle for power involves formal and informal relations of domination and subordination that governs resources, opportunities, and respect within society (Collins, 1991: Fox-Genovese, 1987). The above notion of dress as power does not consist in relations of domination and subordination relative to resources or societal respect. Hence, the notion of dress as power requires explanation.

The purpose of this chapter is to consider the political use of dress in establishing cultural boundaries among African Americans. 'Style,'[3] an aesthetic element found in African American dress is described in terms of its use as a tool in usurping unauthorized power. In order to consider style as power, the concept of power must be clarified. A discussion of the redefinition of power is followed by a discussion of style as power. Examples to illustrate the concept of style as power are provided from recent research, slave narratives, and descriptions of dress in West African countries prior to and during the period of African enslavement in the New World.

## Power

Power is generally defined as the ability to do, capacity to act, capability of performing or producing. However, power is more often seen as the ability to control others or that of having authority or influence. This definition of power carries with it the idea of agency – which creates the system, exercises the power, or both. Raven and Kruglanski (1970) stated that social influence is defined as a change in one person that has its origin in another person or group. Therefore, social influence is a form of power and power is defined as potential influence.

According to Keller (1985), such forms of power operate most successfully in Western cultures where dichotomous thinking characterizes people, things, and ideas in terms of their differences from one another. These dichotomies are positioned in hierarchical arrangements where one element is objectified as the 'Other' and is viewed as an object to be manipulated and controlled. As such, according to Collins (1992), power relationships are formed in which 'legitimate' power is given to one element which attempts to control the other. Social relationships of dominance and resistance are thus formed.

Social relationships of domination operate not only by hierarchies in which power resides at the top but by 'simultaneously annexing the power as energy of those on the bottom for its own ends' (Collins, 1991, p. 228). This requires that the controlling element exert its influence over the subjugated group at various levels: the personal level where values are established and where the definition of self is formed; at the cultural level where definitions of race, social class, and gender take place, and where models for thinking and acquiring knowledge and standards of behavior are formed; and the level of social institutions such as schools where the hegemonic view is propagated (Collins, 1991). By exerting influence over the subjugated group at all levels, the controlling element has unconditional access to the subjugated and according to Frye (1983) the subjugated is powerless. However, when the subjugated excludes the controlling element from some part of the self (e.g., the mind or thought process) the subjugated assumes some degree of control and redefines the relationship. For example, the movie *Roots* illustrates the refusal to relinquish control of the self in Kunta Kente's refusal to accept the name Tobe given by his slave master, thus controlling self-definition. In the context of the twentieth century, I once heard a renown African American scholar speak of his experience of being educated at a prestigious predominately white university and described the necessity of writing two sets of notes in classes – one recording what the professors said and the other, the truth in terms of the reality he lived. He contends that the process prevented him from losing his sanity.

To undertake definition is another face of power. Definitions establish boundaries that govern relationships. They are intentional in that the goal is to normalize notions about that which is, and to direct how one is to relate to that which is defined. Foucault (1980) noted that techniques of power today are subtle and easy to overlook. It is the process of normalization that denotes right and wrong and that gets translated into normal and patho-logical. It is these relationships (e.g., good and bad, right and wrong, black and white) operating in society that aid in localizing power and making power problematic in that there is no one to blame. Thus Foucault noted that

> One should not assume a massive and primal condition of domination, a binary structure with 'dominators' on one side and 'dominated' on the other, but . . . a multiform production of relations of domination. . . . [These] relations of power are interwoven with other kinds of relations (production, kinship, family, sexuality) for which they play . . . a conditioning and a conditioned role. (p.142)

To look for the 'controlling element' or the 'dominators' is to have one's attention deflected from the real issue. Power is technical and power relations are capable of being used in strategies. In fact, politics is simply a strategy for directing power relations (Foucault, 1980).

As a result of a history of slavery, servitude, racism, and discrimination in which notions of African Americans became normalized as the Other, it became necessary for the concept of power to be reconceptualized for the purpose of the survival of a people as well as their culture. According to Collins (1991) power may be usurped through energy fostered by creative acts of resistance. Inherent in this notion of power is the 'sphere of influence which is created and sustained' to ensure that Black people are continuously able to confront oppressive social institutions. This type of power is a creative one used for the good of the community however the community is defined. The intent is to make the community stronger, thus empowering its members. An essential component of this creative power is the ability to resist forms of domination that hinder self-definition and self control. Folb (1980) stated that the most important form of power is power over one's self. This is particularly apparent in an environment where manipulation and control over others have been raised to a fine art.

To cope with the pressures of 'otherness' Majors (1991) stated that many African Americans have channeled their creative talents and energies into the construction and use of particular expressive and conspicuous styles of nonverbal behaviors through demeanor, gestures, clothing, hairstyle, walk, stances, and handshake. Combined with 'attitude,'[4] these behaviors are used to actively construct the self, to keep the dominating individuals and groups off guard about one's intentions, to exercise power and control, and to express pride, among other uses [5] (Majors, 1991). These behaviors represent a deployment of power to define and/or control the situation. To do such is to attempt to alter established relationships, to put into question notions of the norm, and thus, to engage in overt acts of resistance. Foucault (1980) noted that where there are power relations, there is always resistance.

Various kinds of interactions represent a deployment of power, many of which generate resistance. However, resistance is not always reactive, but often proactive in the sense that one does not wait to be acted upon, but finds ways to intentionally influence the outcome that would otherwise occur naturally within the given structure. The identity of resistance may be shaped through the use of dress and various other verbal and nonverbal behaviors.

## Style as Power

Value is placed on personal expressiveness in the African American community. Kochman (1981) described this expressiveness as requiring the exertion of energy and emotion. As a result of a history of oppression and discrimination, African Americans have often found it necessary to engage in behaviors to redefine the self in an effort to control the situation. This often occurs through the shaping of one's own expressive behavior in relation to the condition of his or her life. These expressions are constructed through the creative and energetic use of clothing, hairstyles, and accessories with various gesture and body movements. This 'dramatization' of the self (Majors, 1991) is considered as style, and often has the ability to define the self and/or redefine the situation. Majors (1991) considered this 'performance of emotion' to be a form of dramaturgical role playing used out of necessity for survival. Semmes (1992) defined style as the 'tradition of artfully embellishing movement, speech, and appearance (p. 131). Style is a way of acting, creating and redefining the self in relation to others. It includes attitudes, assumptions, and feelings about the self and others as they are expressed in language, dress, and nonverbal behaviors (Majors & Billson, 1992; Mancini, 1987).

Style is individualistic and personal. In the African American community one does not copy another's style, for to do so is to be pretentious (Hannerz, 1969).

The way you do or say something shows your uniqueness, your individuality, your style. Style is opposed to that which is faked in human behavior. Rather it is a public declaration of who one is. And who one is, is different from who any other is in the universe. (Pasteur & Toldson, 1982, p.180)

Yet, it is not so individualistic that it runs counter to the community's notion of appropriate expression. This form of expression, however, is different from Eurocentric norms of privacy of emotions, impersonal modes of expression, absence of affect and dynamism, and stoic sophistication. Hebdige (1979) saw style as offensive to the 'silent' majority and as challenging to the principle of unity and cohesion [in the dominant culture] because it contradicted the myth of consensus that suggests agreement about acceptable forms of expression. Kochman (1981) stated that:

White culture values the ability of individuals to rein in their impulses. White cultural events do not allow for individually initiated self-assertion or the spontaneous expression of feelings . . . 'showing off,' which would represent individually initiated (unauthorized) self-assertion and more unrestrained self-expression, is viewed negatively within White culture. Black culture, on the other hand, views showing off – in black idiom '*stylin*' . . . – positively. (p. 30)

In the context of the aesthetic of dress in the African American community style is most often simply the display of the unique characteristics of the individual – a free expression of one's essence. Pasteur and Toldson (1982) contend that 'to be divested of essence is to be desensitized to one's impulses or unguided by one's inner signals, the drumbeat of one's inner nature' (p. 181).

Folb (1980) stated that the word style in vernacular usage means to 'show off what you got' (p.109). It makes a statement to the world about who you are and how you wish to be seen. It is used in encoding, often strategically, certain messages about the wearer. When style is used as a tool of persuasion among peers, its level of affect and dynamism may be heightened through the injection of 'attitude', rhythmic strides, and speech. Therefore, style may not be innocent, but purposeful. However, 'In spite of the bombardment of ridicule by whites and middle-class blacks, a bold, humbly arrogant style prevails in the common black folk community' (Pasteur and Toldson, 1982, p.180).

Style is more than just showing off. It functions in African American aesthetic of dress as a transforming element which moves the object of convention (i.e., fashion) to one of culture. Unlike the aesthetic object of Western cultures, technical excellence in objects of dress is insufficient in and of itself to express beauty. As Semmes (1992) stated, 'one must inject beauty, heighten emotion or feeling, and idiosyncratic expression into a product or action' (p.131). Thus, the object as purchased is incomplete and has the potential to become a thing of beauty. The injecting of idiosyncratic expression into objects of dress serves as a customizing agent, which alters the intended meaning of the object. Kirsheblatt-Gimblett (1983) stated that customizing refers to

> the way in which users modify mass-produced objects to suit their needs, interest, and values, and naturalize mass culture items into new systems of meaning and activity. From the consumer's perspective, the mass produced object is not necessarily complete. Nor is it indefinitely tied to its advertised function. (p. 215)

Through customizing, which transforms the mass-produced fashion, African Americans are able to express an aspect of their cultural heritage, thus continuing to resist the notion that all of their history was lost in the Middle Passage.[6] Style, then, becomes a way of rejecting dominant myths, controlling the expressive shaping of one's immediate and everyday life, as well as holding on to one's past history.

Style is also an expression of cultural values, which have their roots in West Africa. Researchers (Asante & Asante, 1990; Baldwin, 1986; Keto, 1991; Mbiti, 1970; Nobles, 1980) agree that a collective consciousness or ethos existed among tribes of West African countries which was manifested through the notion that people are part of the natural rhythm of nature. The individual was believed to be a unique expression of this common power or energy. According to Pasteur and Toldson (1982) it is in the common black folk community that the pulse of Africa is most authentically alive. It is there that 'style and standard go their separate ways' (p.181).

> Self embellishment, with ornament and behavioral nuances, gain distinctiveness in the ways of common black folk. Such adornments and idiosyncrasies seem to reflect the individual's attempt to extend the self, or insure its union with nature, through marking the environment with the blue print of one's essence, one's style. (p. 180)

From these perspectives, style for African Americans is an expression of culture that is often used as a tool in defining the self, redefining interpersonal relations, and exerting influence in the social situation. Thus, style may be a form of resistance, (i.e., the rejection of cultural definitions of the self) and may serve as an instrument in usurping power. When the new definition of the self portrays the notion of nonconformity, altered expectation, or a rejection of the established norms, whether in appearance, manners, or behavior, the interaction situation has been redefined and in many instances control is usurped. In such instances, style is power.

In the context of the African American community, style is an essential element of a cultural aesthetic and consists of an individualistic expression of one's essence. This individual essence may be exaggerated and interpreted as showing off or it may function as a customizing agent for the expression of cultural values and self-definition. These notions of style are seen in research I conducted (see O'Neal, 1998) in which I asked forty-five male and female adults, both old and young, educated, college students and uneducated to describe an African American aesthetic of dress. These informants quickly identified style as an element and gave similar descriptions. For example, the notion of individual expression is seen in a statement from a young female adult:

> African Americans want this flashy look . . . even with hairstyles; it matches their clothes. The clothing is usually . . . something that no one else has or if they have it, they'll change it up . . . we'll always pick something that's really going to make us stand out and be noticed.

A female adult stated:

> I think it manifest itself in our behavior . . . and I think that it goes back hundreds of years. . . . The passion we have for dress. It's unique to us – style, you have to be an individual.

A female college student stated:

> African Americans are more colorful, vibrant, trendy, expressive. [We] will take risk [sic], . . . make statements; we express our concerns about political issues through the way we dress.

A young male adult stated:

> a man can put on a suit, . . . and wear it just like a European, but you have to add that African. . . . It's not what you wear, it's how you wear it. When I walk out, somebody must say, 'This brother knows what he's doing.'

These persons expressed several features described earlier: individual expression, the passion for dress, the completion of the object by that which is brought to it, and the injecting of beauty into an object through heightened emotion or feeling. These African American cultural expressions can also be found in slave dress. For example, writing in her diary between 1838–1839

Frances Kemble, a British woman who married a South Carolina plantation owner stated:

> The passion for dress is curiously strong in these people [enslaved Africans] and seems as though it might be made an instrument in converting them outwardly at any rate, to something like civilization . . .
>
> . . . You cannot conceive anything more grotesque than the Sunday trim of the poor people . . . beads, bugles, flaring sashes, and, above all, little fanciful aprons, which finish these incongruous toilets with a sort of airy grace, . . . (pp. 93–4)

Apparently this passion for dress and the injection of emotion into what was worn predates the period in which Kemble wrote. For example, the South Carolina legislature passed a law in 1740, which strictly regulated the dress of enslaved Africans. However, this attempt was unsuccessful and in 1822 the 'Memorialist of the Citizens of Charleston,' [obviously ignorant of the law] wrote to the legislature the following:

> Your Memorialist also recommends to the Legislature to prescribe the mode in which our persons of color shall dress. Their apparel has become so expensive as to tempt the slaves to dishonesty; to give them the ideas not consistent with their condition; to render them insolent to whites, and so fond of parade and show as to cause it extremely difficult to keep them at home. (as cited in Genovese, 1972, p. 559)

The 'passion for dress,' 'a sort of airy grace' and 'fond of parade and show' suggest the notion of style or personal expressiveness in enslaved Africans. The phrase 'to render them insolent to whites' suggests that the apparel of enslaved Africans must have been worn with a certain 'attitude' or energy that ran counter to established expectation. Similar behavior was also observed among free Negroes in New York City in the late 1820s.

> I have often, particularly on a Sunday, met groups of Negroes elegantly dressed; and have been sometimes amused by observing the very superior air of gallantry assumed by the men when in attendance of their belles, to that of whites in similar circumstances. On one occasion we met in Broadway a young Negress in the extreme of fashion, and accompanied by a black beau, whose toilet was equally studied; eye glass, guard chain, nothing was omitted; he walked beside his sable goddess uncovered, and with an air of the most tender devotion. (Trollope, 1832/ 1984, p. 310)

These descriptions seem to be consistent with the previous notions of style in the African American community. This same apparent 'style' can also be seen among West Africans as indicated in the writings of Barbosa, a Portuguese, in 1517:

> [The Carfes] are black men and go naked saved that they cover their private parts with cotton cloth from the waist down. Some are clad in skins of wild beasts, and some, ... wear capes of these skins with tails which trail on the ground, as a token of state and dignity. They leap as they go, and sway their bodies so as to make tails fly from one side to the other. (as cited in Davidson, 1991, pp. 180–1)

A description of the Gold Coast natives around 1850 indicated the importance of dress and personal expressiveness:

> They are particular in having the part of their dress of the finest texture. It is very frequently of silk, of a showy colour, and they allow the ends of fringes to fall down the side of the leg, that it may occasionally be seen upon any disarrangement of the upper robe, ... These robes are made of all kinds of Manchester goods, of silks, of velvets, and of their own rich country cloths. The patterns and colours are selected according to the taste of the wearer, some preferring a neat modest print, while others delight in gaudy contrasts of colours [sic] ...
> ... The females ... are equally anxious with the men to set off their persons to advantage, and occupy no little portion of their time about their toilets, ... Both sexes make use of beads and gold as ornaments for the neck, wrists, and ankles. ... Their fine smooth skins are, indeed, their principal beauty ... (Cruickshank, 1853, pp. 281–283)

Like the dress of African Americans and that of enslaved Africans, essentially the same principles of style are seen in the descriptions of dress in two West African countries: The Gold Coast and Mozambique in the sixteenth and nineteenth centuries. Phrases such as 'they leap ... and sway their bodies' and 'set off their persons to advantage' again suggest the injecting of energy and the desire to present the self in a unique and favorable manner. African American psychologists Pasteur and Toldson (1982) clarify these links:

> clothing for African people, whether African garb or European designs, is used primarily for a sense of embellishment, accentuating the personality, rather than from a feeling of shame regarding the human body or as protective veneer. Attire as style, then, emerges as a feature of personality, a self-declaration. (p. 185)

Many examples of the congruence between the aesthetic expression found in African American dress and that of enslaved Africans and of West African countries can be illustrated. However these limited numbers are sufficient to establish the links among the aesthetic element of style in the African

American community, enslaved Africans in the New World, and West African countries.


## Conclusion

According to Frye (1983) to undertake definition is a form of power. Collins (1991) stated that it is the role of the controlling element within society to exert its influence at the personal level where the definition of self is formed. Power for Foucault (1980) is a multiplicity of relations of force immanent in the domain in which they are inscribed (p. 187). From Foucault's perspective, the play of power is a technique used in normalizing definitions at all levels of society. The outcome of the normalizing is the same as suggested by Collins (1991) who viewed power in terms of binary structures of dominator and dominated; the result being that of an imposed definition of self on those 'normalized' as the other[7]. Therefore, the acts of defining the self, customizing mass-produced objects into new systems of meaning, and influencing or controlling the situation through the expressive shaping of one's immediate environment, are all acts of resistance or the usurping of power. Such acts serve as strategy for altering or redirecting power relations. Historically these acts helped to preserve elements of a culture whose cultural forms were ridiculed as barbaric.

The slave who injected affect and emotion into prescribed dress was declaring the self not a slave and rejecting the normalized notion of the 'noble savage.' The rejecting of the definition as slave took various other forms as well, and can be seen in the lyrics of the old slave song 'O Freedom:'

O Freedom, O Freedom, O Freedom over me.
And before I be a slave, I'll be buried in my grave
And go home to my Lord and be free.

It was a way of no-saying or an overt way of expressing to other slaves that one still had control of the most essential part of one's being – the mind and spirit, that is, self. This no-saying was a way of also defining the self as African, a person, not just a slave. It was a way of rejecting the form of domination that the prescribed mode of dress depicted.

'Stylin' today may be seen as an act of insubordination (i.e., resistance). For one's dress to be considered 'appropriate' it must conform to European American standards. Thus, to choose fashion and inject into it a new system of meaning which defines the self, and dramatizes conflicting values, is to reject the prescribed, that is, European American dress. Style then, represents the rejection of cultural convention or the 'normal' mode of dress and the unauthorized assumption of control, or the taking of power.

## Notes

1. As this chapter was going to press, a book by Shane White and Graham White was released by Cornell University Press called *Stylin': African American expressive culture from its beginning to the zoot suit*. The entire citation is White, S., & White, G. (1998). *Stylin': African American expressive culture from its beginning to the zoot suit*. Ithaca, NY: Cornell University Press.

2. Dress is considered as a gestalt that includes the body, and all three-dimensional supplements added to it. (See Eicher and Roach-Higgins, 1992).

3. For a discussion of style as an aesthetic element in African American dress see O'Neal, G. S. (1994), (1997), (1998).

4. Attitude as used here refers to the display of emotional qualities through dress and physical movement that stimulate the senses and command attention.

5. While stylin' may be used by adolescents in general and various other groups to gain attention or dominate the interaction, the discussion in this paper is specific to African Americans but does not imply that it is unique to African Americans. Unlike most other groups and individuals, however, style has now been determined as an essential element of a cultural aesthetic which also functions politically to negotiate the strains of marginality resulting from being an American of African descent.

6. Middle Passage refers to the second part of the slave trade circuit, which began with European slave traders sailing to Africa with cargo in exchange for slaves. From there they sailed to the Americas where enslaved Africans were exchanged for money. The ships were then loaded with products such as sugar, tobacco, and coffee and the slavers returned to Europe (Everett, 1991).

7. Although Collins views power in terms of dominator and dominated, she explicates a matrix of domination with multiple levels, all serving as potential sites of resistance.

## References

Asante, M. K. & Asante, K.W. (Eds). (1990). *African culture: The rhythm of unity*. Trenton, NJ: African World Press.

Baldwin, J. A. (1986). African (Black) psychology: Issues and synthesis. *Journal of Black Studies, 16*(3), 235–49.

Collins, P. H. (1991). *Black feminist thought*. New York: Rutledge.

Craik, J. (1994). *The face of fashion: Cultural studies in fashion*. London and New York: Routledge.

Cruickshank, B. (1853). *Eighteen years on the Gold Coast of Africa*. London: Hurst and Blackett Publishers.

Davidson, B. (1991). *African civilization revisited: From antiquity to modern times*. Trenton, NJ: African World Press, Inc.

Davis, F. (1895). Clothing and fashion as communication. In M.R. Solomin (Ed.), *The psychology of fashion* (pp. 15–27). Lexington: Heath/Lexington Books.

Eicher, J. B. & Roach-Higgins, M. E. (1992). Definition and classification of dress. In R. Barnes and J. B. Eicher (Eds), *Dress and gender: Making and meaning in cultural contexts* (pp. 8–20). New York: Berg.

Everett, S. (1991). *History of slavery*. Sacaucus, NJ: Cartwell Books, Inc.

Folb, E. A. (1980). *runnin' down some lines: the language and culture of black teenagers*. Cambridge, MA: Harvard University Press.

Foucault, M. (1980). *Power/Knowledge: Selected interviews and other writings 1972–1977*. New York: Pantheon Books.

Fox-Genovese, E. (1987). The empress's new clothes: The politics of fashion. *Socialist Review, 17*(1), 7–32.

Frye, M. (1983). *The politics of reality: Essays in feminist theory*. Trumansburg, NY: The Crossing Press.

Genovese, E. D. (1972). *Roll, Jordan, roll: The world the slaves made*. New York: Pantheon Books.

Hannerz, U. (1969). *Soulside*. New York: Columbia University Press.

Hebdige, D. (1979). *Subculture: The meaning of style*. New York: Methuen & Co.

Kaiser, S. B. (1990). *The social psychology of clothing symbolic appearance in context*. New York: Macmillan Publishing Company.

Keller, E. F. (1985). *Reflections on gender and science*. New Haven, CT: Yale University Press.

Kemble, F. A. (1961). *Journal of a residence on a Georgia plantation in 1835–1839*. New York: Pantheon Books.

Keto, C. T. (1981*). The African-centered perspective of history: An introduction*. Laurel Springs, NJ: K.A. Publishers.

Kirshenblatt-Gimblett, B. (1983). The future of folklore studies in America: The urban frontier. *Folklore Forum, 16*(2), 175–234.

Kochman, T. (1981). *Black and white styles in conflict*. Chicago: The University of Chicago Press.

Majors, R. (1991). Nonverbal behavior and communication styles among African Americans. In R. L. Jones, (Ed.), *Black Psychology* (3rd ed.) (pp. 269–94). Berkley, CA: Cobb and Henry.

Majors, R. & Billson, J. M. (1992). *Cool pose*. New York: Simon & Schuster.

Mancini, J. K. (1981). *Strategic styles coping in the inner city*. Hanover, NH: University Press of New England.

Mbiti, J. C. (1970). *African religions and philosophies*. Garden City, N Y: Avalon Books.

Nobles, W. (1980). African philosophy: Foundations for Black psychology. In R. L. Jones (Ed.), *Black psychology* (2nd ed., pp. 29–36). New York: Harper and Row Publishers.

O'Neal, G. S. (1994). African-American aesthetic of dress: Symmetry through diversity. In M. R. Delong & A. M. Fiore (Eds), *Aesthetics of textiles and clothing: Advancing multi-disciplinary perspectives.* ITAA Special Publication #7 (pp. 212–23). Monument, CO.

O'Neal, G. S. (1996). Fashioning future fashions. In *Fashioning the future: Our future from our past.* (Museum book Snowden Gallery of the Schottenstein Wing of Campbell Hall) pp. 25–8, 30. The Ohio State University, Columbus, OH.

O'Neal, G. S. (1997). African-American aesthetic of dress: Subcultural meaning and significance. In I. Rauch and G. F. Carr (Eds), *Semiotics around the world: Synthesis in diversity* (pp. 307–10). Mouton de Gruyter.

O'Neal, G. S. (1998). African-American aesthetic of dress: Current manifestations. *Clothing and Textiles Research Journal, 16*(4), 167–75.

Pasteur, A. B. & Toldson, I. L. (1982). *Roots of soul.* New York: Anchor Press/ Doubleday.

Raven, B. H. & Kruglanski, A.W. (1970). Conflict and power. In P. Swingle (Ed.), *The Structure of conflict* (pp. 69–109). New York: Academic Press.

Semmes, C. E. (1992). *Cultural hegemony and African American development.* Westport, CO: Praeger.

Trollope, Mrs. (1832). *Domestic manners of the Americans.* London, Whittaker Thacher & Co.

*7*

# Even Furthur: The Power of Subcultural Style in Techno Culture

## Suzanne Szostak-Pierce

All power, whether it be from above or from below, whatever level one examines it on, is actually represented in a more-or-less uniform fashion throughout Western societies under a negative, that is to say a *juridical* form. It's the characteristic of our Western societies that the language of power is law, not magic, not religion, or anything else. (Foucault, 1980, p. 201)

In Western societies, it is a recurrent view that youth activities must be restrained and/or modified through rules and regulations like music censorship, curfews, and dress codes. One contention of the 'parent' culture,[1] or the culture at large, is that the young are biologically and emotionally immature and therefore incapable of making many of the decisions that affect their lives. Young people are seen as a disenfranchised group without political, economical, and social power (Côté & Allahar, 1996). Because some youth perceive these given roles as incomplete and void of any real meaning, subcultures emerge by developing their own culture in an attempt to find worthwhile identities (p. 20). Youth subcultures are generational groups that differentiate themselves from the culture at large through distinct activities, values, particular uses of material artifacts, and social spaces (Clarke, Hall, Jefferson, & Roberts, 1997). Style is 'the active organization of objects with activities and outlooks, which produce an organized group-identity in the form and shape of a coherent and distinctive way of "being-in-the-world"' (p. 108). Subcultural style is manifested through look, sound, and performance, yet dress is a subculture's most powerful means of communication because of its high visibility. For youth subcultures, power is the negotiation of style within given cultural parameters. In this chapter, I explore the relationship of style and power in the rave subculture located in the Midwestern region of the United States. My approach to this topic is interdisciplinary. I draw from diverse writings on youth and style in the fields of clothing and textiles, cultural studies, sociology, and youth studies in order to present a multi-faceted interpretation. The data collected from my fieldwork in the rave scene provides the primary basis for my discussion on one particular rave event, *Even Furthur.* [2]

## Style as Power

During the life period of youth, style is a powerful means of giving a sub-culture an alternative approach to status attainment. Dick Hebdige (1997) maintains that while anonymity is a common characteristic of the powerful, subcultures respond to observation by posing and displaying themselves. He argues that this act feeds our voyeuristic tendencies by allowing us to gaze at strange appearances and activities from the safety of our own social locales. He concludes: 'Power is inscribed in the looks of things, in our looking at things' (p. 404). Youth subcultures define their spaces through styles of music, dance, dress, and rituals that are first unfamiliar and subsequently portrayed as threatening through media distortion. Moral panics may result because the meanings being communicated by the subculture through dress and appearance programs do not coincide with the meanings assigned by the viewer in their review of the programs (Stone, 1962). It is through deliberate aesthetic reconstruction of mainstream cultural practices that it is possible for subcultural groups to achieve a sense of empowerment. The symbolic power of style is a subculture's ability to symbolize otherness.

For example, bell hooks (1990) believes in willfully choosing the margin as a site of resistance rather than accepting it as a place of imposed oppression. By making this distinction, it is then possible for marginalized groups to live in spaces of creativity and power. Through her lived experiences as a Black woman, hooks describes how a powerless position can be transformed to one of strength through aesthetic evolution. hooks writes:

> We are transformed, individually, collectively, as we make radical creative space, which affirms and sustains our subjectivity, which gives us a new location from which to articulate our sense of the world. (p. 153)

The power of cultural expression distinguishes subcultures from the main-stream, the un-hip, and the inauthentic. Metaphorically, it releases them from the authoritative grips of commerce and media. Most youth with subcultural membership will emphatically deny any connection with the conventional, and will often discard a style if they feel it has been commodified. Hebdige (1989) contends that commodification is an attempt to control and tame the subculture; that the diffusion of style leads to the defusion of the subculture's subversive power. It is at this point that subcultures negotiate their styles so they can re-authenticate their appearances (Thornton, 1996). Authentication can be viewed as a means to protect the original ideologies associated with a subcultural style. Although fluid relationships in reality, subcultures prefer to view themselves as separate, elitist entities in order to authenticate what they view as unique existences. The radically baggy and long look of skateboarding style has now been commodified by the Levi-Strauss clothing brand in their *Wide* label jeans. One skateboarder in Minneapolis, MN confided to me that he is now choosing to wear a less baggy pant since skatestyle has been diffused into mainstream culture. When his style was incorporated by the mainstream, he experienced a loss of power. As this skater's style evolved to maintain the authenticity of his subculture, there was another shift in power. Power, then, is a process of negotiation for a subculture.

Style is a subculture's most immediate form of communication, yet the meanings are complex constructions because how youth experience style is subject to various interpretations across time and space. One example of hip-hop dress of the 1980s, which consists of knock-off designer emblems[3] such as Gucci and Chanel, is stylistically different than the current fashion trend of wearing Tommy Hilfiger clothing or other phat gear.[4] Likewise, the politics of gangster rap are understood differently by a Black, urban youth as opposed to a White, suburban youth. The meanings forged from such sights and sounds are understood clearly when attention is given to gender, ethnicity, and socio-economic background.

In *Black Noise*, Trisha Rose (1994) explores rap music and Black culture in American society, and is particularly interested in the power struggles that exist between male youth and female youth within the rap community. She contends that the hip-hop appearance of Black women rappers is reflective of a working class, Black youth aesthetic. Their distinctive dress is an attempt to resist images of sexual objectification seen in music videos, and to claim cultural visibility within the dominant popular culture (p. 170). In this instance, the visual presence produces a subcultural space that is empowered by female youth in relation to both members and non-members.

The particular subcultural moment I explore is rooted in the contemporary spaces of techno culture. A culture characterized by technological and conceptual advances, the current techno culture experience is described as being fractal; a nonlinear means of constructing one's reality through computers, appearance, electronic music, psychedelic drugs, and pagan-like rituals (Rushkoff, 1994). While the culture at large is suspect of such postmodernist thought, this culture is embracing alternative ways of seeing their world. The subcultural group that practices these tenets is most popularly referred to as the rave community.

## Interpretive Inquiry

In 1995 and 1996, I acted as a participant and as an observer at several raves in the Midwest region of the United States. Entering a person's lifeworld by participating and gathering anecdotes is referred to as close observation (van Manen, 1990). I also regularly explored Internet web sites, discussion lists, and chat lines devoted to rave culture to deepen my understanding of how this subculture reflects a techno culture. Because understanding the ways people subjectively experience style is the basis for my inquiry, I choose to use an interpretive science perspective as my mode of inquiry. When I attempt to understand how style is integrated in the experiences of youth, the descriptions I receive are an interpretation of the lived experience of the event of understanding through discourse. As a participant, my own lived experiences become a valid component in the interpretation. During a rave, it is not possible to conduct formal interviews because documentation would not be possible in the existing conditions of dim light and loud music. In addition, the weather conditions at *Even Furthur* were not conducive to taking photographs or recording conversations. My interpretation of this particular event uses close observation as the method, and the technique of field notes to record information.

## Raving in the United States

During the two years of my fieldwork, I observed various subcultural configurations, which made each rave I attended unique. Although what is produced and consumed at each rave is similar, the fusion of elements varied. The Internet web site, Hyperreal.com, is a techno culture resource created and maintained by its members. They describe the rave concept as:

a party, usually all night long, open to the general public where loud 'techno' music is mostly played and many people partake in a number of different chemicals, though the latter is far from necessary. The number of people at the event is unimportant; it can range from 50 people to 25,000 people. The cost of attendance is also unimportant – there have been good raves and bad raves at both end of the cost spectrum (though in practice, the higher the price, the more commercial the event, and the lower the quality). At a rave, the DJ is a shaman, a priest, a channeller of energy – they control the psychic voyages of the dancers through his or her choice in hard-to-fit music and their skill in manipulating that music, sometimes working with just a set of beats and samples, into a tapestry of mindbending music. A large part of the concept of raves is built upon sensory overload – a barrage of audio and very often visual stimuli are brought together to elevate people into an altered state of physical or psychological existence. (Behlendorf, 1994)

Raving is also regarded as a spiritual revolution and many participants continuously pursue the activity as a hopeful vision of what might ultimately be possible for the future of humankind. While this really represents a synergy between the abstract and the physical, four ideals make up an acronym that is followed by some ravers: P.L.U.R., Peace, Love, Unity, and Respect (Fogel, 1993). One of the guidelines of *Even Furthur* illustrates the concept of P.L.U.R.: 'Through kindness and positive attitudes we can help in the process of change that makes everyone open minded' (Promotional Flyer, *Even Furthur*, 1996). A rave then, cannot be easily defined, but rather described by the elements of music, dance, dress, drugs, and the ideology that comprise the ritual experience of rave.

The rave is a ritual of style and philosophy that has been growing for over ten years throughout the world since its birth in Europe and the United States in the late 1980s. Like the origins of techno music, ravers debate whether the first rave was held in Spain, the U.K., or various cities throughout America. The largest rave I attended during my fieldwork is what I regard as the quintessential example of this creative evolution – *Even Furthur*. Next, I describe the Midwest raver's most prized techno culture gathering, and explore how this style experience empowered 4,000 youth.

Like lovers we close our eyes not to be disturbed, anxious for a most exquisite avalanche of sweet consciousness. We have again set the stage for creativity, serenity, and irony – to   poetically frolic in the passionate bloom of youth . . . it's time to hurry up and start living, people; hurry up and start staring at flowers until butterflies appear; and hurry up, with gushing detail, and start preparing to assemble. (Promotional Flyer,[5] *Even Furthur*, 1996)

A celebration of the Midwest's rave scene, *Even Furthur* is a four-day electronic festival promoted by Milwaukee, Wisconsin's techno lavel, Drop Bass Network (Figure 7.1). A Memorial weekend tradition since 1994, I attended the third *Furthur* that was held in a camp ground in Gotham, Wisconsin from May 24th to May 27th in 1996. I can best describe *Furthur* as a place where technology and nature converge. Thousands of youth were immersed in rain and mudslides as they danced and listened to various genres of electronica[6] music (techno, house, acid, gabber, jungle, trance, hardcore,

**Figure 7.1.** Flyer of the *Even Furthur* rave event promoted by Drop Bass Network.

ambient). Throughout the camp, cars, trucks, and vans outlined the tents and campfires. Some people set up trampolines for playtime as they watched intellebeams, or laser lights beamed from projectors, lighting up the sky in sheets of green rain. Also visible was cigarette smoking, the drugs Ecstasy, Acid, and nitrous-filled balloons. There were constant hugs and kisses between new friends and old friends, and dress ranging from hip-hop to hippy.

*Furthur* reflected the indefinable nature of the rave as well as the dogma of the culture, as it was an intersection of many types of youth and styles. The *New York Times* (Strauss, 1996) reported that *Even Furthur* was a mixture of people ranging from age twelve to thirty who displayed both rave gear and dress of the Grateful Dead fans. However, dress was not limited to the standard phat pant and tie-dyed shirts commonly associated with ravers and hippies. Fashion at raves consists of unique ensembles that are highly volatile. On display at this particular event were body-conscious clubwear paired with platform shoes and elaborately applied make-up for both male and female youth. Extremely baggy pants and jeans; many of them homemade or re-inventions of store-bought apparel, were worn in wide and long lengths to effectively drag on the ground, while simultaneously covering expensive athletic shoes. Hooded sweatshirts, skate shirts adorned in graffiti-style illustrations, Hilfiger and Polo shirts, tiny-tees, and athletic logos such as Nike and Adidas were also visible in cotton, metallic, and knit fabrics. Ravers had various parts of their bodies pierced, tattooed, and painted. Hair was worn short or long, styled in Afros, and was dyed a variety of colors including blues, pinks, and oranges. Others wore wigs, baseball caps, or hoods to cover their head. A variety of backpack styles were used to carry supplies such as food and drink, candy, cigarettes, illegal drugs, toilet paper, glo sticks for viewing and dancing, and many toys. Many *old skoolers*, [7] or those who have been in the rave scene for a number of years, wore dress that was appropriate to the natural environment: layers of clothing, rain gear, hiking boots, and rolled-up jeans.

Although the campsite was filled with hills and paths of deep mud (everyone I spoke to told me it had been the same in previous years), most ravers opted to wear their personal uniforms, choosing fashion over physical comfort. Being a raver is a complete transformation of the everyday as temporalities and corporealities are challenged. When the music changed to softer ambient sounds in the late morning, the ravers went to sleep until late afternoon and arose again to scrape off the mud from the bottoms of their pants and shoes in preparation for another night of dance and music. Many ravers informed me that dancing and the use of drugs like Ecstasy also influenced their dress. They asserted that loose, cotton clothing is more comfortable to wear in intensive dance, and the euphoria caused by such a drug makes textured fabrics feel desirable on the body. On display was not a group style of dress, but a mixture of vernacular style unique to each individual. Dress style was influenced by other lifestyle choices outside weekend raving such as skateboarding, clubbing,[8] and hip-hop culture.

In *streetstyle*, Polhemus (1994) describes this kind of hybrid of subcultures in the nineties as 'the gathering of the tribes' (p. 128–9). He argues that all subcultures have shared media intrusion, and have thus united together to fight the establishment in order to maintain the authenticity of their cultures. In doing so, he believes that styles and ideologies inevitably fused together to produce new subcultures like the rave scene. In *stylesurfing*, Polhemus (1996) further states that subcultural style has evolved to the deliberate presentation of confusing and complex appearances in order to avoid the categorization and labels that are characteristic of a modern ethos. This type of appearance management signifies a departure from homogeneity, and allows an individual to both conceal and reveal meanings that must be negotiated through visual and verbal discourse (Kaiser, Nagasawa, & Hutton, 1991). Visually, *Even Furthur* reflects this ambivalence. Although each person appeared at the festival under the umbrella of raves and electronica music, their experiences with style varied. From choice of dress to choice of music tents visited, each festival participant was able to construct his or her own realities in these four days, without regard to the rules and regulations enforced by the culture at large.

This massive display of style exhibited at *Furthur* took place in a more private than public arena, transforming it into a space of resistance and acting as a metaphor for social change. Hebdidge (1997) proposes that we are currently seeing an evolution in the activities of youth subcultures. He writes:

> We are witnessing the formation of new collectivities, new forms of social and sexual being, new configurations of power and resistance. . . . All these shifts in power mean that older cultural traditions which provided the basis for collective forms of identity and action are being disrupted and eroded and that new ones are beginning to emerge. As power is deployed in new ways, so new forms of power-lessness are produced and new types of resistance become possible.
>
> They can be seen as attempts to win some kind of breathing space outside the existing cultural parameters, outside the zone of the given. They can be seen as collective responses on the part of certain youth fractions and factions to dominate value systems, as forms through which certain sections of youth oppose or negotiate, play with and transform the dominant definitions of what it means to be powerless, on the receiving end. (p. 403)

It can be argued that subcultural empowerment emerges in new aesthetic expressions like those observed at *Even Furthur.* In her discussion of fashion and postmodernism, Morgado (1996) writes that youth subcultures 'might be explained as expressions of postmodern culture's rejection of authority and its embrace of the principle of pure difference.' She continues 'this condition could hold promise for inclusion and empowerment of excluded groups and oppositional movements, and for the revitalization of culture' (p. 49).

Taking control of social space through a rave style also indicates a shift from modernism to a postmodern interpretation of aesthetics, with dress being the most visible evidence. Morgado (1996) asserts that there are identifiable features of postmodern dress. First, the end of progress and original design is being suggested in contemporary appearances that seem to be recycled from the past and chronologically are confusing. Fashion change is interpreted as volatile, as compared with the rhythmic cycles of modernism. Aesthetic codes and traditions are challenged about how dress is worn and co-ordinated. There is disharmony in styles and fabrics and emphasis on ornamentation, as compared with simplicity and unity. Finally, the cultural categories of age, gender, race, and status are distorted, allowing a number of styles, including those previously marginalized, to coexist (p. 48).

At *Even Furthur*, elements of subcultural and historical fashion styles were worn such as the tie-dye shirts inspired by the Grateful Dead movement; phat gear that was first used by skateboarders and hip hop followers; and danceclub dress such as hip-huggers and platform shoes modified from the fashion of the 1960s. Many people wore pacifiers around the neck or in the mouth; some held stuffed animal toys and backpacks; others continuously consumed lollipops and other candy, borrowing from what is usually thought of as infant and toddler identities.

Fashion change at rave parties is accelerated, making a fashion cycle difficult to assess. Each person chooses an eclectic mix of dress that is purchased, reconstructed, or homemade, making the act of dressing similar to choosing a separate costume for each event. Traditional rules of fit are challenged in the wearing of shirts that are several sizes too small, and pants that are several sizes too large. Other Western aesthetic codes are challenged in adorning the body with multiple piercings and painting the face with lavish makeup and glitter. The dress I describe did not appear to be gender-specific or disclose a particular ethnicity.

Dress style is interwoven with the other elements of the rave. Like dress, electronic music is an arrangement of recycled music samples and original sounds that span a variety of rhythms and beats. The event is also perceived to have roots in ancient ceremonies as ravers participate in the ritual of individual dance and soul-searching to reach what they define as a collective pulse. The location of *Even Furthur* combined aspects of the physical and synthetic worlds in the interplay of technology and the natural environment. I posit that the experience of these combined conditions is empowering to a social group who is seeking transcendence.

## Summary and Conclusions

Power is a function of all cultural production. Youth interpret their social positions as powerless, so their marginality becomes a place of creative development and fashion innovation. The postmodern perspective of aesthetic expression, as illustrated through the style of *Even Furthur*, is a time of subcultural empowerment as these ravers continue to break away from the tenets of modernism and seek new ways of constructing their realities. Nonlinear assemblages of dress and music, combined with the spiritual practices of dance, drugs, and ritual, represent elements of a techno culture.

Although rave philosophy proposes that members act as a collective whole, I would suggest further research that explores power relations, specifically those involving gender within the rave culture. Because raving is limited to weekend commitments, tensions may also exist between rave space and the return to everyday life. Researching youth subcultures and their highly visible styles enables us to learn new cultural perspectives, and better prepares us for a future that seems to be mapped through a *bricolage* of elements. Power through youth style, then, can be viewed as one cultural indicator of social change as we look towards the new millennium.

## Notes

1. The parent culture refers to the culture of which a smaller culture is a subset of so that these youth are seen in terms of their relation to the wider societal networks. See Hall & Jefferson, (1993 pp.13–17) for further explanation.

2. Furthur is intentionally misspelled. The name is inspired by the same word printed on the bus Ken Kessey and the Merry Pranksters drove around in during the 1960s (Strauss, 1996).

3. The subcultural identity of hip hop has generated a variety of styles in music, dance, and dress since the late 1970s. In 1987, rap artists Erik B. and Rakim could be seen wearing upscale brands of sportswear like Gucci and Louis Vuitton. This fashion was soon reflected in the street trend of wearing t-shirts printed with designer emblems.

4. The term phat is used to describe an extremely baggy style in pants in both rave and hip-hop speak.

5. Flyers are a popular means of promoting an upcoming rave event through innovative, graphic design.

6. Electronica is a music type that consists of many genres that are generally defined by their beats per minute.

7. The term, *old skoolers*, is a phonetic spelling of the word school. The term is used to distinguish between participants who have been raving for many years and those that have recently entered the scene.

8. Clubbing is an expression given to youth who frequent dance clubs. They also refer to themselves as 'club kids.'

## References

Behlendorf, B. (1994, May 8). *Hyperreal*. [Online]. Available: http://www.hyperreal.com/raves/altraveFAQ.html [1995, January 15.]

Clarke, J., Hall, S., Jefferson, T., & Roberts, B. (1997). Subcultures, cultures and class. In Gelder, K. & Thornton, S. (Eds), *The Subcultures Reader* (pp. 100–11). London and New York: Routledge (originally published in 1975).

Côté, J.E. & Allahar, A.L. (1995). *Generation on hold: Coming of age in the late twentieth century*. London & New York: New York University Press.

*Even Furthur* promotional flyer. (1996).

Fogel, L. (1993). The spirit of raving archives. Hyperreal WWW site. http://www. hyperreal.com/raves/spirit of raving.html [World Wide Web Publication.]

Foucault, M. (1980). *Power/knowledge: Selected interviews and other writings 1972– 1977* (C. Gordon, L. Marshall, J. Mepham, & K. Soper, Trans.). New York: Pantheon.

Hall, S. & Jefferson, T. (Eds) (1993). *Resistance through rituals: Youth subcultures in post-war Britain.* London: Routledge.

Hebdige, D. (1989). *Subculture: The meaning of style.* London: Routledge (originally published 1979).

Hebdige, D. (1997). Posing . . . threats, striking . . . poses: Youth, surveillance and display. In K. Gelder & S. Thornton (Eds), *The Subcultures Reader* (pp. 393– 405). London & New York: Routledge (originally published in 1983).

hooks, b. (1990). Choosing the margin as a space of radical openness. *Yearning: Race, Gender, and Cultural politics*, pp. 145–53. Boston: South End Press.

Kaiser, S. B., Nagasawa, R. H. & Hutton, S. S. (1991). Fashion, postmodernity and personal appearance: A symbolic interactionist formulation. *Symbolic Interaction, 14*(2), 165–85.

Morgado, M. A. (1996). Coming to terms with *postmodern*: theories and concepts of contemporary culture and their implications for apparel scholars. *Clothing and Textiles Research Journal, 14*(1), 41–53.

Polhemus, T. (1994). s*treetstyle: From sidewalk to catwalk.* London, New York: Thames and Hudson.

Polhemus, T. (1996). *stylesurfing: What to wear in the 3rd millennium.* London: Thames and Hudson.

Rose, T. (1994*). Black noise: Rap music and black culture in contemporary America.* Hanover, NH: Wesleyan University Press.

Rushkoff, D. (1994). *Cyberia: Life in the trenches of hyperspace.* San Francisco: Harper Collins.

Stone, G. (1962). Appearance and the self. In A.M. Rose (Ed.), *Human Behavior and the Social Processes: An Interactionist Approach* (pp. 86–116). New York: Houghton Mifflin Co.

Strauss, N. (1996, May 28). All-night parties and a nod to the 60's (rave on!). *New York Times*, pp. B1–B2.

Thornton, S. (1996). *Club cultures: Music, media and subcultural capital.* Hanover, NH:Wesleyan University Press.

van Manen, M. (1990). *Researching lived experience.* Albany, NY: State University of New York Press.

# 8

# Social Power and Appearance Management among Women[1]

## Nancy A. Rudd and Sharron J. Lennon

Socially constructed ideas about beauty manifest themselves through the ways in which individuals and groups create their appearances. Personal and cultural factors affect how we evaluate our appearances and our subsequent feelings of self-worth, as well as our feelings of social power. Researchers interested in the broad area of appearance and human behavior study the processes by which the body is modified through appearance-management behaviors.

The body is experienced as a reflection of the self (Fallon, 1990) and it contributes strongly to overall self-esteem (Cash, Winstead, & Janda, 1986; Lennon & Rudd, 1994; Striegel-Moore, Silberstein, & Rodin, 1986). Body image, the mental image we hold of our bodies and our affective response to it, has received attention by researchers (Brown, Cash, & Lewis, 1989; Jackson, Sullivan, & Rostker, 1988; Lerner & Javonovich, 1990; Thompson & Heinberg, 1993); distortions in body image play a major role in body-image disturbances that affect many women.

Given the incidence and prevalence of harmful appearance-management behaviors, it is clear that the rewards for maintaining or striving after an attractive appearance may come at a high price. From pre-adolescence, girls learn how important appearance is to their success and their influence over others; they learn how to monitor their appearances as they attempt to approximate a cultural ideal (Orenstein, 1994) and thus reap some rewards that their appearances may bring. For example, about 66 per cent of all adolescent girls are dissatisfied with their weight (Moore, 1993), which may lead to the development of eating disorders (Nasser, Hodges, & Ollendick, 1992), and low self-esteem (Orenstein; Pipher, 1994). Among college women, researchers estimate that between 28 per cent (Rudd & Lennon, 1993) and 60 per cent (Mintz & Betz, 1988) practice risky behaviors related to body image. Furthermore, the incidence of anorexia, bulimia, and other body image related disorders is on the rise in the U.S. (Halmi, Zleifield, & Wagner, 1997). For example, the sharpest increase in anorexia among women occurs between the ages of fifteen and twenty-four (Hill, 1997) and fasting has been reported in 20 to 40 per cent of teenage girls (Moore, 1988; Whitaker et al., 1989). Concern with body image is lifelong, and is likely shaped by these early experiences of body monitoring and appearance-management during child-hood and adolescence.

'Feeling powerful and feeling good about oneself are closely connected' (Freedman, 1986, p. 75). Therefore, if most women feel dissatisfied with their bodies, as research shows, then perhaps they feel powerless in social situations. In this chapter, we explore perceptions of power in relation to appearance-management behaviors of women such as dieting, exercise, cosmetics use, hair grooming, use of clothing, and cosmetic surgery. In general, behaviors undertaken to manage one's appearance run the gamut from mild (e.g., daily grooming) to extreme (e.g., eating disorders). We demonstrate that feelings of power are acquired by conforming to an ideal appearance through these appearance-management behaviors. For some who may feel powerless in many aspects of their lives, controlling their eating and activity levels, and thus their body size, is one way of gaining a sense of power and control. However, the desire for such power may cause severe damage to mental and physical health, and perhaps even total self-destruction. While quantitative methods have been used by researchers to examine the intricate relationship between body image and variables such as peer pressure, gender-role ideology, cultural influences, and disordered behaviors, very few qualitative approaches are reported in the literature. Taking a qualitative approach allowed us to explore the complex feelings women had about their bodies and to isolate any motivations related to power. Specific objectives for this research with women were (a) to explore body-image satisfaction and appearance-manage-ment behaviors, (b) to explore motivations for appearance-management behaviors, including those related to feelings of power, and (c) to examine relationships between appearance and self-esteem.

## Theoretical Framework

### Importance of Attractiveness

In the U.S. in the late twentieth century, people are reinforced and rewarded for having attractive appearances, which for women is commonly understood to mean being thin or at least not overweight, and possessing a narrow range of physical characteristics such as facial attractiveness. As compared to unattractive people, attractive people are preferred for hiring (Cash & Kilcullen,

1985), are preferred for dating partners (Walster, Aronson, Abrahams, & Rottman, 1966), and are evaluated higher in terms of task performance (Landy & Sigall, 1974). Furthermore, attractiveness affects social interactions. Attractive people are more successful at selling (Reingen & Kernan, 1993), are more influential (e.g., Chaiken, 1979; Pallak, 1983), and are more likely to elicit help from others (e.g., Benson, Karabenick, & Lerner, 1976) than unattractive people. Finally, in large national surveys, annual salaries reported by people objectively rated as attractive are significantly higher than those of people objectively rated as unattractive (Hamermesh & Biddle, 1994; Roszell, Kennedy, & Grabb, 1989). Thus, in a variety of ways people show preferences for those who are attractive.

According to Hatfield and Sprecher (1986), there are at least three reasons for such preferences. First, attractive people have an aesthetic appeal; in other words, just like people find it pleasant to live in a beautiful environment, they also find it pleasant to associate with beautiful people. Second, appearances affect what we infer about people's inner characteristics. Attractive people are perceived to have many positive characteristics, simply because they are attractive (Miller, 1970). Third, we like to accompany attractive people because our self-esteem and status are increased when beautiful people associate with us. This is especially true for men who associate with beautiful women (Sigall & Landy, 1973), but not necessarily for women who associate with attractive men (Bar-Tal & Saxe, 1976). Thus, beautiful women have important exchange value for men, and women who provide that exchange value may enjoy social power.

## Social Power

Probably the best known framework for studying interpersonal power is the typology outlined by French and Raven (1959) and later updated by Raven (1965; 1992; 1993). Accordingly social power is defined as the potential to change a person's beliefs, behaviors, or attitudes as a result of the actions of an influencing agent. The typology delineates the resources that the influencing agent can use to affect change in the other person. The source of reward power is the ability to reward others, either with something tangible such as a bonus or with something intangible such as personal approval. The source of coercive power is the ability to punish; for example, highway police can stop drivers and issue traffic citations. The source of legitimate power stems from a belief that the influencing agent has the legitimate right to influence; for example, a small child is obliged to accept the influence of parents. The source of both expert and informational power is knowledge possessed by the influencing agent. With expert power, the person being influenced is compliant due to the belief that the influencing agent has expertise, although the person being influenced may not understand that expertise. For example, particularly in the past, a physician told patients to discontinue certain behaviors because said behaviors were unhealthy and the patients usually complied because the doctor was the expert. With informational power, the person being influenced is compliant because a presentation of information leads to persuasion. Today, to induce compliance physicians explain why behaviors are unhealthy and if patients choose to change, they do so presumably because the presentation of information makes sense to them. The source of referent power is the fact that the influencing agent is desirable in some way; for example, a sports hero has referent power over youngsters with sports aspirations.

One of these, reward power, is germane to a discussion of attractiveness. In dating and mating relationships, men consider the physical attractiveness of women to be highly desirable (Buss, 1989; Buss & Barnes, 1986). Thus, when a beautiful woman accompanies a man, the woman's attractiveness may be rewarding for her male companion. Because of this value for men, attractiveness may function as a type of indirect power for women.

**Sources of Power**

Freedman (1986) points to the conflict women feel in using beauty to acquire social power. While attractiveness may enhance the indirect power a woman has over her social environment, it may also cause her to be taken less seriously by others, resulting in her having less direct power. Freedman distinguishes between two types of power: agonic power is direct influence over others, and may involve aggression; hedonic power is indirect influence over others, and is acquired by virtue of one's appearance, charm, exhibition, or political savvy. Hedonic power is often viewed as manipulative and is mistrusted (Freedman) because it is enhanced through adornment or display. 'Real' (e.g., direct or agonic) power is not accrued from simply being attractive and attracting, but rather is accrued from being important, competent, strong, or wealthy.

In the animal kingdom, agonic power might be demonstrated through threat, while hedonic power might be achieved by becoming conspicuous, thereby attracting attention. Among humans, aggressive or threatening activity is considered masculine and is therefore not valued in women, while submissive activity is considered feminine and consequently not valued in men (Freedman, 1986). Agonic power is readily available to men through physical strength, money, or authority, while hedonic power is readily available to women through attractiveness and charm. Thus, attractiveness can become a woman's primary source of social power or influence over others. Even if she possesses agonic power, because this type of power historically has been considered to be unfeminine, she may feel it necessary to compensate for having this power with attention to her beauty (hedonic power). For example, a women who is chief executive officer of a company or a college dean may feel she must pay particular attention to dressing fashionably, styling her hair, and wearing perfect makeup in order to appear attractive (hedonic power), even though she clearly possesses the intelligence, motivation, and expertise to hold such a responsible position (agonic power). She may feel that she is not really powerful unless she also looks good in the eyes of her peers. Such confusing expectations regarding beauty can contribute to mixed feelings about the beauty women perceive themselves to have, as well as mixed feelings about enhancing beauty in order to acquire power in a gender-biased world where men hold high status.

The problem with Freedman's interpretation of power is that it uses the ubiquitous 'reasonable man' (e.g., universal, normal male) as a standard for judging women's behaviors. In U.S. culture men define the norms and it is their behaviors that are the standard by which women are judged (Tavris, 1992). In other words, we perceive the behavior of women as something to be explained in relation to the behavior of men. For example, we might lament that women have lower self-esteem and less self-confidence than men, although we could also describe these same relationships by saying that men are more conceited and tend to overvalue what they do in comparison to women (Tavris). It is worth comment that although the definition of social power is the ability to influence, as a society we tend to judge direct (agonic) power more positively, better, or as more 'real' than indirect (hedonic) power, which we define somewhat negatively (Raven, 1992). In fact, women are discouraged from adopting assertive behaviors traditionally considered to be masculine. For example, in a sexual discrimination case (*Price Waterhouse* v. *Hopkins*, 1989) which reached the Supreme Court, Ann Hopkins was rejected for a partnership in the accounting firm for which she worked. Her behavior was described as macho, harsh, and aggressive. In an attempt to be helpful, the partner who explained the decision to Hopkins advised her to 'walk more femininely, talk more femininely, dress more femininely, wear makeup, have her hair styled and wear jewelry' (*Price Waterhouse* v. *Hopkins*). Hopkins, who eventually won her case, was rejected for exhibiting the same kinds of behaviors for which male colleagues were made partners. Because any power is better than no power, and behaviors rewarded for men are not rewarded for women, women may pursue the main avenue open to them for achieving power or influence over others, attraction through beauty and charm.

This is not necessarily an easy route to social power. U.S. culture equates female beauty with worth and establishes narrow and unrealistic standards of beauty. As a result, women may be very dissatisfied with the attractiveness of their faces and their bodies (Sanford & Donovan, 1984) and engage in harmful appearance-management behaviors as a consequence. Davis (1995) has outlined an interesting theory to explain how women can exert power while living in a socially-gendered world. After interviewing many women about their decisions to undergo cosmetic surgery, she concluded that they did so, more to normalize their appearances with other women than to achieve an ideal standard of beauty. Even though these women were acutely aware of the cultural standards of beauty that oppressed them, they demonstrated agency or control of their social circumstances by taking charge of their appearances in a rather dramatic way. They believed that their decisions would bring them social power. Rudd (in press) found this desire for social power via appearance-management behaviors explained women's purchase and use of cosmetics; in addition, cosmetics use contributed to both personal and social identity for women, thereby giving them a greater sense of social power.

To connect Freedman's (1986) and Raven's (1992) discussions of social power related to appearance, Freedman says that hedonic power is that which comes from the display of beauty and is the primary source of power available to women. Raven would call hedonic power one type of reward power, whereby the individual benefits from being attractive. Freedman's agonic power, derived from characteristics other than attractiveness, would include the other types of power (e.g., coercive, legitimate, expert) that Raven discusses.

## Method

We were interested in women's experiences with appearance management and perceptions regarding their body image. The purpose of the focus-group technique is to explore participants' understanding of and perspectives on an issue of interest (Millward, 1995). Therefore, seven focus-group interviews were conducted with a total of forty-two women for the purpose of further defining the significance of the body-image concept. A flexible interview schedule was used, following a fairly structured set of questions. The purpose of this research was not initially to study power and no questions directly addressed power. However, in the course of the interviews participants generated comments that related their level of perceived attractiveness to social power. As a result, we were able to investigate relationships among appearance-management behaviors, attractiveness, and power. Participants addressed questions regarding the nature of their appearance-management behaviors, their definitions of beauty, who and what influenced their perceptions of beauty and appropriate appearance-related behaviors, and how body image affected their feelings of self-worth and power.

Interviews were conducted over a period of nine months, in various public settings such as libraries and civic centers, with groups ranging in size from four to nine. Participants were women, who ranged in age from twenty-four to sixty-nine, with body-image concerns. They were solicited through flyers, requests to social organizations, and personal referrals. Participants included Caucasian American, African American, Asian American, and Hispanic American women. They were paid a small honorarium, funded through a grant from the Vanity Fair Corporation. Recorded focus groups lasted about one hour, yet allowed for discussion of related topics. Two assistants transcribed tapes and subsequently, we analyzed responses. Using an interpretive approach to analyze qualitative data, we looked for similarities among responses and arrived at several distinct categories. We agreed not only on the meaning of the categories, but also on the verbatims that were placed within the categories. Verbatims are used to illustrate our findings.

## Overall Findings

Negative feelings concerning appearance came early to many participants, in elementary school, and to all participants by puberty. Participants were well aware of comparisons made by themselves and others to siblings, classmates, grade levels, and best friends. Comments from those who recognized these feelings in elementary school tended to focus on general comparisons such as height or attractiveness, while comments reflecting feelings during puberty tended to focus on specific events such as onset of menstruation and changes accompanying puberty (e.g., size of breasts, hips, and thighs, and weight gain). Significant others, including family members, peers, and people in positions of authority, exercised social power over participants. Often the influence of others served as a catalyst to engage in appearance-management behaviors, yet at other times this influence acted to suppress self-worth. Family members often teased participants about their weight or general appearance. Friends, peers, and boys were strong influences during eighth and ninth grades. Teachers and school nurses made comments, sometimes public, about weight. Physicians commented on hip size, need to lose weight, and perceived ability to bear children related to body size; to the women, these comments seemed more to reflect physician's personal preference than anything medical. One respondent experienced job discrimination on the basis of body size. Significant others also influenced the 'appropriateness' of certain appearance-management behaviors. Dieting was a near universally accepted behavior to try to tame unruly bodies, with many participants mentioning mothers who dieted or comments from friends and family about the wisdom of dieting. Thus, controlling eating and activity levels was viewed as important, thereby contributing to feelings of control and the illusion of agonic power. Being in control is at least an active response to the influence of others, although ultimately the type of power it confers is hedonic.

The women perceived that body image affected their feelings of self-worth and power, primarily in their quest to be accepted. Self-worth reflected both real (i.e., verbalized) and imagined appraisals of others. If participants could not control the reactions of others to their appearances, then there was a shared feeling that they could at least control their own behaviors. For example, feelings of control were exhibited through comments about controlling weight and feeling good about it, or engaging in yo-yo dieting despite its recognized danger, or not buying any new clothes until one respondent could fit into a size 12 again (even though it had been four years since she had been this size). One might question whether such feelings of control have positive or negative consequences. For instance, these women may have believed that greater control over eating and exercising, thus influencing body size and shape, might result in greater hedonic power, but this belief carries the risk of incurring health problems.

Examples of hedonic power were seen when participants reported that their appearances made others feel comfortable or garnered attention, or when they exerted control through personal decisions about appearance management. For example, recognizing that one's smile makes others feel comfortable and at ease represents power. Women, who thought their appearances negatively influenced or repelled others, felt a lack of hedonic power. Body size, amounts of fat, and body proportion changes due to aging or childbirth were examples typically mentioned. Other characteristics that were presumed to carry negative value were small breasts, buttocks and hips (including one respondent who wanted to be 1" smaller), hair, wearing glasses, and eyelashes falling out with age.

Based on the questions asked, the following themes were identified: definitions of beauty, early feelings of body image, body image and influence, body image and acceptance, body image and self-worth, appearance-management behaviors, power and appearance management, and power conflict.

**Definitions of Beauty**

Participants defined beauty as comprised of both inward characteristics and outward appearance. However, definitions of beauty focused on general characteristics of the self such as health, personality, energy, self-acceptance, maturity, and childbearing, rather than specific physical aspects of appearance. Inward characteristics are identified in the following sample verbatims:

I think so much of your attractiveness comes out in your personality. ($R_{52}$)

I think my humor is some certain kind of energy. ($R_{54}$)

To me, looking attractive . . . I have finally come to the vast conclusion that it means feeling good about yourself. You must have that self-esteem that you are beautiful, that you have accomplished things in life, that you have a goal, you know you're going somewhere. ($R_{55}$)

Other women commented on external physical characteristics of beauty such as body size, facial features, or muscle tone as important to their definitions of beauty.

If I could describe it, it would be slim body, sultry face, cheekbones. ($R_{44}$)

When I was growing up, we were all supposed to look like Twiggy. ($R_{42}$)

### Early Feelings of Body Image

The effects of social power on appearance management began early in life. When participants were asked when they began to experience the impact of their appearance on others (potential hedonic power), feelings of body image were traced to an early age. Experiences recounted in early elementary school included comparisons to older siblings, classmates, and even school weigh-ins announced publicly. Puberty, which for some women began in second or third grade, was also a critical time as the participants began to develop breasts and compare themselves and be compared to their peers. Teasing by peers was common, suggesting the potential effects of coercive power (Raven, 1992). The literature on teasing suggests that young girls engage in eating disturbances such as dieting and bulimia to reduce teasing about body weight and size (Fabian & Thompson, 1989; Thompson & Heinberg, 1993). Edicts from family members regarding appearance and food also reflect coercive power attempts. The onsets of menstruation and gaining weight were other aspects that were important to their feelings about their bodies. Participants' comments elicited strong feelings.

I can remember back in elementary school and I had a big stomach back then. I remember a specific skirt I hated. It was a straight skirt and my mother would make me wear it, and the last time she made me wear it, the kids teased me so bad . . . they teased me all day. I went home from school crying. ($R_{11}$)

In 2nd grade I had to start wearing a training bra. When I was in 3rd grade I had breasts. I used to get teased a lot and I was taller. I just felt like a little big person. ($R_{33}$)

I was always referred to as the fat middle child. ($R_{36}$)

## Body Image and Social Influence

Friends, media images, parents, and spouses were all considered influential, thus wielding social power over participants. Supermodels and fashion publications in general were loathed, although the influence of advertising claims was well recognized. Some influences were intentional and some were incidental. Intentional influences were targeted toward a specific individual with the intent to motivate her toward a certain behavior. It was not always easy to determine from comments the type of social power wielded, but in general peers tended to wield coercive power and informational power, and family members wielded reward power.

When I was in nurse's training, we had very strict rules about weight. We couldn't be over or under . . . I lost 20 pounds because I had a very perfectionist attitude. I weighed 140 when I went in from high school. ($R_{42}$)

My aunt has been married 29 years and she wanted to cut her hair and her husband said no. Before they got married, she had to agree to keep her hair long, never going to bed in rollers and always on their anniversary being able to fit into her wedding dress. ($R_{72}$)

Incidental influences, on the other hand, were not targeted toward specific individuals, but still exerted a profound influence on the individual. Incidental influences often focused on unwitting comments made by others and on commercial influences. Media images wielded referent and expert power for participants.

[Social influence came] from magazines, TV, movie stars, commercials. ($R_{32}$)

As a child I was nice and heavy. When I think back on it, I don't think I was really that fat. But I do remember wearing chubbies. I remember one of my Mom's friends coming over and saying, 'Oh, does Carol wear chubbies?' She asked that and it was like something private you don't want people to know. ($R_{52}$)

Any risk I have felt previous to this point, it is in the magazines. Like you have to wear a size 3 or 4 to be a model. ($R_{53}$)

## Body Image and Acceptance

Feelings of self-acceptance were evident as women discussed specific aspects of their appearance, or as they related how their feelings as adults were more self-accepting than they were as adolescents. Lived experience in their bodies, such as consistency of body size or giving birth to children, seemed to give a certain perspective of acceptance. It therefore seemed that, among these women, body acceptance provided a sense of power, a point Freedman (1986, p. 96) makes, as well as a sense of peace.

> I think that I have finally adjusted to being heavier. I've been like this for about three or four years. ($R_{52}$)

> I think there's only so much you can do. I have wide hips. I ran through high school, 15 miles a day through cross-country season. I still had wide hips compared to the rest of my body, no matter what I did. ($R_{57}$)

> I used to resent being a stocky little Scottish person. I guess I've come to appreciate the size of the proportions that I am . . . Maybe I made some peace with my body image. ($R_{56}$)

> I'm 40 now, and I gained 15 pounds in the last 3 years. It nags on me a little bit, but I never made any effort (maybe a little exercise) to work at it. I'll be damned if I'm going to watch what I eat. If I want a candy bar or a piece of cake, I'll eat it. ($R_{51}$)

> As I get older, I am becoming comfortable with my child-bearing hips. ($R_{56}$)

However, several women were not very accepting of their bodies and made comments that suggested they felt little hedonic power because of their appearance.

> I thought until I get closer to that (slim body), I'm not going to be womanly. ($R_{44}$)

> I'm everything women aren't supposed to be . . . strong, capable, muscular. ($R_{42}$)

## Body Image and Self-Worth

There were strong connections between body image and self-worth. Most women acknowledged that self-worth increased when they were satisfied with their weight and appearance, yet it plummeted when weight increased or body parts changed with age or childbirth. Self-worth reflected real as well as imagined appraisals of others, as in the case of the woman who assumed she was not hired by any of the companies she had interviewed with because she was 'fat.' Hedonic power gained through attractive appearances was important to many participants. When asked to give a figure for the amount of self-worth accounted for by their appearance, responses varied from none to 90 per cent. Specific incidents were often reported with great emotion, including tears and anger; these women seemed to feel the least social power.

> You know, as far as they were concerned I was perfect for the job, and when I didn't get it, the thing that kept going through my mind is I'm fat. (R$_{23}$)

## Appearance-management Behaviors

Participants considered dieting to lose weight normative; all women reported dieting at some point. According to Freedman (1986), all forms of appearance-management behaviors, including dieting, can be classified as attempts to gain hedonic power. Two women reported bingeing and purging. Participants had tried a variety of commercial weight loss programs. These behaviors suggest that appeals by the diet industry wielded some power, in this case probably expert power or informational power over some participants.

> I remember being on Weight Watchers ... I have done like Slim-Fast. Other than that, in college I did the Stillman (diet). It was only cottage cheese and high protein. I stayed on that for months. (R$_{52}$)

> I've been on Jenny Craig, Nutra System; I've been on Slim-Fast; I've been on Weight Watchers. What's that one – Diet Center? I've been on all of them. (R$_{53}$)

Increasing physical activity was a popular strategy to control weight. Exercise routines or plans to increase exercise were also common. One woman exercised by walking up and down every aisle at the grocery store.

> I hated the (Jazzercise) class. I didn't like to sweat. If I can't win at it, then I don't want to sweat. But now I play tennis. (R$_{53}$)

Participants engaged in numerous grooming activities. They also discussed hazardous surgical procedures they might consider having if they could be sure of physical safety. Such comments suggest that these women would feel attractive with these changes and might experience reward or hedonic power.

> I'd have to have on a little mascara, curl eyelashes, cover up the circles under my eyes, a little blush, lipstick ... otherwise you look washed out. (R$_{54}$)

I would probably . . . if it were perfectly safe, I would do it (breast implants). (R$_{47}$)

Color my lips . . . permanently. (R$_{51}$)

I like for my hair to look ok . . . that is the minimum. (R$_{53}$)

## Power and Appearance Management

Social power, or the potential to influence another person, was seen in relation to appearance management. Other people had power in influencing participants' appearance-management behaviors or attitudes, as these sample verbatims attest.

> I have friends who are uncomfortable with the way I dress. I'm not comfortable looking like a complete slug, but half of the times I have exercise class, I just wear my sweats . . . They [friends] are uncomfortable with my appearance. (R$_{53}$)

> Then as I got older, and my kids started to get older, my kids would tell me, 'Mom, you are one of the better looking moms'. So it made me feel good as I got older. (R$_{51}$)

> My aunt used to tell me all the time that I was fat. It was a big deal for her. (R$_{34}$)

> I am married and I want my husband to continue to think I'm attractive. (R$_{51}$)

> I like it when people tell me I look young. (R$_{33}$)

Some women also commented on their ability to influence the beliefs, attitudes, or behaviors of others through their appearance. Such influence might arise from making others feel comfortable (reward and hedonic power), in gaining attention from others (hedonic power), or in exerting control over others through their own decisions (coercive power).

> My smile makes people feel comfortable. (R$_{53}$)

> I have big calves . . . but I noticed as I went through high school, people were envious because I had such nice legs. (R$_{31}$)

> Every once in a while, my husband will say, 'Wow, I notice you don't do that anymore. Why not? I like that.' (R$_{51}$)

Participants also reported feelings of personal power about appearance. This power sometimes meant educating others (informational power) and withstanding pressure to change one's or others' appearances. Withstanding this pressure implies that one is in control and that others are powerless with respect to their influence attempts.

I diet by verbalizing that I'm dieting, but I never do. (R$_{52}$)

I'm not going to question everything I put into my mouth. I'm not going to say . . . I can't have this candy bar, or oh gee I'm going out to dinner with friends, so I'm not going to have the wine. (R$_{53}$)

Then she (my aunt) started in on my children. And I said, 'Don't you tell my children what you told me.' I was very nice about it, but also very assertive. She got kind of quiet. I told her size doesn't matter; they are what they are. (R$_{34}$)

One woman, forced through divorce to be resourceful and strong (i.e., agonic power), expressed related feelings of tension between agonic and hedonic types of power.

I've often struggled with the feminine and unfeminine. I struggled with . . . I feel stupid trying to be feminine because I feel there is nothing feminine about me. (R$_{42}$)

**Power Conflict**

Some participants verbalized a sense of powerlessness that many women may feel, which is conflict between subscribing to the cultural appearance norms and wanting to change, and feeling that they are just fine the way they are. Comments suggested that women want to be taken seriously for the many personal characteristics they possess (agonic power), instead of being valued on the basis of how closely they meet narrow norms of physical beauty (hedonic power).

I want to lose weight, but I also want to be proud of the way I look. Do you go for losing weight, or go for feeling good about yourself? . . . If you feel you have to lose weight, then you obviously don't feel good about your body. The way I see it is if you have problems with your weight, then you have problems with yourself. (R$_{32}$)

The whole thing makes me mad where women are expected to wear makeup. I'm mad at myself every time I put it on because I think it is adding to my wrinkles. . . . It makes me mad that I have to put it on every day, so that the people I see don't think I'm a scumbag. I think I look better this way because society says I look better this way. (R$_{55}$)

## Summary and Synthesis

Participants seemed to enjoy the opportunity to discuss their feelings and lived experiences regarding appearance, body image, and appearance-management behaviors. They clearly understood the social power derived from being perceived as beautiful. The ability to influence others through some aspect of one's appearance (reward power) was commonly acknowledged, as was being influenced by others regarding appropriate or desirable appearance-management behaviors (coercive, expert, referent, and informational power). Many harmless appearance-management behaviors and some with harmful potential (e.g., dieting) were accepted as normative. Appearance-management behaviors that these women engaged in ranged from mild to extreme. Mild behaviors were seen in daily grooming procedures such as cosmetics use (ranging from a little lipstick to full makeup) and styling the hair 'just right,' as well as regular physical exercise such as aerobics classes, taking the steps at work, playing tennis, jogging, and eating healthy foods. Dieting and monitoring food intake were typical; in addition, extreme behaviors were exemplified by bulimia and by many formal diet regimens that advocate questionable practices. Several women reported their interest in having cosmetic surgery (breast implants, tattooed cosmetic color); one woman reported she had her spider veins dissolved for cosmetic reasons.

Social expectations to maintain a certain appearance sometimes created conflict in participants; some decided to suit themselves rather than maintain such appearances. Social acceptance and self-worth were often mentioned as important corollaries of appearance management.

From interviews with these forty-two women, it is clear that women have very strong perceptions of and attitudes about their bodies. Body image was of great importance to them, as evidenced by the liveliness of the discussions, the emotion with which some women shared their experiences, and the myriad ways in which body image was connected to feelings of self-worth and power. All participants had thoughts they wanted to share, underscoring the importance of body image in the lived experience of all women. However, the women did not seem to be aware that they were connecting their appearance management with ways to increase their social power. We did not specifically ask them to discuss social power in relation to their appearance because we wanted to examine motivations for appearance-management behaviors in general, and they may have only addressed motivations that they thought were socially desirable. Power is not traditionally thought to be socially desirable for women. We might have had different results if we had directly asked about the desire for social power as a motivation for doing what these women did to their bodies.

Overall, these women clearly recognized the hedonic power that can come from being beautiful to others, either naturally or through judicious appearance-management behaviors. Engaging in appearance-management activities that they believed enhanced their attractiveness may have given women the feeling that their appearances allowed them to compete with others favorably, to be noticed and therefore considered, and to be taken seriously. While some participants did in fact try to achieve the cultural ideal of female beauty, most undertook cosmetic, weight monitoring, and exercise regimens to try to normalize their appearances or level the playing field with other women, the strategy Davis (1995) described.

Yet, deciding not to diet and concentrating on one's accomplishments rather than one's appearance represented a focus on agonic power. These examples were rare among these women. Considering this relative absence of agonic power, and considering that hedonic power is thought by some to not be 'real' or direct social power (Freedman, 1986), we might ask if the women felt powerless overall. While we did not ask this question directly, through their responses it was clear that most women in the focus groups certainly did not feel good about themselves. They did not express much self-confidence about their appearances. Although participants clearly understood the power of beauty, few indicated they felt such power due to their own appearances. Rather, they engaged in a variety of appearance-management behaviors in a quest for hedonic power. We deduce that they did not feel powerful, based on Freedman's supposition that hedonic power is the source of power most readily available to women yet does little to enhance self-esteem. She argues that feeling powerful and feeling good about oneself are closely connected. If women believe they come up short on the measuring stick of attractiveness, they likely do not feel good about themselves nor feel socially powerful regardless of other positions they hold such as parenthood or careers.

When women wanted to feel pride in their normal appearances, yet worried about meeting cultural standards of attractiveness, conflicts arose. If women carry constant mental reminders about how they 'ought' to look in relation to idealized standards, and are surrounded by media images as well as significant others who support these idealized standards, it becomes difficult indeed to reaffirm that their 'real' body shapes and features are good and attractive. These nagging feelings detract from the powerful effects of being pleased with one's appearance, which may occur momentarily, as it did for some participants after weight loss or a new hairstyle or after receiving compliments from significant others.

## Conclusions

Based on this research, three main conclusions were formulated. First, for most women in this study, their appearances were not a strong source of social power as indicated by their criticisms of appearance. However, they recognized that an attractive appearance could confer power. Being socially accepted was important for nearly everyone, whether by siblings or family members during childhood, by peers or the opposite sex during adolescence, or by significant others and professional peers during adulthood. Participants recognized that attractiveness brings social rewards, and tried through a variety of appearance-management behaviors to increase their own attractiveness as much as possible.

Second, while we could not measure the actual social power any of the women had, they were engaged in endless rounds of appearance-management behaviors in an attempt to gain hedonic or reward power. Women who controlled body size by eating and exercise, and women who took pains with hair and cosmetic grooming, seemed to feel that they possessed the power to favorably impress others or at least to garner attention they might not otherwise receive. Thus, it seems plausible that if one *believes* she has the advantage or at least a fair playing edge through her total physical packaging, her self-worth is strengthened and she may handle herself in a more self-confident way than if she *believes* she is disadvantaged by her appearance. Of course, it is one thing to spend some time and effort in harmless grooming behaviors to construct an appearance that meets the mental expectations of looking one's best, and it is quite another to jeopardize one's physical health in pursuit of these expectations as did the two women who were bulimic. It may be a very fine and easy line for many women to cross, compounded by the fact that some appearance-management behaviors are socially acceptable even though they are harmful (e.g., chronic dieting, bingeing, purging). It was surprising and encouraging to find that participants acknowledged so few harmful behaviors related to their appearance-management. While most women did not express feelings of acceptance toward their bodies or general appearance, some certainly did. Such self-acceptance and self-confidence in one's physical packaging is a clear indication that one feels social power.

Third, Freedman (1986) raises the question of the real purpose behind the beauty myth and concludes it is one of division among women, using the divide and conquer strategy. If women can support one another in expressing their natural beauty and challenge the narrow expectations for appearance, as some of our participants did, then we begin to stretch the beauty boundaries and thereby, as Freedman says, alter the norm. 'As we judge others, so will we be judged, and so will we judge ourselves' (p. 238). Such gender-neutral expectations of beauty will undoubtedly lessen the conflict many women feel with their bodies, and provide multiple avenues for social power based on personal characteristics other than appearance.

## Note

1. This research was funded by a VF Corporation Research Grant, International Textiles and Apparel Association.

## References

Bar-Tal, D., & Saxe, L. (1976). Perceptions of similarly and dissimilarly attractive couples and individuals. *Journal of Personality and Social Psychology, 33,* 172–281.

Benson, P. L., Karabenick, S. A., & Lerner, R. M. (1976). Pretty pleases: The effects of physical attractiveness, race, and sex on receiving help. *Journal of Experimental Social Psychology, 12,* 409–15.

Brown, T., Cash, T., & Lewis, R. (1989). Body-image disturbances in adolescent female binge-purgers: A brief report of the results of a national survey in the U.S.A. *Journal of Child Psychology and Psychiatry, 30,* 605–13.

Buss, D. M. (1989). Sex differences in human mate preferences: Evolutionary hypotheses tested in 37 cultures. *Behavioral and Brain Sciences, 12,* 1–49.

Buss, D. M., & Barnes, M. (1986). Preferences in human mate selection. *Journal of Personality and Social Psychology, 50,* 559–70.

Cash, T. F. & Kilcullen, R. (1985). The aye of the beholder: Susceptibility to sexism and beautyism in the evaluation of managerial applicants. *Journal of Applied Social Psychology, 15,* 591–605.

Cash, T. F., Winstead, B. A., & Janda, L. H. (1986, April). The great American shape-up. *Psychology Today,* 30–7.

Chaiken, S. (1979). Communicator physical attractiveness and persuasion. *Journal of Personality and Social Psychology, 37,* 1387–97.

Davis, K. (1995). *Reshaping the female body: The dilemma of cosmetic surgery.* New York: Routledge.

Fabian, L. & Thompson, J. K. (1989). Body image and eating disturbance in young females. *International Journal of Eating Disorders, 8*(1), 63–74.

Fallon, A. (1990). Culture in the mirror: Sociocultural determinants of body image. In T. F. Cash and T. Pruzinsky (Eds), *Body images: Development, deviance, and change* (pp. 80–109). New York: The Guilford Press.

Fallon, A. & Rozin, P. (1985). Sex differences in perception of desirable body shape. *Journal of Abnormal Psychology, 94,* 102–5.

Favazza, A. (1987). *Bodies under siege: Self-mutilation in culture and psychiatry.* Baltimore: Johns Hopkins University Press.

Freedman, R. J. (1986). *Beauty bound.* Lexington, MA: Lexington Books.

French, J. R. P., & Raven, B. H. (1959). The bases of social power. In D. Cartwright (Ed.), *Studies in social power* (pp. 150–67). Ann Arbor, MI: Institute for Social Research.

Halmi, K., Zleifield, E., & Wagner, S. (1997). *Eating disorders scientific advisory group training manual: Anorexia nervosa, bulimia nervosa, binge eating.* Washington, D.C.: National Institutes of Mental Health.

Hamermesh, D. S., & Biddle, J. E. (1994). Beauty and the labor market. *The American Economic Review, 84,* 1174–94.

Hatfield, E., & Sprecher, S. (1986). *Mirror mirror: The importance of looks in everyday life.* Albany: State University of New York Press.

Hill, L. (1997, April 18). *Are eating disorders increasing? Now more than ever?* Paper presented at the Conference on Co-occurrence of eating disorders and clinical depression: Signs, symptoms, and treatment. Harding Hospital and Ohio Department of Mental Health, Columbus, OH.

Jackson, L., Sullivan, L., & Rostker, R. (1988). Gender, gender role, and body image. *Sex Roles, 19,* 429–43.

Landy, D., & Sigall, H. (1974). Beauty is talent: Task evaluation as a function of the performer's physical attractiveness. *Journal of Personality and Social Psychology, 29,* 299–304.

Lennon, S. J., & Rudd, N. A. (1994). Linkages between attitudes toward gender roles, body satisfaction, self-esteem, and appearance management behaviors in women. *Family and Consumer Sciences Research Journal, 23,* 94–117.

Lerner, R. & Javonovic, J. (1990). The role of body image in psychosocial development across the life span: A developmental contextual perspective. In T. F. Cash and T. Pruzinsky (Eds), *Body images: Development, deviance, and change* (pp. 110–27). New York: Guilford Press.

Miller, A. G. (1970). Role of physical attractiveness in impression formation. *Psychonomic Science, 19* (4), 241–3.

Millward, L. J. (1995). Focus groups. In G. M. Breakwell, S. Hammond, and C. Fife-Schaw (Eds), *Research methods in psychology* (pp. 274–92). Thousand Oaks, CA: Sage.

Mintz, L. & Betz, N. (1988). Prevalence and correlates of eating disordered behaviors among undergraduate women. *Journal of Counseling Psychology, 35*(4), 463–71.

Moore, D. (1993). Body image and eating behavior in adolescents. *Journal of the American College of Nutrition, 12*(5), 505–10.

Nasser, C., Hodges, P., & Ollendick, T. (1992). Self-concept, eating attitudes, and dietary patterns in young adolescent girls. *The School Counselor, 39,* 338–43.

Orenstein, P. (1994). *School girls: Young women, self-esteem, and the confidence gap.* New York: Doubleday.

Pallak, S. R. (1983). Salience of a communicator's physical attractiveness and persuasion: A heuristic versus systematic processing interpretation. *Social Cognition, 2,* 156–68.

Pipher, M. (1994). *Reviving Ophelia: Saving the selves of adolescent girls.* New York: Ballentine Books.

*Price Waterhouse v. Hopkins,* 490 U.S. 228 (1989).

Raven, B. H. (1965). Social influence and power. In I. D. Steiner and M. Fishbein (Eds), *Current studies in social psychology* (pp. 371–81). New York, NY: Holt, Rinehart, and Winston.

Raven, B. H. (1992). A power interaction model of interpersonal influence: French and Raven thirty years later. *Journal of Social Behavior and Personality, 7*, 217–44.

Raven, B. H. (1993). The bases of power: Origins and recent developments. *Journal of Social Sciences, 49*, 227–54.

Reingen, P. H., & Kernan, J. B. (1993). Social perception and interpersonal influence: Some consequences of the physical attractiveness stereotype in a personal selling setting. *Journal of Consumer Psychology, 2*(1), 25–38.

Roszell, P., Kennedy, D., & Grabb, E. (1989). Physical attractiveness and income attainment among Canadians. *The Journal of Psychology, 123*(6), 547–59.

Rudd, N. A. (in press). Cosmetics comparison and use among women: Ritualized activities that construct and transform the self. *Journal of Ritual Studies.*

Rudd, N. A., & Lennon, S. J. (1993). Body image and appearance-altering behaviors in college women [abstract]. In C. Ladisch (Ed.), *Proceedings of the 1993 meeting of the International Textiles and Apparel Association* (p. 107). Monument, CO: International Textiles and Apparel Association.

Sanford, L., & Donovan, M. (1984). *Women and self-esteem.* Garden City, N.Y.: Anchor Press/Doubleday.

Sigall, H., & Landy, D. (1973). Radiating beauty: Effects of having a physically attractive partner on person perception. *Journal of Personality and Social Psychology, 28*, 218–24.

Striegel-Moore, R., Silberstein, L., & Rodin, J. (1986). Toward an understanding of risk factors for bulimia. *American Psychologist, 41*, 246–63.

Tavris, C. (1992). *The mismeasure of woman.* New York, NY: Simon & Schuster.

Thompson, J., & Heinberg, L. (1993). Preliminary test of two hypotheses of body image disturbance. *International Journal of Eating Disorders, 14*(1), 59–63.

Walster, E., Aronson, V., Abrahams, D., & Rottman, L. (1966). Importance of physical attractiveness in dating behavior. *Journal of Personality and Social Psychology, 4*(5), 508–16.

Whitaker, A., Davies, M., Shaffer, D., Johnson, J., Abrams, S., Walsh, T., & Kalikow, K. (1989). The struggle to be thin: A survey of anorexic and bulimic symptoms in a non-referred adolescent population. *Psychological Medicine, 19*, 143–63.

# 9

# *Obesity and Powerlessness*

## Betsy Covell Breseman, Sharron J. Lennon, and Theresa L. Schulz

Christina Corrigan, a 680-pound thirteen-year-old, died on November 19, 1996, when her heart gave out ("Weight Issue," 1997). As a result, her mother was charged with felony child abuse.[1] According to a spokesperson from the National Association to Advance Fat Acceptance, a fat activist group, the charge would not have been brought if Christina Corrigan were not obese. Although the prosecutors pointed out that Christina had not been to a doctor in over four years, the defense attorney argued that the girl may have had a rare disease (Prader-Willi Syndrome) in which raging hunger is combined with a very slow metabolism. An endocrinologist testified that dieting would likely have caused Christina's metabolism to slow further, and probably would have only led to weight gain ("Weight Issue," 1997). This case illustrates the extent to which contemporary U.S. society expects weight to be controlled, if not by the individual then by a parent. This case also reflects prejudice toward those who are obese or associated with the obese, stereotyping about obese individuals, and ideas about power and obesity.

In this chapter we document relationships among stereotypes, prejudice, and discrimination as they relate to power among obese[2] individuals. We argue that obese women are powerless as a result of stereotyping, prejudice, and discrimination. Most of the research relating to obesity and human behavior demonstrates stereotyping and prejudice, but a few research studies demonstrate discrimination. As evidence of discrimination we discuss specific instances reported in the workforce, in public accommodation[3] and transportation, and in education. Issues of health care, provision of goods and services, and social discrimination (i.e., dignity and human rights) are addressed. In so doing, we rely on some reports appearing in the popular press. Finally, we examine ways in which obese women seek empowerment, including legal solutions to discriminatory practices.

According to Baron and Byrne (1991), stereotypes are defined to be cognitive frameworks that consist of knowledge and beliefs about particular social groups. Prejudice is an attitude, often negative, about members of a particular social group. Discrimination occurs if negative actions are taken with respect to a particular social group. Social power is the potential to change the beliefs, attitudes, or behaviors of a person resulting from the action or presence of another (Raven, 1992). Based on these definitions, an individual with social power has the potential to change stereotypes, prejudice, and discrimination.

Obese[4] women in American society are targets of one of the last remaining 'acceptable' prejudices (Crandall & Biernat, 1990). Obese women encounter social discrimination in finding jobs (Fraser, 1994; Kennedy, 1988) or in getting adequate health care ("Overweight," 1994). Obese women are frequently insulted or humiliated by physicians (Burgard & Lyons, 1994). Some obese women have experienced physical discrimination in restaurant seating (Lampert, 1994; Polaneczky, 1994) or have had to pay for more than one seat on an airplane (Polaneczky, 1994). The obese are ridiculed daily by those around them (Grilo, Wilfley, Brownell, & Rodin, 1994; Polaneczky, 1994). Obese women are likely to be ascribed character traits generally considered negative, such as lazy, stupid, and unfriendly, which are likely assigned to them based solely on their relative body size. This practice often leads to stereotypical attitudes toward the obese (Crandall, 1994; DeJong, 1980; Jasper & Klassen, 1990b; Lundberg & Sheehan, 1994). They are perceived to be 'slow moving,' which people often associate with 'slow thinking' (Kennedy, 1988, p. 152).

It is a common misconception that obese people lack discipline and are responsible for their size (Goodman, 1995). They are perceived as unable to control their own behaviors (e.g., eating and exercise). If being thin and physically fit is 'a metaphor for success and power' in the U.S. (Rodin, 1992, p. 224), then being obese equals failure and a lack of power. We contend that obese women lack power to control situations or attitudes when their size is a factor contributing to others' perceptions of them. Subsequently, when one's opinions and abilities are ignored, one is powerless to influence his or her destiny.

## Discrimination and Lack of Power for Obese Women

Historically, many groups in U.S. society have experienced discrimination based on race, religion, lifestyle, and gender.[5] Until they began to seek their legal and civil rights, people within these groups suffered from a lack of power or control over consequences in their lives. Although prejudice against these groups has not disappeared entirely, there are now regulations and laws to help protect certain groups from becoming targets of discrimination[6] and attempts have been made to educate society about members of these groups. However, obesity discrimination, or 'sizism,' as it is sometimes called, remains a strong force in American society (Crandall & Biernat, 1990). Numerous people, including many of the 'victims' themselves (Crandall & Biernat, 1990) accept prejudice and discrimination based on body size as 'politically correct.' Perhaps this can be attributed, in part, to a lack of information in general about what causes obesity and to the lack of laws to protect and assert the rights of people based on body size.

## Social Discrimination and Prejudice in the Workplace

Popular press sources reveal discrimination in employment is widespread and blatant regarding obese women. Prospective employers often fear that obese people are a health risk, have low energy, will repulse the buying public, and cannot perform well on the job; 'this is a perception rather than a real problem, but perception is often accepted as truth' (Jonas, 1997, p. 39). For instance, in a case that began in 1988, Bonnie Cook (5 feet 2 inches, 320 pounds) reapplied for a position she had held previously as an institutional attendant for mentally retarded persons at the Ladd Center (Murphy, Barlow, & Hatch, 1994), operated by the Rhode Island Department of Mental Health, Retardation and Hospitals (MHRH). She was denied the job upon reapplication because the routine pre-hire physical examination found her 'morbidly obese,' although no limitations on her ability to do the job were specified. MHRH maintained that Cook would be unable to evacuate patients in an emergency and refused to rehire her.

Appearance, including body size, plays a major role in decisions to hire. Brad W. Harper of Nelson, Harper, and Associates stated, 'Appearance constitutes 80 per cent of a first impression. Any applicant with an attribute that makes her different – like excess weight – will have to try harder and work harder' (cited in Kennedy, 1988, p.152). Harper told the story of an insurance company personnel office from which department managers, looking through the window, could see the applicants entering the building. Managers signaled their supervisors with a thumbs up or down before the applicant entered the office for her interview. If her appearance was judged negatively, the applicant had an unlikely chance to overcome the first, long-distance, and visual impression she had made. Kennedy (1988) also suggested that while many jobs in technical or educational settings may not use appearance as a criterion for employment, in most settings in which the applicant will have contact with the public it is likely that obesity and a perceived unattractive appearance will be used as a criterion.

Obese men and women both may have negative perceptions with which to contend if they desire to work in field sales. Martin Everett (1990) recounted the case of several obese individuals in sales. He wrote that obese salespeople are perceived as unhealthy and are thought to reflect poorly on a company's image. Often obese salespeople are denied opportunities to prove their ability to sell and are unfairly rejected for positions in which they would meet the public; in other words, obese people tend not to be hired for positions for which they are 'visible.' However, they may find employment in jobs such as telephone sales in which customers would not see them.

Denial of job opportunities can distinctly impact the self-esteem of the obese. An article appearing in a recent issue of *Big Beautiful Woman* magazine related the story of an obese communications manager who had gained weight since her job interview (Jonas, 1997). The board that hired her later rejected her, when she reported for work weighing more than she did at her interview. This woman had also received a rejection from the Peace Corps because of her size. She apparently internalized the prejudice and discrimination directed against her since she now refuses to do on-camera interviews because she feels she does not project a desirable image. Due to her size, she has ceased actively looking for work (Jonas, 1997).

Many job applicants and employees have been ordered to lose weight in order to keep their jobs. Fraser (1994) recounted the story of a 230-pound director of public relations for a major East Coast medical center who, upon arriving at her first day of work, was greeted by her new boss with exclamations that she had gained weight since her interview. The employee's size had not interfered with her performance as a manager in a previous position. To keep her new job she was pressured daily to lose weight, enduring humiliating comments and advice from co-workers; her new boss recommended that she only wear navy or black to work. She had to promise that she would go on a diet and get counseling. After working at her new job for over a year, successfully implementing award-winning programs and raising money, she was fired on the grounds that 'things that should have changed did not change' (p. 54). The implication was that she had not lost the weight she had been ordered to lose. She did not file a lawsuit because she felt it would hurt her chances of getting another job. Apparently she felt powerless to defend herself against such obvious prejudice and discrimination. In another similar incident a minister was offered a position by an attorney but only if she would agree to lose 10 pounds a month and be weighed on his office scales (Fraser, 1994).

Researchers working in academic settings find results that support popular press accounts of job discrimination (i.e., social discrimination). In a study of young adults, Koretz (1994), discovered that 10 per cent of sixteen-year-old women who were the most overweight of all the subjects, relative to their height, earned an average 7 per cent less than their peers by age twenty-three. Other researchers investigating personal characteristics and perceptions of unethical salesforce behavior found that extremely overweight salespeople were judged harshly for engaging in hypothetical unethical selling behavior (Bellizzi & Norvell, 1991). Respondents suggested termination of the obese salesperson. The overweight salespeople were also judged less self-disciplined, less ambitious, less clean cut, less healthy, less serious, lazier, more insecure, and more untidy than the normal weight salespersons. Jasper and Klassen (1990a) discovered undergraduate students held negative attitudes toward obese salespeople. Students had read descriptions (including height and weight information) of a fictitious employee on an 'employee's summary sheet.' The students were asked to indicate how much they would like to work with the person and how effective the person would be in selling them something they wanted. As the researchers expected, the students reading about a nonobese person indicated greater desire to work with that person than did the students reading about an obese person. In addition, as compared to students who read about the sales effectiveness of the obese person, students who read about the nonobese person indicated greater confidence in that person's ability to sell them a product. In a related study, Jasper and Klassen (1990b) reported that subjects described potential obese co-workers as sloppy, messy, lazy, unambitious, unhealthy, and insecure.

In other research concerning evaluations of the job performance of obese people, subjects compared characteristics of 'overweight males/females,' 'average-weight males/females,' and 'underweight males/females' based on verbal descriptions (Larkin & Pines, 1979). The overweight persons were judged less competent, less productive, less industrious, less successful, more disorganized, more indecisive, and more inactive, than the average and underweight persons.

Other studies of hiring practices in general include an examination by Brink (1988) in which undergraduate students evaluated descriptions of applicants (including weight) for the position of psychology professor. Subjects discriminated on the basis of weight, rejecting the heavier applicant. Pingitore, Dugoni, Tindale, and Spring (1994), in a mock employment interview study investigating differences between moderately obese and normal weight women, found that bias existed for the obese women significantly more frequently than for the normal weight women.

In the airline industry hiring practices traditionally enforced rigid and narrow restrictions in which airline flight attendants were required to adhere to strict weight and height guidelines; these have relaxed somewhat in recent years. In one study no obese flight attendants were hired and those who gained weight were likely fired if they did not lose weight (Lynch, 1996). In summary, it is clear obese people are treated differently in actual and hypothetical employment situations and, relative to thinner people, have fewer chances to take advantage of opportunities for which they are equally qualified.

## Social Discrimination in Education

Because obese people are subject to many negative social stereotypes in both interpersonal situations (Goodman, 1995) and in employment-related situations, they might also expect to be discriminated against with respect to education. Writers in the popular press document several accounts of social discrimination toward the obese in educational settings. In 1985, a nursing school student, Sharon Russell (5 feet 6 inches, 306–315 pounds), was dismissed from Salve Regina College in Rhode Island, despite her good grades and Red Cross certification, when she was unable to lose weight (Creighton, 1988). Earlier and under pressure from administration at the college, she had signed a contract promising to lose at least two pounds a week and to report for weekly weigh-ins. She was dismissed in spite of high praise from her supervisor at the college-affiliated hospital, who described Ms Russell as a professional with good attendance and performance, and as someone he would be happy to hire.

Researchers provide additional examples of social discrimination and prejudice in educational settings. In a study of elementary school principals, more than half of the respondents attributed obesity in children to lack of self-control and psychological problems (Price, Desmond, & Stelzer, 1987); such negative attributions demonstrate prejudice and could prove detrimental to the students. Canning and Mayer (1967) revealed that educators discriminated in their recommendations for students, while Hendry and Gillies (1978) revealed discrimination by physical education teachers. Obese individuals are perceived as lacking at least two characteristics thought to be necessary for success in school. For example, obese individuals are judged as less intellectual (Lennon & Miller, 1984–5) and less intelligent (Harris, Harris, & Bochner, 1982) than smaller individuals. Specifically, obese individuals are expected to be less successful in graduate school than thinner individuals (Benson, Severs, Tatenhorst, & Loddengaard, 1980). Finally, in large nationwide surveys, obese women (Gortmaker, Must, Perrin, Sobol, & Dietz, 1993) and both obese men and women (Sargent & Blanchflower, 1994) were found to actually complete fewer years of education than thinner people. In summary, not only must obese individuals contend with prejudice regarding their potential to do well in school, if existing research is used as a guideline, they will likely complete fewer years of education than their peers. As is the case with other groups who suffer social discrimination (e.g., racial or ethnic minorities), obese individuals' power over all aspects of their lives, including future success, is jeopardized by the constant struggle to overcome prejudice and social discrimination.

## Social Discrimination in Health Care

Frequently obese women find going to the doctor a frustrating and humiliating experience. Many instances of obese prejudice and discrimination that exist in health care are documented in popular press accounts. For instance, obese women are often admonished for being fat or overweight during doctor's visits for medical concerns that have little or nothing to do with their size, such as one woman who was reproached about her weight when she went to pick up her glasses (Burgard & Lyons, 1994). When one woman sought birth control from her gynecologist, she was asked pointed and impertinent questions regarding her options in sexual partners ("Overweight," 1994).

Many health care professionals defend their weight prejudice and subsequent discrimination of patients as being in the best interests of the patient (Grodner, 1995). Packer interviewed women more than 30 per cent overweight ("Overweight," 1994); one interviewee reported that prior to surgery for a malignant ovarian cyst, her doctor asked if she would like to have her stomach stapled in conjunction with the surgery. In another case, a woman, who had been raped, was told to lose weight by the doctor at the hospital where she was taken for semen samples ("Overweight," 1994). Fear of humiliation and abuse could result in many obese women not seeking proper medical care when they need it. Burgard and Lyons (1994) reported on a woman who had recently had a mastectomy. The woman, 'despite her apparent risk for cancer . . . would not undergo routine Pap smears because' of past humiliation 'by a physician who said she was too fat for a proper exam' (p. 214–15). Burgard and Lyons also related the incident of a physician who knew of 'a 60-pound abdominal tumor that was overlooked because the thought of palpating a very fat abdomen was abhorrent to the examining physician' (p. 215). When professionals in the health care industry harbor prejudice toward obese people, that prejudice is likely to affect how they perform on the job (Goldborough, 1970). Consequently, prejudice may lead to discrimination since the treatment received by obese patients could be affected. Unfortunately, such treatment may also affect the extent to which professional advice is followed (Prewitt & Rogers, 1987). In a study of 234 registered dieticians and sixty-four dietetics students, both groups were found to hold negative attitudes toward obesity (Oberrieder, Walker, Monroe, & Adeyanju, 1995). Other researchers found that health care professionals receiving continuing education on obesity tended to agree that obese individuals were self-indulgent and had family problems (Maiman, Wang, Becker, Finlay, & Simonson, 1979).

In a study of negative attitudes toward obese people and their treatment, nearly two-thirds of school nurses labeled obese children as lazy and sad (Price, Desmond, Ruppert, & Stelzer, 1987). In other research with nurses, common attitudes held that self-control can prevent obesity, hospitalized obese adults should be dieting, and providing care for an obese patient is exhausting (Maroney & Golub, 1992). In a study of 335 pediatricians, many had attitudes that could impair their treatment of childhood obesity (Price, Desmond, Ruppert, & Stelzer, 1989). Recommendations to lose weight included reducing calories (84 per cent) and joining Weight Watchers (66 per cent), which, although seemingly reasonable, may be contrary to medical and clinical research that emphasizes using caution with diets that do not provide good nutrition or simply are not effective (Allen & Beck, 1986; Coates & Thoresen, 1978; Ernsberger & Haskew, 1987; Kassirer & Angell, 1998; Roberts, Savage, Coward, Chew, & Lucas, 1988). Mental health professionals may also be prejudiced against obese people. A study by Young and Powell (1985) revealed that counselors and therapists were more likely to attribute negative psychological symptoms to obese models than to overweight and normal weight models in case histories with which photographs were included. In summary, medical and mental health professionals are entrusted with providing the most up-to-date diagnostic and treatment skills possible. It is therefore discouraging and frustrating to many obese women that control over their health is subverted by advice and opinions based on prejudice and outright discrimination by their doctors, nurses, and therapists. Thus many obese women are likely to feel powerless to assert themselves in the context of medical and mental health services.

### Social Discrimination in the Provision of Goods and Services

Discrimination based on body size occurs in the marketplace, especially with apparel retailers and designers. Obese women are faced with far fewer choices from which to select clothing than 'normal' sized women. Although stores such as Lane Bryant, Forgotten Woman, Sizes Unlimited, and T. Deane offer moderately priced, mainstream apparel and accessories to women who wear size 14 or larger, they are rare and a small percentage of the whole when compared to the clothing choices and stores available to women who wear smaller sizes. More choices exist now than in prior decades, but those stores providing apparel for obese women are sparsely scattered across the country.

It is puzzling that there are not more stores catering to obese women because popular sources of fashion and apparel information such as trade and fashion publications report that approximately 31 per cent of all American women nationwide are size 16 or larger and spend over $10 billion on clothing annually (Daria, 1993). Furthermore, at least 45 per cent of such women are 24 to 35 years old, making them the 'most powerful clothes-purchasing segment of the U.S. population' (Daria, 1993, p. 149). Even a high fashion, mainstream publication like *Vogue* magazine, reported an estimated 7.5 million readers, 20 per cent of whom wore a size 16 or larger (Dunn, 1986). In addition, at least half of the readers of *Vogue* wore a size 12 or larger (Dunn, 1986).

One apparent explanation for the scarcity of high fashion garments for obese women begins with the attitudes of designers and company principals. According to Daria (1993), top apparel companies such as Calvin Klein, Ralph Lauren, Anne Klein, and Donna Karan regard large sizes as 'fashion poison' (p. 149). The general attitude expressed is that it is not fair to a smaller woman, who supposedly works hard to maintain a good figure, to be confronted by an obese woman wearing the same outfit. Designers claim that targeting large-size women would severely damage their business (Daria, 1993). Fortunately, not all high fashion designers or stores avoid large sizes. Vittadini, Saks Fifth Avenue, Arnold Scaasi, and Mary McFadden are a few of the designers and stores offering high-priced larger sizes, but the selections are small and hard to locate outside of New York City.

The perception exists that obese women have little interest in clothing aesthetics; however, Chowdhary and Beale (1988) determined that large women were interested in color, fabric, fashion, fit, selection, size, and style of clothing. Shim and Kotsiopulos (1990) also suggested that tall/large women were just as interested in clothing, shopping, and fashion as petite and average-sized women. Although obese women have the power to express their need for fashionable clothing through their spending habits, this power is limited in view of the small market that currently targets them. As this market for large-sized apparel continues to expand, it seems likely that company profit or lack thereof will be a greater motivator for targeting large-sized women than simply the recognition that this market needs choices.

Not only do obese people seem to have trouble finding clothing, their actual shopping experiences may be frustrating because of the treatment they receive in retail stores. For example, in a study of salespersons' response time toward obese and nonobese customers, salesclerks were rated by observers as to how quickly they attended to the target customers (Pauley, 1988). Obese customers were approached significantly and consistently more slowly than their non-obese counterparts.

## Social Discrimination in Interpersonal Situations

Affronts to the dignity of obese people abound in numerous settings and situations. For instance, an obese woman was told by a male co-worker at an office party that he was surprised that an obese person could dance (Fraser, 1994). Bonnie Cook and her children endured endless taunts from strangers, who commented on her eating habits ("Tipping the scales," 1993, p. 99). Regarding eating in restaurants, an obese woman said, 'I've grown very careful about what I order in public and often feel self-conscious about eating, period' (Gregory, 1994, p. 110). In a supermarket, an obese woman encountered a four-year-old who repeatedly marched around her and screamed 'You are fat. You are fat. You are fat' (Millman, 1980, p. 9).

The respect received while growing up may impact self-image as adults. Indeed, 'the frequency of being teased about one's weight and size while growing up is associated with the degree of body image concerns during adulthood' (Grilo, Wilfley, Brownell, & Rodin, 1994, p. 447), as teasing increases so does dissatisfaction with the body. Grilo and associates also discovered that early onset of obesity was positively related to greater body dissatisfaction. In other words, someone who is obese and is teased about body size as a child may develop a negative self-image early in life, which might carry over into adulthood. For example, twelve-year-old Samuel Graham (5 feet 4 inches, 174 pounds) hanged himself from a tree in his backyard rather than face the weight-related teasing and humiliation he anticipated receiving from his classmates on the first day of school (Sharp, 1996; Wann, 1998). This is not the only case of suicide provoked by obesity-related teasing. A high school sophomore declared that he could not take it anymore one day when other kids were teasing him about being fat; he pulled out a gun and shot himself in the head (Wann). Kelly Yeomans overdosed on sleeping pills after three years of constant teasing from bullies who threw food at her windows and shouted insults about her weight outside her house at night (Wann).

The humiliation and lack of respect can even continue after death, as in the case of Patricia Mullen, an obese woman and Chicago Chapter member of the National Association to Advance Fat Acceptance ("Chicago PD,"1996). Responding to an emergency call from Ms Mullen's children, Chicago police officers arrived to find her unclothed body in the bathroom where she had died. One officer told Ms Mullen's niece that the body was too fat to take to the coroner. According to the local media, the body was allowed to lay uncovered in the house for several hours while the police played video games and ate from Ms Mullen's refrigerator. Allegedly, a police officer offered snacks to curious neighborhood children while they stared at the body ("Chicago PD,"1996, p. 10). Police were said to have kicked the body and to have made jokes about how the fat jiggled. Ms Mullen's corpse was finally dragged outdoors, still uncovered.

The ability to command respect is denied to those who are victims of teasing and disrespect; this is detrimental to self-concept and confidence. Power and respect are reciprocating; they co-exist. Without power, people lack the ability to achieve their desires and goals; without respect their opinions and needs are not taken seriously. When self-confidence is undermined, people doubt themselves and fail to assert independence of thought and will.

## Physical Discrimination in Public Accommodations and Transportation

Discrimination against obese people is not always social, physical discrimination exists as well. Popular press accounts of access difficulties to public accommodations and transportation such as airplane, train, and restaurant seating are common. Physical discrimination of obese women is illustrated in numerous examples of attempts to fit into seats that are too small (e.g., dentist chairs, theater and airline seats), and of struggles with seatbelts that do not fit comfortably (Polaneczky, 1994). When people must contend daily with public accommodations that restrict ability to be seated, it is clear that discrimination exists and that social power is lacking in the discriminated-against group.

Leslie Lampert (1993), a 'normal' sized reporter on an assignment to study obesity, experienced eye-opening instances of both social and physical discrimination. She donned a 'fat suit' to make herself appear 150 pounds heavier; and encountered various types of humiliation, including a taxi driver who laughed as she tried to get in and out of the cab, and two women who whispered and glared angrily at her as she took up a seat and a half on a commuter train. Lampert (1993) discovered that she had difficulty going through the revolving door at Bloomingdale's, in maneuvering the aisles in grocery stores, and in sitting behind the wheel of her own car (she adjusted the seat to accommodate her size, but then her feet would not reach the pedals). At an upscale restaurant, Lampert requested a table near the front, but, instead, was seated in the back; her perception was that she was considered too unsightly to be seen seated in the front of the restaurant. In a similar restaurant incident, an obese woman and her average-sized companion were obliged to accept a table for four in the restaurant's bar (the smoking section) because booths were too narrow and tables for two were too small to accommodate them (Polaneczky, 1994).

Seating in classrooms, in which the chairs or desks are apt to be only 14 inches wide, frequently pose problems for obese women (Fisher, 1997). One frustrated woman (500 pounds) recounted her experiences with college seating and obese prejudice (McAfee, 1997). Delaying college until her middle years because her high school guidance counselor had told her 'not to bother to apply because [she] was too fat' (p. 7), she arranged special seating for her classes prior to each semester. Arriving for an exam one night, she discovered that her special chair had been moved to another room. She found the chair and asked the young man sitting in it to please let her have it so that she could take it back where it belonged; he refused to give up the seat. The woman was forced to notify the campus police for help getting the seat returned. Unfortunately, by the time the chair was returned to the proper room, her exam was already underway and she missed some important announcements concerning the exam. This woman not only had the responsibility of arranging her own seating each semester, but had to contend with the blatant disrespect of the young man, the inconvenience of finding the chair, and missing part of her exam. As she said in reference to the young man and the incident, 'You limit my opportunities by your prejudice and you demean me by your assumptions of superiority. You debase my very existence by actions and attitudes that perpetuate the sense of shame that all obese people are supposed to have' (McAfee, p. 9).

Weight-based discrimination incidents regarding public accommodations and transportation are cited in research studies and in legal reviews as well. For instance, obese passengers have little power over airline seating and have often been required to purchase two seats on a flight (Polaneczky, 1994). At 5 feet 10 inches, a 400-pound man sued Denny's Restaurants because, when he could not fit into the tiny booths or a too-small chair with armrests which prevented him from sitting, an employee ridiculed him in front of other customers (O'Hara, 1996). In a case involving theater seating accommodations, in which most seats are a mere 18 to 20 inches wide, (O'Hara; Polaneczky), a Tennessee woman (5 feet 4 inches, 360 pounds) sued the owners of a movie theater for denying her the opportunity to set up her own chair in the handicapped section; the case was settled out of court (O'Hara).

## Social Solutions to Obesity Discrimination

Many obese individuals are taking an active role to change the way they are treated (Goodman, 1995); they are beginning to voice their opinions and demand respect. Organizations such as the National Association to Advance Fat Acceptance (NAAFA) support legislation that could protect the obese from discrimination; they publish a newsletter for members with updates on legal actions and news items of interest to obese people. NAAFA also sponsors protest demonstrations and national conferences in an effort to inform government and the public about obesity issues (Smith, 1995).

In an attempt to assert some amount of power and control many obese women have taken the initial steps of demanding respect by speaking out against the social abuse they endure. For example, some are responding to insensitive physicians by writing letters to them and to their health providers to express their displeasure with unnecessary weigh-ins and dieting advice on a routine basis (Burgard & Lyons, 1994). In these letters, women point out that they pay the same rates as thin women and are entitled to the same level of respect and care. Ultimately, 'the power of consent rests with the individual receiving care' (Burgard & Lyons, p. 216). In addition, health care providers should also take the initiative to ensure appropriate and reasonable treatment. Educating health care providers is the first step in guaranteeing adequate and fair medical treatments for obese women. For example, an editorial in the *New England Journal of Medicine* (Kassirer & Angell, 1998) urged doctors to help end discrimination against obese people by condemning preoccupation with thinness, by realizing that many obese individuals are healthy, and by using caution in admonishing patients for being obese and pressuring them to diet because 'the cure for obesity may be worse than the condition' (p. 53).

Scholars have also begun to advocate for fat acceptance with such organizations as NAAFA.[7] Dr. Laura Brown, a feminist therapist and psychology professor, states

> Fat oppression, which can be defined as the fear and hatred of fat people, particularly fat women, and the concomitant presence of oppressive and discriminatory practices aimed toward fat people, has become one of the few 'acceptable' prejudices still held by otherwise progressive and aware persons (cited in Ouellette, 1991, p. 22).

Other obesity-rights organizations include the Council on Size and Weight Discrimination of Maryland and the Association for the Health Enrichment of Large People in Virginia (Fraser, 1994). The supporters of the fight against obese discrimination and the activists for change in attitudes and practices are addressing the prejudices toward and lack of respect for obese people; they are speaking out about concerns of image, diet, and misinformation regarding the obese. The beliefs that obese people are somehow not normal may contribute to fear of becoming obese and a resultant rise in eating disorders, low self-esteem, and depression. The size acceptance movement hopes to change commonly held attitudes toward obese people, which may in turn help to reverse the discrimination faced by the obese. Only by exposing the negative stereotypes directed toward obese people as untrue of most obese people, by demonstrating that obese people make positive contributions to society, and by acknowledging that the obese will no longer tolerate the social prejudice and discrimination inflicted on them simply because they are a different size, can society begin to appreciate and accept obese people as normal members of society.

## Legal Solutions to Obesity Discrimination

Obese individuals are discriminated against with respect to employment, public accommodation (theaters, restaurants), transportation (airlines, trains), and education. There are currently no federal statutes (laws passed by Congress) and very few state statutes (laws passed by state legislatures) that specifically bar discrimination of obese individuals with respect to hiring. However, some states and cities have enacted laws to protect individuals based on their physical appearance and federal laws are beginning to be interpreted by the courts in such a way that they also may protect obese individuals from discrimination.

In 1990, Congress passed the Americans with Disabilities Act (ADA) which prohibits discrimination in employment by state and local governments and private employers with at least twenty-five employees (that number was reduced in 1994 to only fifteen employees). The ADA was patterned after the Rehabilitation Act passed in 1973 which forbids discrimination by federal contractors and recipients of federal financial assistance. Although the ADA does not protect employees of the federal government, the Rehabilitation Act covers them. Because the ADA and the Rehabilitation Act are so similar, courts generally interpret and apply the provisions of the two acts in the same way (Rothstein, 1994). The Department of Labor is responsible for enforcing the Rehabilitation Act and the Equal Employment Opportunity Commission (EEOC) is responsible for enforcing the ADA.

According to the ADA, employment discrimination against 'qualified individuals with a disability' is forbidden. Qualified individuals with a disability are defined as those 'who meet the skill, experience, education, and other job-related requirements of a position held or desired, and who, with or without reasonable accommodation, can perform the essential functions of the job.' This definition is complicated and best analyzed when broken down into its components. First, the individual must be disabled. The ADA (like the Rehabilitation Act) uses a three-prong test to determine disability. A disabled person is one who: (a) has a physical or mental impairment that substantially limits one or more major life activities; (b) has a record of such an impairment; or (c) is regarded as having such an impairment. A 'physical impairment' is further defined by the ADA as 'any physiological disorder, or condition, cosmetic disfigurement, or anatomical loss affecting one or more of the following body systems: neurological, musculoskeletal, special sense organs, respiratory (including speech organs), cardiovascular, reproductive, digestive, genito-urinary, hemic and lymphatic, skin, and endocrine' (ADA, 1990, p. I–26).

A person's physical impairment is determined without regard to whether medicine is taken to control the impairment (such as epilepsy) or an assistive device (such as a prosthetic) is utilized. Thus, the epileptic is still considered disabled under the ADA even if medication is taken to reduce the impact of the impairment. The EEOC has promulgated regulations to lend some interpretive guidance and explain that an impairment must be a disorder, not a simple physical characteristic ("Technical Assistance Manual," 1992). Thus, height or weight of an individual, if within normal range, is not in itself an impairment under the ADA ("Technical Assistance Manual," 1992). The phrases 'major life activity' and 'substantially limits' under the first prong of the disability test can also be confusing. The ADA does not define a 'major life activity,' but several examples are walking, speaking, breathing, performing manual tasks, seeing, hearing, learning, caring for oneself, sitting, standing, and lifting ("Technical Assistance Manual," 1992, p. II–3).

To determine whether an impairment 'substantially limits' a major life activity, it is necessary to consider the nature and severity of the impairment, how long it will last or is expected to last, and its permanent or long-term impact, or expected impact. Thus, a broken leg may substantially limit the major life activity of walking, but is not a disability because it is temporary. However, if the broken leg did not heal properly and permanently left the individual with a significantly restricted ability to walk, it would be a disability ("Technical Assistance Manual," 1992, p. II-5).

The second prong of the ADA disability definition protects those from discrimination that have a history of a disability, whether or not they currently are substantially limited in a major life activity. For example, a person with cancer that is in remission, one with a history of cocaine addiction who has been successfully rehabilitated, or one who was previously misdiagnosed as being mentally retarded, are all individuals with a history of a disability that are protected by the second prong.

The third prong of the ADA disability definition protects those from discrimination who are not substantially limited in a major life activity but are perceived as having such a limitation. The U.S. Supreme Court has stated, and Congress has reiterated, that such protection is necessary because 'society's myths and fears about disability and disease are as handicapping as are the physical limitations that flow from actual impairments' ("Technical Assistance Manual," 1992, p. II–10). This third prong protects against stereotypes, fears and misconceptions of society; in other words, it is protecting against social prejudices ("Technical Assistance Manual," 1992, p. II–11). This is the prong that has been relied upon by a number of obese people who have suffered discrimination in employment. The EEOC has described three situations in which this third prong of the disability definition is implicated: (a) the individual may have an impairment that is not substantially limiting, but is treated by the employer as an impairment that is substantially limiting; (b) the individual has an impairment that is substantially limiting because of attitudes of others toward the condition; and (c) the individual may have no impairment at all, but is regarded by an employer as having a substantially limiting impairment ("Technical Assistance Manual," 1992, pp. II–10 – II–11). If an employer makes an adverse employment decision based on a fear or stereotype that a person's perceived disability will cause problems in attendance, safety, productivity, accessibility, and acceptance by co-workers and customers, and if the employer cannot show a legitimate, nondiscriminatory reason for the action, the employer has violated the ADA.

After determining that an individual is disabled under the three-prong ADA definition, the person must also be shown to be qualified to be protected under the ADA. A 'protected individual with a disability' is one who meets the necessary prerequisites of the job (education, training, work experience, license) and can perform the essential functions of the job either with or without a reasonable accommodation by the employer. Determining the 'essential functions of the job' and 'reasonable accommodations' are also complicated issues under the ADA and will not be discussed herein. However, it is important to note that an obese person could lawfully be discriminated against if the particular job requires a specific physical ability or agility (e.g., firefighters, police officers, rescue workers) that the obese person could not perform due to his/her obesity.

The federal laws, including the Rehabilitation Act and the ADA merely set minimum levels of protection for employees. States and localities can enact laws that provide an even greater level of protection. For example, the ADA only prohibits discrimination by employers with fifteen or more employees, but some state human rights laws prohibit similar discrimination by employers with as few as one employee. That 'obesity discrimination remains a fluctuating and non-cohesive area of law' (Dunworth, 1994, p. 537) is due in part to the fact that federal and state laws offer differing degrees of protection from obesity discrimination, and also due in part to the fact that different courts interpret similar statutes in different ways.

With regard to state statutes, Michigan is the only state that specifically prohibits discrimination on the basis of height and weight (Mich. Comp. Laws Ann., 1991). The District of Columbia has enacted a statute (D.C. Human Rights Act, 1981) that prohibits discrimination on the basis of 'personal appearance.' According to the D.C. statute, 'personal appearance' includes bodily conditions or characteristics, dress, hairstyle and facial hair. The City of Santa Cruz, California, has passed a law (Santa Cruz Ordinance 92–11, 1992) prohibiting discrimination on the basis of 'physical characteristics.' Massachusetts (Massachusetts House Bill No. 3972, 1997) and New York (New York Assembly Bill No. 588, 1997; New York Senate Bill No. 1600,1997) also have bills pending in their respective state legislatures that make it unlawful to discriminate on the basis of height and weight.

In addition, a number of states have their own disabilities laws that may protect obese individuals. For example, in the case of *Gimello* v. *Agency Rent-A-Car Systems, Inc.* (1991), an obese person was considered handicapped for the purposes of the New Jersey laws against discrimination and won a case in which his employer fired him from his position as office manager due to his size and weight, although he could perform the 'unctions of the job. Likewise, in the case of *State Div. of Human Rights* v. *Xerox Corp.* (1985), obesity was considered a disability under New York's Human Rights Law and a computer programmer (5 feet 6 inches, 249 pounds) who was denied a job solely due to her obesity was found to have been unlawfully discriminated against. The employer in that case tried to justify its actions by pointing to statistical evidence that the plaintiff's obese condition could produce impairments in the future, leading to an adverse impact on disability and life insurance programs offered by the employer. In the case of *Cassista* v. *Community Foods, Inc.* (1993)[8] however, a court decided that obesity is a handicap or disability under the applicable California state law only if medical evidence demonstrated that it resulted from a physiological condition that limited a major life activity. The plaintiff (5 feet 4 inches, 305 pounds) in that case could not demonstrate that she had, or was perceived as having, a physiological disorder that affected basic bodily systems and limited her ability to participate in major life activities, as required under the state law. Thus, the court concluded that the employer did not unlawfully discriminate against her. In other words, the plaintiff's weight was not considered attributable to a condition beyond her control. Likewise, in the case of *Greene* v. *Union Pacific R.R. Co.* (1981), a court held that obesity is not a handicap under Washington law because it was not an immutable condition, such as blindness.

Like the state courts that have deemed obesity to be a disability under state anti-discrimination laws, the federal courts have recently begun to consider whether obesity can be protected as a disability under the ADA and the Rehabilitation Act. In *Cook* v. *Rhode Island* (1993), for example, a woman (5 feet 2 inches, 320 pounds) applied for a job as an institutional attendant for the mentally retarded, completed all required tests and interviews, including passing a pre-hire medical examination. She was not hired, however, due to the employer's beliefs that, because of her size, she (a) would not be able to evacuate patients in case of an emergency and (b) would be at greater risk of developing serious ailments which could then lead to absences and workers' compensation claims. The plaintiff brought suit under the Rehabilitation Act's 'regarded as' prong, and a jury verdict was upheld in her favor. The fact that the two cases of *Cook* and *Cassista* were decided differently is not unusual in that *Cook* was a case decided by a federal court interpreting federal law and *Cassista* was a case decided by a state court interpreting state law. It is also not unusual for federal courts in different districts to decide cases differently, because one district court decision does not bind another district court. There are eleven districts in the federal court system and each one could conceivably interpret the same federal statute differently from the others. Thus, although the situations of the two women were similar in *Cook* and *Cassista,* the cases were heard in different court systems and under different laws, which is why they produced different results.

In a case brought under the ADA as well as state law, *Nedder* v. *Rivier College* (1995), an assistant college professor (5 feet 6 inches, 380 pounds) was terminated from her employment and claimed that it was due to unlawful disability discrimination. This case is interesting because it was brought under the first prong of the ADA's definition of disability, rather than the third. The plaintiff claimed that her obesity was a disability that substantially limited her in the major life activity of walking and working (participating in commencement and convocation exercises). The court found that based on the evidence in that case, plaintiff was not substantially limited by her obesity in walking or working as an associate professor.

In a more recent case, *EEOC* v. *Texas Bus Lines* (1996), a woman applied for a position as a passenger van driver, passed all necessary interviews and employment tests, but failed a medical test because she was obese (5 feet 7 inches, 345 pounds), and was denied the position. The physician who performed the medical examination expressed concern that the woman's obesity would affect her mobility based upon his observation of her trouble getting out of her chair in the waiting room and the fact that she 'waddled' into his office. The woman brought suit under the ADA, contending that she was not actually disabled due to her obesity, but that the employer regarded her as disabled. The federal court agreed, allowing the plaintiff to bring her case to trial. Whether or not this case was settled or has gone to trial is uncertain[9] at this point. However, it appears that in this case an employer made an adverse employment decision based on stereotypical thinking which the ADA prohibits.

The ADA does not extend to disabled airline travelers because Congress had previously enacted the Air Carrier Access Act (1986) (ACAA) to protect that group of individuals from discrimination. Created from the Federal Aviation Act of 1958 as an attempt to overturn a Supreme Court ruling in which commercial airlines were declared outside the influence of federal assistance and therefore not obligated to provide access to disabled passengers, the ACAA 'covers all air carriers by its provision, regardless of their status as recipients of federal financial assistance' (Lynch, 1996, p. 234). Essentially, the ACAA requires airlines to provide transportation to all individuals, regardless of handicap, unless allowing such individuals air transportation would compromise the overall safety of the flight (Lynch, 1996). Legal scholars have suggested that airline passengers who are discriminated against by airlines due to their obesity may find legal recourse under the ACAA (Lynch, 1996). For this to be a viable remedy, however, the courts must determine that obesity qualifies as a valid handicap under the ACAA. As courts and state legislatures begin to define obesity as a disability under the ADA and Rehabilitation Act, perhaps obesity will also be defined as a handicap under the ACAA.

## Conclusions

The review of state and federal statutes and cases shows that social and physical discrimination against the obese is not uniformly prohibited by law, but depends upon the particular statute at issue, if any, and the court that is interpreting the statute. The Rehabilitation Act and the ADA are the most all-encompassing statutes forbidding discrimination, but as the cases demonstrate, these statutes do not always prohibit discrimination against the obese. In addition, while some state statutes clearly forbid discrimination based upon weight or physical appearance, those states are in the minority. The remaining states may have general human rights or civil rights acts, but it is not clear that these always protect discrimination against the obese.

Consequently, legislation may be a necessary, but not sufficient means of dealing with discrimination of obese people. Serious study is needed to develop strategies to combat both prejudice and discrimination of the obese. Many stories and incidents related in this chapter appeared in popular press publications such as newspapers, newsletters, and magazines. Although academic research in the areas of obesity discrimination and prejudice exist, an understanding of obesity discrimination, people's reactions to the obese, and methods to alter attitudes and behaviors toward the obese are rare outside the popular press. Carefully designed and executed research could provide necessary assessments that might serve as a foundation (a) for the development of proactive strategies to deal with obesity prejudice and (b) for a better understanding of the experiences of obese individuals.

In a society in which 'thinness is an index of success' (Fraser, 1994, p. 93), obesity discrimination will be difficult to reverse. Too often power is denied to those who are not considered physically attractive by arbitrary societal standards. Without the ability to exert influence and control over their lives, people lose their individual and collective voices in deciding matters of concern. Obese people are judged by their relative size. Until society can come to understand that it is acceptable for people to come in all shapes and sizes and that 'beautiful' and 'thin' do not necessarily equal 'good' or 'intelligent' anymore than 'fat' and 'obese' equal 'bad' or 'stupid,' it will be an uphill struggle to demonstrate that positive traits, competencies, and abilities are not related to size. Success in this endeavor will mean power and control for obese people to make choices and to enjoy the same opportunities and respect as nonobese people.

## Notes

1. Marlene Corrigan, Christina's mother, was convicted of the lesser charge of misdemeanor child abuse on January 9, 1998. She was sentenced on February 24, 1998 to three years probation, 240 hours of community service, and a $100 fine ("Marlene Corrigan," 1998).

2. Obesity is defined in the medical literature as 30 per cent over one's normal weight. Unfortunately, what constitutes 'normal' weight is not unambiguously defined in the literature. For example, the Metropolitan Life Insurance Company's table of ideal weights has been scaled upward several times since 1959 (Metropolitan Life Insurance Company, 1983).

3. A public accommodation is 'a facility, operated by a private entity, whose operations affect commerce' as defined by Title III of the Americans with disabilities act (The Americans with Disabilities Act, 1990).

4. The terms, 'obese' and 'fat,' are often used interchangeably. Some feel that the term 'fat' is generally more descriptive and accurate (e.g., National Association to Advance Fat Acceptance). However, the term 'fat' may be used by individuals of any body size or shape as a self-perception of their appearance; 'obese' can be clinically defined in terms of levels of obesity (e.g., morbid obesity).

5. For example, women, African Americans, Hispanic Americans, Mormons, Jews, gay men, and lesbians have all experienced some level of discrimination.

6. The Civil Rights Act of 1964 outlaws discrimination on the basis of race, sex, color, religion, or national origin (Hartnett, 1993).

7. For example, academic members of the Advisory Board of NAAFA include Dr Paul Ernsberger, of Case Western University Medical Center, and chair of the board; Dr Ester Rothblum, psychology professor at University of Vermont; and Dr O. Wayne Wooley and Dr Susan Wooley, psychology professors at University of Cincinnati College of Medicine.

8. Toni Linda Cassista applied for a position at Community Foods, a health food

store. She was asked back for a second, in-depth interview, but was not hired. Cassista claimed she was told they were concerned about her ability to navigate narrow aisles and ladders because of her weight, but Community Foods insisted that they had hired people with more experience than Cassista (Dunworth, 1994).

9. This court decision was based on a summary judgment motion, in which it was argued that the plaintiff's case did not have sufficient merit to proceed to trial, but the court decided that it did. Thus, it is known that the plaintiff was allowed to bring the case to trial. Whether the case was tried or whether it settled cannot be determined from computerized legal databases. Unless the matter is appealed to the Appellate Court level, it will not be recorded in the legal research databases.

# References

Air Carrier Access Act of 1986. 49 U.S.C. 1374(c) (1994).

Allen, D. O., & Beck, R. R. (1986). The role of calcium ion in hormone-stimulated lipolysis. *Biochemical Pharmacology, 35,* 767–72.

Americans with Disabilities Act of 1990, 42 U.S.C. section 12101, et. seq.

*Americans with Disabilities Act handbook.* (1991). Washington, D.C.: U.S. Equal Employment Opportunity Commission and the U.S. Department of Justice.

Baron, R. A., & Byrne, D. (1991). *Social psychology: Understanding human interaction* (6th ed.). Boston, MA: Allyn and Bacon.

Bellizzi, J. A., & Norvell, D. W. (1991). Personal characteristics and salesperson's justifications as moderators of supervisory discipline in cases involving unethical salesforce behavior. *Journal of the Academy of Marketing Science, 19*(1), 11–16.

Benson, P. L., Severs, D., Tatenhorst, J., & Loddengaard, N. (1980). The social costs of obesity: A non-reactive field study. *Social Behavior and Personality, 8,* 91–6.

Brink, T. L. (1988). Obesity and job discrimination: Mediation via personality stereotypes? *Perceptual and Motor Skills, 66,* 494.

Burgard, D., & Lyons, P. (1994). Alternatives in obesity treatment: Focusing on health for fat women. In P. Fallon, M. A. Katzman, & S. C. Wooley (Eds), *Feminist perspectives on eating disorders* (pp. 212–30). New York: The Guilford Press.

Canning, H., & Mayer, J. (1967). Obesity: An influence on high school performance. *American Journal of Clinical Nutrition, 20,* 352–4.

*Cassista v. Community Foods, Inc.,* 5 Cal. 4th 1050 (1993).

Chicago PD desecrates body: Chicago NAAFA stages protest. (1996). *National Association to Advance Fat Acceptance (NAAFA) Newsletter, 26*(2), 1, 10.

Chowdhary, U., & Beale, N. V. (1988). Plus-size women's clothing interest, satisfactions and dissatisfactions with ready-to-wear apparel. *Perceptual and Motor Skills, 66,* 783–8.

Coates, T. J., & Thoresen, C. E. (1978). Treating obesity in children and adolescents: A review. *American Journal of Public Health, 68,* 143–50.

*Cook v. Rhode Island,* 10 F. 3d 17 (1st Cir. 1993).

Crandall, C. S. (1994). Prejudice against fat people: Ideology and self-interest. *Journal of Personality and Social Psychology, 66*(5), 882–94.

Crandall, C., & Biernat, M. (1990). The ideology of anti-fat attitudes. *Journal of Applied Social Psychology, 20*(3), 227–43.

Creighton, H. (1988). Dismissal of obese woman from school of nursing: Actionable? *Nursing Management, 19*(4), 26–31.

Daria, I. (1993). Truth in fashion: Why more designers are designing large-size clothes – and why some still won't. *Glamour, 91*, 149–50.

D.C. Human Rights Act § 1–2512 (1981).

DeJong, W. (1980). The stigma of obesity: The consequences of naïve assumptions concerning the causes of physical deviance. *Journal of Health and Social Behavior, 21*, 75–87.

Dunn, W. (1986, August). Selling to big Americans. *American Demographics, 8*, 38–40, 55–6.

Dunworth, K. B. (1994). *Cassista v. Community Foods, Inc.:* Drawing the line at obesity? *Golden Gate University Law Review, 24*, 523–46.

*EEOC v. Texas Bus Lines*, 923 F.Supp. 965 (S.D. Tex. 1996).

Ernsberger, P., & Haskew, P. (1987). Health implications of obesity: An alternative view. *The Journal of Obesity and Weight Regulation, 6*, 1–137.

Everett, M. (1990, March). Let an overweight person call on your best customers? Fat chance. *Sales & Marketing Management, 142*, 66–70.

Federal Aviation Act of 1958 (FAA) (Pub.L. 85-726, Aug. 23, 1958, 72 Stat. 731).

Fisher, E. (1997). School's in! *National Association to Advance Fat Acceptance (NAAFA) Newsletter, 27*(1), 6, 9.

Fraser, L. (1994, June). The office F word. *Working Woman, 19*, 52–4, 88, 90–1.

*Gimello v. Agency Rent-A-Car Systems, Inc.*, 594 A.2d 264 (N.J. App. Div. 1991).

Goldborough, J. D. (1970). On becoming nonjudgmental. *American Journal of Nursing, 70*, 2340–3.

Goodman, W. C. (1995). *The invisible woman: Confronting weight prejudice in America*. Carlsbad, CA: Gürze Books.

Gortmaker, S. L., Must, A., Perrin, J. M., Sobol, A. M., & Dietz, W. H. (1993). Social and economic consequences of overweight in adolescence and young adulthood. *The New England Journal of Medicine, 329*, 1008–12.

*Greene v. Union Pacific R. R., Co.* 548 F.Supp. 3 (W.D. Wash. 1981).

Gregory, D. (1994, August). Heavy judgment: A sister talks about the pain of 'Living Large'. *Essence, 25*, 57–58, 105, 110–12.

Grilo, C. M., Wilfley, D. E., Brownell, K. D., & Rodin, J. (1994). Teasing, body image, and self-esteem in a clinical sample of obese women. *Addictive Behaviors, 19*(4), 443–50.

Grodner, M. (1995). Size discrimination. *Journal of Nutrition Education, 27*(1), 3.

Harris, M. B., Harris, R. J., & Bochner, S. (1982). Fat, four-eyed, and female: Stereotypes of obesity, glasses, and gender. *Journal of Applied Social Psychology, 12*(6), 503–16.

Hartnett, P. (1993). Nature or nurture, lifestyle or fate: Employment discrimination against obese workers. *Rutgers Law Journal, 24*, 807–45.

Hendry, L. B., & Gillies, P. (1978). Body type, body esteem, school, and leisure: A study of overweight, average, and underweight adolescents. *Journal of Youth and Adolescence, 7*, 181–95.

Jasper, C. R., & Klassen, M. L. (1990a). Perceptions of salespersons' appearance and evaluation of job performance. *Perceptual and Motor Skills, 71*, 563–6.

Jasper, C. R., & Klassen, M. L. (1990b). Stereotypical beliefs about appearance: Implications for retailing and consumer issues. *Perceptual and Motor Skills, 71*, 519–28.

Jonas, R. (1997, Spring). Sizing up the job market: Is plus a minus? *Big Beautiful Woman*, 39–41.

Kassirer, J. P., & Angell, M. (1998). Losing weight: An ill-fated new year's resolution. *New England Journal of Medicine, 338*, 52–4.

Kennedy, M. M. (1988, March). Discrimination against fat women: A reality in the workplace. *Glamour, 86*, 152.

Koretz, G. (1994, November 21). Physical traits can hurt pay: Fat women and short men suffer. *Business Week*, 22.

Lampert, L. (1993, May). Fat like me. *Ladies Home Journal, 110*, 154–155, 214–215.

Larkin, J. C., & Pines, H. A. (1979). No fat persons need apply: Experimental studies of the overweight stereotype and hiring preference. *Sociology of Work and Occupations, 6*(3), 312–27.

Lennon, S. J., & Miller, F. (1984–5). Attire, physical appearance, and first impressions: More is less. *Clothing and Textiles Research Journal, 3*(1), 1–8.

Lynch, D. M. (1996). The heavy issue: Weight-based discrimination in the airline industry. *Journal of Air Law and Commerce, 62*, 203–42.

Lundberg, J. K., & Sheehan, E. P. (1994). The effects of glasses and weight on perceptions of attractiveness and intelligence. *Journal of Social Behavior and Personality, 9*(4), 753–60.

Maiman, L. A., Wang, V. L., Becker, M. H., Finlay, J., & Simonson, M. (1979). Attitudes toward obesity and the obese among professionals. *The Journal of the American Dietetic Association, 74*, 331–6.

Marlene Corrigan convicted. (1998, January/February). *National Association to Advance Fat Acceptance (NAAFA) Newsletter, 27*(5), 8.

Maroney, D., & Golub, S. (1992). Nurses' attitudes toward obese persons and certain ethnic groups. *Perceptual and Motor Skills, 75*, 387–91.

Mass. House Bill No. 3972 (1997).

McAfee, L. (1997). College, chairs, and fat pride. *National Association to Advance Fat Acceptance (NAAFA) Newsletter, 27*(1), 7, 9.

Metropolitan Life Insurance Company. (1983, Jan–June). Comparison of 1959 and 1983 Metropolitan height and weight tables. *Statistical Bulletin*, 6–7.

Mich. Comp. Laws § 37.2202 (1991).

Millman, M. (1980). *Such a pretty face: Being fat in America*. New York: W. W. Norton & Company.

Murphy, B. S., Barlow, W. E., & Hatch, D. D. (1994). Discrimination against the obese violates rehab act. *Personnel Journal, 73*(2), 35–6.

*Nedder v. Rivier College*, 908 F.Supp. 66 (D. N.H. 1995).

New York Assembly Bill No. 588 (1997).

New York Senate Bill No. 1600 (1997).

Oberrieder, H., Walker, R., Monroe, D., & Adeyanju, M. (1995). Attitude of dietetics students and registered dietitians toward obesity. *Journal of the American Dietetic Association, 95*(8), 914–16.

O'Hara, M. D. (1996). "Please weight to be seated": Recognizing obesity as a disability to prevent discrimination in public accommodations. *Whittier Law Review, 17*, 895–954.

Ouellette, L. (1991, March/April). As fat as they wanna be: Large women are calling for an end to size discrimination. *Utne Reader*, 21–2.

Overweight: Dr. Fat-Attack. (1994). *Psychology Today, 27*(2), 10.

Pauley, L. L. (1988). Customer weight as a variable in salespersons' response time. *Journal of Social Psychology, 129*(5), 713–14.

Pingitore, R., Dugoni, B. L., Tindale, R. S., & Spring, B. (1994). Bias against overweight job applicants in simulated employment interview. *Journal of Applied Psychology, 79*(6), 909–17.

Polaneczky, R. (1994, July). More of her to love. *Philadelphia, 85*, 48–51, 85–7.

Prewitt, T., & Rogers, M. (1987). Giving weight-loss advice that patients will heed. *Contemporary OB/GYN, 30*, 81–2, 87, 90.

Price, J. H., Desmond, S. M., Ruppert, E.S., & Stelzer, C. M. (1989). Pediatricians' perceptions and practices regarding childhood obesity. *American Journal of Preventive Medicine, 5*, 95–103.

Price, J. H., Desmond, S. M., Ruppert, E.S., & Stelzer, C. M. (1987). School nurses' perceptions of childhood obesity. *Journal of School Health, 57*(8), 332–6.

Price, J. H., Desmond, S. M., & Stelzer, C. M. (1987). Elementary school principals' perceptions of childhood obesity. *Journal of School Health, 57*(9), 367–70.

Raven, B. H. (1992). A power interaction model of interpersonal influence: French and Raven thirty years later. *Journal of Social Behavior and Personality, 7*, 217–44.

Roberts, S. B., Savage, J., Coward, W. A., Chew, B., & Lucas, A. (1988). Energy expenditure and intake in infants born to lean and overweight mothers. *New England Journal of Medicine, 318*, 461–6.

Rodin, J. (1992, May). The new meaning of thin. *Glamour*, 224–7.

Rothstein, M. A. (1994). *Employment law*. St. Paul, MN: West Publishing Co.

Santa Cruz, Calif., Ordinance 92–11 (April 28, 1992).

Sargent, J. D., & Blanchflower, D. G. (1994). Obesity and stature in adolescence and earnings in young adulthood: Analysis of a British birth cohort. *Archives of Pediatric and Adolescent Medicine, 148*, 681–7.

Sharp, D. (1996, August 27). Boy fears teasing on his weight, kills self. *USA Today*, p. 4A.

Shim, S., & Kotsiopulos, A. (1990). Women's physical size, body-cathexis, and shopping for apparel. *Perceptual and Motor Skills, 71*, 1031–42.

Smith, S. E. (1995). Size acceptance: Building bridges in the movement between past and future. *Healthy Weight Journal*, 53–4.

*State Div. Of Human Rights v. Xerox Corp.*, 480 N.E.2d 695 (N.Y. Ct. App. 1985).

*Technical assistance manual on the employment provisions of the Americans With Disabilities Act.* (1992, January). Equal Employment Opportunities Commission: Washington, D.C.

The Civil Rights Act, 42 U.S.C. § 1975a–1975d, 2000a–2000h (1964).

The Rehabilitation Act, 29 U.S.C. § 701–797 (1973).

Tipping the scales of justice. (1993, December 13). *People Weekly*, 99.

Wann, M. (1998, January/February). Save the fat kids. *National Association to Advance Fat Acceptance (NAAFA) Newsletter*, 27(5), 4, 10.

Weight issue on trial. (1997, December 29). *Columbus Dispatch*, p. 6A.

Young, L. M., & Powell, B. (1985). The effects of obesity on the clinical judgments of mental health professionals. *Journal of Health and Social Behavior*, 26, 233–46.

# Index